INVENTING
NEW ENGLAND
REGIONAL TOURISM
IN THE
NINETEENTH CENTURY

DONA BROWN

SMITHSONIAN INSTITUTION PRESS
Washington and London

This book is dedicated to my grandmother, Lucille Ruppel Hinds.
I still have alot to learn from her.

Copy Editor: Jennifer Lorenzo
Production Editor: Jenelle Walthour
Designer: Janice Wheeler

Library of Congress Cataloging-in-Publication Data
Brown, Dona
   Inventing New England : regional tourism in the nineteenth century / Dona
   Brown.
      p.   cm.
   Includes bibliographical references and index.
   ISBN 1-56098-473-2 (acid-free)
   1. Tourist trade—New England—History.   I. Title.
   G155.U6B76   1995   94-23220
   338.4´791740443—dc20

British Library Cataloguing-in-Publication Data is available

Manufactured in the United States of America
02 01 00 99 98 97 96 95   5 4 3 2 1

(∞) The paper used in this publication meets the minimum requirements of the
American National Standard for Permanence of Paper for Printed Library Materials
Z39.48-1984.

CONTENTS

Acknowledgments

My work on this book began (more years ago than I want to count) with a summer at the American Antiquarian Society in Worcester, Massachusetts. A Frances Hiatt Fellowship made it possible for me to begin to explore one of the most outstanding historical collections in the country with the help of a staff whose professionalism, knowledge, and enthusiasm have never wavered. They have made a research home for me, as for many others. Barbara Trippel Simmons and Keith Arbour, who have since gone on to other things, helped to shape the initial direction of my research. John Hench, Diane Schoen, Joyce Tracy, Georgiana Barnhill, Tom Knoles, and Jenny Cope made their special provinces accessible to me; Marie Lamoureaux and Joanne Chaison, on the front lines, were unfailingly welcoming and patient with my endless requests.

Out on the road, too, I incurred many traveler's debts. John Kendall, the head of Special Collections at the University of Massachusetts, first directed me to the university's guidebook collection. The staff members of the Dukes County Historical Society, the Vermont Historical Society, and the Nantucket Historical Association were all extremely helpful. At the Old

York Historical Society, I was privileged to be part of an ambitious and highly successful project spearheaded by Sarah Giffen and Kevin Murphy. The book they edited, *A Noble and Dignified Stream: The Piscataqua Region in the Colonial Revival, 1860–1930,* is only the most tangible product of a lengthy and fruitful collaboration among a wide variety of scholars whose work was not only coordinated but also substantially enriched by the editors. Chapter 6 of this book grew out of my work on that project. It benefits directly from the research skills and imagination of the editors, the other authors, and the staff at the Old York Historical Society.

Gary Kulik's work on the "invention of New England" initially suggested the dissertation topic that grew into this book; since the early days of the dissertation he has been a supportive and perceptive reader. Paula Baker raised important questions and contributed valuable information to Chapter 5. Kathy Peiss, David Glassberg, and Kevin Sweeney gave the dissertation the benefit of their own unique insights. Robert Gross has been generous with his time and energy from the beginning, both as a scholar of exceptional insight and as a friend. I hope the book shows clear signs of his influence.

During the years I was revising the manuscript, I taught in the history department at the University of New Hampshire, as supportive an environment as anyone could want. Among the many kind and helpful colleagues there, Charles Clark and Laurel Ulrich have been particularly generous with scarce time. The students of History 600, Topics in Tourism, shared the results of their work on local vacation spots with me. Jim O'Connell of the Cape Cod Commission helped to shape my understanding of contemporary vacation issues on the Cape. Janet Schulte shared her own work on family vacations and collaborated with me on several panels that deepened my understanding of my own work. Mark Hirsch has gone above and beyond the duty of an acquisitions editor; his enthusiastic support of the book kept me working in spite of a series of disruptions that ranged from mononucleosis to changing jobs. Jennifer Lorenzo was the perfect copy editor: sensitive and efficient.

I have been equally lucky in my family network. Charles and Claudia Brown, and Margaret and Dietrich Stroeh, provided the moral support (not to mention the more practical forms of support) I needed to get through this project. From my family in Massachusetts, I received the same unstinting support. Rosalind Cuomo is the best of "best friends": Always in my corner, she never hesitates to let me know when I've gone off the deep end. Sarah Darling has shared with me her intellectual integrity and curiosity since our college days together. This book—and all my work—is inspired by her commitment to the things that really matter. Both Sarah and Roz know that this book reflects their work and commitment as well as mine.

Stephen Nissenbaum has been both my most sensitive and most demanding critic from the beginning. His imagination and high standards have shaped this work at every step. I hope the book reflects a little of his insight, and something of his commitment to the craft of writing. And I hope, too, that his next vacation will be considerably more carefree, without the heavy analytical baggage his traveling companion has been lugging around for so long.

INTRODUCTION

Most Americans know a lot about tourism. Even if they never leave home, the tourist industry comes to them. From Manhattan to the most rural counties of the West, private promoters and government agencies work hand in hand to create and market all kinds of "attractions." No place is immune. The Texas town I grew up in would have been an unlikely tourist destination thirty years ago. As central Texas went, it was prosperous but hardly glamorous: It had cotton mills, and stores that catered to farmers in the surrounding hill country. These days, though, it has become a popular tourist spot. Promoters discovered a gold mine in its spring-fed river—and in the quaintness of its German heritage. Now an amusement park lines the riverbanks; thousands of visitors crowd the town during its annual "Oktoberfest."

The town I live in now is a thousand miles away from the Texas hill country, as its green fields and tree-lined streets reveal. This town makes its living (and preserves its classic New England landscape) not by tourism but by another "clean" postindustrial business—colleges. But this town, too, has its tourist attractions. Here they are genteel and inconspicuous, like Emily Dickinson's house, but one need only inquire at the local chamber of commerce to find out how much such local attractions mean to area businesses.

No area is passed over, no matter how isolated or economically marginal. Indeed, tourism now often appears to be the answer to all economic problems great and small, from declining farm profits to deindustrialization. In the face of economic uncertainty, disruption, or downright disaster, local governments turn to tourism for financial salvation. The city of Flint, Michigan, its economy devastated by General Motors' massive plant shutdowns during the 1980s, launched an aggressive promotional campaign to bring tourists to a rebuilt Disneyized version of the downtown area of Flint, a theme park called Auto World. (The real downtown, with its boarded-up storefronts and burned-out buildings, was no place for tourists.)[1] With a similar disregard for reality, New Haven, Connecticut, the nation's seventh-poorest city, attempted to cash in on the free-flowing wealth of the 1980s by launching a campaign to train its cab drivers to be more courteous to tourists. Even areas already overrun by tourists compete for more. Massachusetts' Cape Cod is facing severe environmental problems: its water sources strained to the limit, overbuilt as far as the eye can see, hosting world-class traffic jams every summer weekend. But here, too, local alliances work to bring ever more people across the crowded bridges to the Cape.

In spite of all this enthusiasm for the tourist industry, it is not a business that is held in high repute. Heavily touristed areas are all too clearly no heaven on earth. Tourism is *not* the ultimate clean industry, as anyone who has ever lived near a popular beach can testify. And everyone has seen signs that tourists are not always welcome where they would like to go. The signs are not limited to outright physical assaults on tourists, like the recent incidents in Jamaica, Cairo, and Florida. Dissatisfaction with visitors can also be expressed more gently, with humor and ingenuity. On the central turnpike leading back to Boston from Maine, the locals hang out a sign on Labor Day: "Next time, just *send* the money!" Cape Codders wear T-shirts advertising, "I cheat drunks and tourists." Such local protests thrive in many heavily traveled communities, in spite of attempts by local governments and chambers of commerce to squelch them.

These are relatively lighthearted gestures, but they often disguise deep conflicts—conflicts over money, class, and power. In some places, where tourists seek out "local color" through an encounter with a genuine "native," such gestures can signal a profound discomfort with being "toured." More generally, they express the submerged anger of people at work toward the people at play whom they serve. And such gestures can also play a role in concrete struggles over what we now call "sense of place." How, for example, should a town arbitrate between two groups of lake users— one made up of year-round residents with motorboats, the other of wealthy summer people with sailboats? What price does a community pay when local farmers are driven out of business by the skyrocketing property values brought on by ski-resort development? Tourism complicates the questions of ownership and control that lie at the heart of "sense of place"—questions about the meaning, value, and uses of actual places.

Not one of these conflicts is new. Nearly two centuries have gone by since commercial tourist industries first appeared in the northeastern United States. In all these years, tourism has shaped the region's landscape, influenced (and at times invented) its culture, and played a crucial role in its economy. As early as the construction of the mills of Lowell, Massachusetts, and the beginnings of mass production in the workshops of Rochester, New York, and Paterson, New Jersey, the business of tourism began to take shape. Sometimes it took the form of big business, with all the infrastructure and capitalization of a major corporation. At other times and in other places, tourism became a kind of "cottage" industry, more like palm leaf hat-making, for instance, than like textile manufacturing. But whatever their scale, tourist businesses have often been on the cutting edge of capitalist development.

When foreigners toured the United States in the early nineteenth century, they were struck by the mushrooming growth of industry in many parts of the Northeast. They saw sawmills and gristmills clustered by waterfalls in the smallest villages; they testified to the rapid destruction of the woodlands. They scrupulously investigated and evaluated the experiment in industrial relations taking place in the mills of Lowell. But they were equally attentive to another part of the American scene, something they did not see as industrialization but which accompanied it everywhere. Every dramatic waterfall had its lumber mill or factory. And everywhere, on the other side of the falls, was a staircase, built by a nearby hotel keeper to cater to his guests' enthusiasm for scenery.

Tourism had a way of showing up in the areas with the fastest industrial and technological growth. A route called the fashionable tour, the subject of Chapter 1, became the first commercial tourist region to develop in the 1820s. The tour followed quite closely the path of the most rapid economic development in the region: up the Hudson River from New York City to Albany and west along the Erie Canal as it broke new ground on the way to Niagara Falls. In some places, tourism not only followed the trail of industrial growth but forged it. In the White Mountains of New Hampshire, for example, travelers in the 1830s encountered a country on the edge of the frontier. Farmers were still clearing old-growth forest, no accurate maps existed, and the only accommodations were rude inns built for lumberjacks and peddlers. But this primitive country was soon the site of a booming tourist industry.

Like the mills and factories that were transforming nearby areas, the tourist industry brought the countryside, piece by piece, into its own complex network of trade. The popularity of the White Mountains soon attracted an extensive railroad system that allowed tourists from Boston to reach the heart of the region in nine hours. By the 1850s, the mountains were a study in contrasts. Much of the area was still sparsely settled: There was "scarcely a dwelling to be seen except for the hotels," but those mountain hotels had become part of an urban social network. They were filled with elegant tourists playing cards, drinking champagne, and comparing notes on the latest fashions.[2]

Part of my purpose in writing this book is to examine the economic impact of nineteenth-century tourist industries like those in the White Mountains. But from the very beginning tourism had an impact that cannot be measured solely in economic terms. Chapter 2 explores how the White Mountains were drawn into a national cultural industry as well as a national commercial network. Travelers were familiar with the region's scenic wonders long before they ever got there. They had seen them in paintings (or reproductions) and engravings, read about them in guidebooks and poetry. Indeed, many of the most popular representations of the region were produced by painters and writers on their way to professional success. Both Nathaniel Hawthorne and Thomas Cole traveled the White Mountains in search of material, using what they found there as the basis for stories like Hawthorne's "The Great Stone Face" and paintings like Cole's *Notch of the White Mountains*.

Scenic touring provided much more than a vacation for nineteenth-century travelers. It also helped them to stake claims to a genteel status by demonstrating their good taste and sensitivity.[3] The pursuit of scenery linked a crucial pair of nineteenth-century "isms." For the consumer, scenic tourism softened the hard features of an industrializing society with a veil of romanticism. Standing on a mountaintop quoting poetry was as close as many genteel young men and women could get to emulating the romantic Byronic heroes with whom they often identified. On the other hand, the business of scenery was capitalism, pure and simple. Indeed, it was the cutting edge of capitalism, marketed with the most advanced techniques, served by the highest of high-tech transportation systems and building methods. For the entrepreneur, scenic tourism offered an intangible but very real product, one that could be exploited as easily as lumber or farm acreage. Romantic travelers could turn to Nature as an escape from the crude commercialism of their society—but not before they had purchased the railroad ticket, the trunks, the hotel room, the elegant bound journal, and the guidebook.

When Ralph Waldo Emerson published his famous essay on "Nature" in 1836 (four years after his own trip to the White Mountains), he used a phrase that articulated the new intangible "product" that was being marketed in scenic regions. Farmers owned the usual sort of property in land: "Miller owns this field, Locke that, and Manning the woodland beyond." But none of these farmers owned "the landscape." That was "a property in the horizon," as Emerson called it, "which no man has but he whose eye can integrate all the parts, that is, the poet." Emerson was arguing that the "poet's" sort of property was *not* for sale. But he was wrong. By the 1830s, any Miller, Locke, or Manning with enough imagination and capital could speculate in such scenic property.[4]

The tourist industry came to specialize in intangible products like scenery in the mid-nineteenth century. But it operated under special restrictions. Nineteenth-century tourists (like twentieth-century tourists) liked to think of some things as "private," apart from the world of buying and selling, and those experiences were precisely what tourism often sold. Some items of the tourist trade could be marketed openly. Stagecoach tickets, bathing machines, hotel rooms: Those things had prices and were appropriate for market transactions. But romantic scenery must not appear to be tainted by buying, selling, and speculating. It had to exist, as Emerson imagined it, in the world of the "poet." It had to appear untouched by marketplace transactions.

Tourist businesses were not unique in that regard. Market transactions—and a simultaneous denial of their existence—shaped the production and consumption of nineteenth-century culture itself, the conditions under which writers, painters, publishers, and printers worked. And women's unpaid work in the home, although deeply influenced by market forces, also operated behind a veil that seemed to distance it from open contact with the marketplace. The society that separated home from work, women from men, and aesthetic experience from work and daily life also created a "separate sphere" for tourist experiences. But that did not make the business of selling those products any less profitable.

Romantic scenery was not the only "property in the horizon" discovered by nineteenth-century entrepreneurs. Tourist promoters came to specialize in a whole array of such intangible consumer goods. In fact, tourism played a key role in *creating* a consumer-oriented society and economy. The tourist experience was crucial to the transformation of old-fashioned middling artisans, shopkeepers, and professionals into a new middle class, converting them from a tradition of self-denying soberness and frugality to a consumer ethic that sought liberation and fulfillment in purchases.

For those who still clung to the abstemious life of hard work and simplicity, tourism was often the crowbar that pried them away from their convictions. Methodist artisans in southern New England rejected ostentatious display, embraced their preindustrial mixed-class religious communities, and abhorred the luxurious excesses of their "betters." But they, too, broke down in the 1860s and began to make their camp meeting grounds into vacation communities. One such transformation took place on Martha's Vineyard and is the subject of the third chapter. A soul-searching marketing campaign conducted by some of the Methodist campers themselves was responsible for the changeover. Supporters of vacations took on the work of reassuring themselves and others that relaxation and leisure could be shorn of their traditional associations with vice. The product of this particular tourist industry was not simply a cottage on the shore but a justification for leisure, as well as an environment that guaranteed the morality of spending money on pleasure.

One way or another, tourism lured tourists into a world where all experiences were for sale: culture and gentility for the Unitarian minister in the White Mountains, community and religion for the Methodist grocer on Martha's Vineyard. Precisely because these products were intangible, because they disguised the commercial relationship, they were well calculated to overcome residual resistance to consumer relations. Tourists were able to see themselves, not as consumers purchasing goods, but as sensitive lovers of scenery or loyal members of a religious community.[5]

Tourist promoters were not the only ones who played this game, but they played it consummately. By mid-century they had been phenomenally successful in expanding their trade. Tourist businesses became increasingly large and complex. Investment corporations and railroads poured money into hotels and large-scale resort developments that dwarfed the efforts of small-scale entrepreneurs. Geographically, the tourist industry spread far beyond its original specialized regions. From Newport, Rhode Island, all the way up to Bar Harbor, Maine, coastal resorts sprang up along the railroad lines. Rural communities in the hill towns of western Massachusetts and Connecticut, in the "lake country" of southern New Hampshire, and on the peripheries of cities, faced a growing influx of vacationers each summer.

New investors in tourism were equally successful in expanding their potential market beyond its original boundaries. More people than ever found it necessary and desirable to allocate part of their income to a vacation or trip. Urban professionals—doctors, lawyers, ministers—came to regard a month in the country as an absolute necessity. Influential religious leaders like Henry Ward Beecher came down on the side of vacations. Beecher insisted to his young, upwardly mobile parishioners in Brooklyn Heights that such vacations were crucial to their mental and spiritual well-being. Even office clerks and journalists, small shopkeepers and teachers found it possible to take a week or two away from home in summer. By the mid-nineteenth century, everyone with even a remote hope of achieving middle-class status understood that a vacation was as essential to that status as owning a piano and a carpet.

Far from signaling a "democratization" of tourism, however, the industry's growth enforced profound class divisions. It widened the gulf between the growing minority who could aspire to such leisure and the great majority for whom a week away from work would mean unemployment and a slide into poverty. Vacations did not unite middle-class tourists, either. Vacation communities were divided by extremely fine distinctions of class, religion, family, and ethnicity; they were far more segregated than most urban neighborhoods.

Indeed, for many tourists, their very identity might come to depend on their vacation choices. Too flamboyant a stay at Newport might bankrupt a respectable businessman, but Nantasket Beach might be too plebeian for a wealthy family. (William Dean Howells's fictional character, the nouveau riche Silas Lapham, was one who discovered the social shortcomings of Nantasket, to his family's great misery.) Ambitious young men and women in search of the right mates might have to change their images to suit the resort: What was appropriate for the sporting crowd at Mount Desert might not be acceptable among the exclusive Beacon Hill families who summered at Nahant. Little wonder that William Dean Howells himself put so much feeling into a mock complaint about the difficulties of vacationing. In an essay titled "The Problem of the Summer," Howells lamented the vacationing predicaments of people "with some measure of money, ease, and taste." Families were torn apart by their conflicting demands for both "society and solitude, mountain-air and sea-bathing." "For most people," as Howells put it, "choice is a curse."[6]

Despite its attendant complications, tourism grew rapidly in mid-century. And according to the testimonies of dozens of New England local histories, it came not a moment too soon. "It was certainly at a fortunate time," wrote one local historian, "that the summer business began." His region had been facing economic disaster: "The herring fisheries were becoming less and less profitable, the coasting trade was slack, the hills had been stripped of the last trees suitable for sawing, the thin soil of the farms was practically exhausted." Then, miraculously, the tourist industry had appeared like the cavalry on the horizon: "With the coming of the new population," he wrote, "the whole aspect of affairs changed."[7]

This upbeat account celebrates the good fortune of Mount Desert, an island on the coast of Maine, where a fashionable resort sprouted up in the town of Bar Harbor in the 1860s. The same might have been written, though, in almost any account of a New England coastal town in the last third of the nineteenth century. Without the reference to herring, it would serve as well for many upcountry rural areas. Scores of declining New England towns and villages had reason to welcome tourism: Farming had become unprofitable, lumbering was exhausted, the whale fisheries had been destroyed, harbors were silting in.

Tourism helped to forge a new landscape out of the economic and social crisis that loomed over much of the Northeast in the late nineteenth century. Before the Civil War, tourists who had contemplated a trip to New England had envisioned it as a great hive of invention and progress. They had hoped to get a look at the imposing educational edifices at Harvard and Yale, to tour the technological and social innovations of Lowell, perhaps even to encounter some of the notoriously radical theologians, political theorists, and reformers around Boston. Southerners had always been drawn to the spots sacred to the American Revolution in Boston—and to the cool weather in the mountains. (Jefferson Davis himself was in the foothills of the White Mountains only months before the Civil War broke out.)

But by the last quarter of the century, an entirely new kind of tourism was shaping the region. This new tourism was driven by a profound "sentimentalization" of New England, a new vision of the region expressed in an extensive literature—from history and journalism to novels and short stories—and in architectural and landscape reforms that began to transform the appearance of many towns and villages. Out of these diverse cultural movements emerged a mythic region called Old New England—rural, preindustrial, and ethnically "pure"—a reverse image of all that was most unsettling in late nineteenth-century urban life.[8]

Much of New England by the last quarter of the century was in fact highly urbanized, industrial and ethnically diverse. Its city landscapes were dominated by huge brick factories where immigrants from every part of Europe sought work. But tourists sought out the isolated or remote parts of New England, looking for an imagined world of pastoral beauty, rural independence, virtuous simplicity, and religious and ethnic homogeneity. In these years, a trip to New England came to mean an escape from the conditions of modern urban industrial life, the very life New Englanders a generation earlier had been praised (and sometimes blamed) for creating.

When late nineteenth-century consumers grew uneasy with the world they had helped to make, tourism offered an escape from that world. Novelist Edward Bellamy was dazed and exhausted by the rapid pace of his work as a journalist in New York City. His doctor ordered him to Nantucket, where he could enjoy the almost ghostly silence the island had acquired after the demise of the whaling industry. William Dean Howells took his family to a Massachusetts farm for the summer, hoping to give his children the good food, fresh air, and simple joys he associated with rural life. Thomas Bailey Aldrich was profoundly uncomfortable with the side effects of industrialization. Appalled by the poverty and violence of the cities, but even more disturbed by the crowds of Italian, Irish, and Jewish laborers who thronged the streets, Aldrich made his summer home in the quiet and dignified old seaport of Portsmouth, New Hampshire, far from those alien crowds.

For the communities that became involved in this kind of tourism, the new image of New England made another kind of sense. Wherever they could, local promoters put their dilapidated buildings and grass-grown streets to work, creating "old Deerfield" or "romantic Marblehead." The last three chapters of the book explore the process by which tourism spread into the backwaters of New England, transforming the economic hardship and dislocations of those places into a powerful marketing device.

On the island of Nantucket, nostalgia for the golden age of whaling linked up with a desperate need for a new industry. Together, the two forces generated a vision of Nantucket that attracted affluent vacationers who yearned for the exoticism of a preindustrial island fantasy. In northern New England, state promotional campaigns attempted to play on the heart-strings of city people, evoking their fond memories of simpler childhood days to bring them "back home" to the farm for the summer. In dilapidated old coastal towns and villages like York, Maine, the aging "colonial" architecture attracted wealthy summer people eager for a piece of the past. Tourism thus played a crucial role in organizing relations between isolated backwaters and industrial centers, not only in the first stages of commercialization, but in its later stages as well, both for the countryside of the early nineteenth century and for failed port cities and abandoned farms at the end of the century.

By the end of the nineteenth century virtually the whole region had become a part of the tourist's landscape. And whatever entered the tourist's landscape also entered the terrain of the marketplace. This book is therefore a study of the spread of market relations—into the landscape, and even into regions of human consciousness. Each chapter tells a tale of a different kind of experience in the process of being transformed into a commodity. First, tourism itself became a commercial pursuit; then tourist industries brought natural scenery, leisure time, history, and even childhood memories and personal ancestry into the world of market transactions. Linking these chapters, too, is a single overriding narrative: the story of how tourism brought New England itself into the marketplace.

That is why I have chosen to make the region of New England the focus of this book. The Northeast is a good place to study tourism because its early and rapid economic development fostered the precocious growth of a wide variety of industries, including tourism. Before the last quarter of the century, however, tourists had paid little attention to New England as a region. The White Mountains had not, for example, been marketed as "New England" mountains, nor were any special "New England" qualities attributed to northern beaches. In the late nineteenth century, all that changed. Tourists discovered—indeed, they helped to invent—a new myth of Old New England, a vision of the region that has proved to be extraordinarily tenacious and attractive.

The process described here is by no means unique to New England. On the contrary, the late nineteenth century's reimagining of the region appears to be only one among several such transformations. The literature of the southern states reveals a similarly romanticized vision of the Old South already being fully articulated in the first half of the nineteenth century, and embellished by myths generated by the Civil War and Reconstruction.[9] A distinctly identifiable region of Appalachia emerged out of the turn-of-the-century explorations of local color writers, missionaries, and progressives.[10] My book is thus a kind of case study in itself: a case study of the process of "inventing" a region.

What about my choices of the individual case studies? Clearly, some very well-known places are not included here. Cape Cod, for example, New England's preeminent vacation region today, appears only briefly, in the epilogue. There is a simple explanation for that choice: Until very late in the nineteenth century, Cape Cod was regarded as a kind of New England outback, inhabited by unschooled savages with almost no contact with the outside world. Henry David Thoreau (who went out of his way to visit places no other tourist would go) visited Cape Cod in the 1850s. Writing about Nauset Beach, now one of the most popular beaches on the Cape, Thoreau reported only "a vast *morgue*, where famished dogs may range in packs." Thoreau knew what he was talking about when he predicted that "for a long time, [fashionable visitors] will be disappointed here."[11] The outer Cape remained more or less untouched by tourism for decades. Not until the age of the automobile did Cape Cod really come into its own.

A few other choices were equally easy to make. The first commercial tourist region in the country, the "fashionable route" to Niagara Falls and Saratoga Springs, was clearly the place to begin. The White Mountains were both the earliest and the most popular scenic region of New England before the 1870s.[12] After that the issues became more complex. The tourist industry became far more diverse and widespread in the second half of the century. At that point, the case studies become my own choices, reflecting the sorts of questions that have most intrigued me.

This book deals exclusively with middle-class tourists, for example, even though nineteenth-century tourist industries were by no means confined to a middle-class market. Newport, for instance, was the most famous of all American summer resorts for the rich. Among the pastoral retreats of the 1890s were palatial Berkshire "cottages" at Lenox and Stockbridge, as well as Vermont farm boarding houses catering to schoolteachers and saleswomen. Middle-class resorts up and down the coast were flanked by equally popular and successful resorts like Salisbury Beach on the north shore of Massachusetts, whose clientele was drawn from the working classes of the great industrial cities of the Merrimack

River. These places and people deserve study in their own right, and will amply repay any attention devoted to them.

My focus here, though, is on middle-class tourism. That apparently straightforward social category embraces a great deal of diversity—more than enough for one book, in fact. It includes a wide variety of people whose interests, values, and experiences were by no means identical: the artisanal families of Wesleyan Grove and the investors of Nantucket; the genteel tourists of the White Mountains and the speculators who housed them; the Vermont farm families and their city boarders; even the wealthy professionals who restored old houses in southern Maine. Tourism played a crucial role in the creation of a coherent middle class out of these diverse groups and in the negotiations that shaped the shifting boundaries of class over the century.

Moreover, tourism offers a way of looking deep into the heart of middle-class culture. Nineteenth-century tourists, like their twentieth-century counterparts, sometimes yearned for a world of beauty, harmony, order, and peace—even while they clung with both hands to the harsh, chaotic, and competitive world that had brought them prosperity. Sometimes that longing took forms that respectable tourists now repudiate: Today's wealthy patrons of Maine's southern coast do not speak as freely as their ancestors did of the "taint" of other races, for example. It is an easy task to expose the internal contradictions at the heart of tourism, to lay bare the naked social ambition beneath the scenic rhetoric of the 1840s, or the fear and racism beneath the nostalgia of the 1890s. But my aim here is not simply to expose these tourists' longings as racist, reactionary, or just misguided. It is to explore what is perhaps the ultimate contradiction of middle-class life in capitalist societies, in their century or ours.

Tourism offered tourists satisfaction through acquisition (in this case, the acquisition of *experiences*), emotional fulfillment through spending money. Throughout the nineteenth century, the product that tourism offered most consistently was some form of antidote to industrial capitalism. (In the 1830s and 1840s, marketing strategies were built around a set of perspectives that historians have called sentimentalism; later on, they made use of feelings we might refer to as antimodernist, or simply nostalgic.) Tourism offered remedies for crass commercialism, urban blight, labor conflict, the loss of permanence, the loss of community—every misery ever detected in the new industrial order. But far from opposing that order, tourism was an integral part of it.

From its beginning, industrial capitalism has been able to encompass the buying and selling of cultural experiences that seem to be outside it, or even in direct conflict with it. In spite of how scenic tourists saw it, tourism did not protect nature from commercialization; it intensified the commodification of both art and nature. Whatever nostalgic tourists thought, tourism was no more a return to idyllic preindustrial class relations than were the mills of Fall River. That was the ultimate irony of the industry: not that people hid selfish motives behind lofty rhetoric (which is after all not much of a discovery), but that they inevitably bought what they did not want. Nineteenth-century tourists turned away from the allure of the marketplace to travel straight into the arms of the marketplace. And that is a route that has become well-traveled indeed in the past two centuries.

1
TOURS, GRAND AND FASHIONABLE

The Origins of Tourist Industries in the United States, 1815–1830

The travelers, two young college students on summer vacation, were approaching Niagara Falls on horseback when they sensed something looming in the distance. "With mounting enthusiasm," they increased their speed in pursuit of the "tall misty cloud" in front of them. But the great white phantom was not the falls at all; it was "a vast white—hotel!" The hotel actually blocked their route: The travelers could not even reach the falls without going through it. "A long fence on either side the immense building cut [us] off from all approach. . . . there was no access to Niagara except through the back-door" of the "vast white hotel."[1]

This deliberately anticlimactic scene comes from a short story by the popular American writer Nathaniel P. Willis. The story was published in 1835, but the events it describes had actually taken place seven years earlier, when Willis was a college senior. Despite its title ("Niagara—Lake Ontario—the St. Lawrence") and its romantic beginning, the story was not about scenery. It was about tourism. The characters were not romantic travelers wandering through the wilderness. They were embarked on what was already well-known by the 1820s as the "fashionable tour."

15

The rage of the 1820s, the "fashionable tour" was a string of attractions that brought travelers from New York City up the Hudson River to Albany and "the Springs," then west by way of the Erie Canal to Niagara Falls. The latest transportation innovations, the beautiful scenery of the Hudson, the sublime experience of Niagara Falls, and the glamour of Saratoga and Ballston Springs all became part of a fashionable itinerary that enticed thousands to travel the "northern route." Perhaps in 1827 the great hotel at Niagara might really have taken Willis by surprise; in 1835 it could already have become an inside joke for the American reading public. By then no traveler would have come upon either Niagara Falls or the "vast white hotel" (which Willis's readers would have recognized as the Pavilion Hotel, on the Canadian side of the falls) by accident. The fashionable tour had become thoroughly institutionalized and familiar, as Willis knew; he had already reported in another story that the tour was "taken by almost every 'well-to-do' citizen of the United States."[2]

The fashionable tour offered few experiences that were entirely new. But Willis's story gave prominence to its most unsettling and intriguing novelty: the "vast white hotel" looming in the landscape. All along the fashionable route, new ways of organizing and marketing tourism were transforming both the tourist's experiences and the countryside that was being toured. Faster transportation, more luxurious lodgings, and above all, a new awareness of the tourist as a consumer—these were precisely what distinguished the fashionable tour from the traditional tours that preceded it, and that still existed in the rest of the country.

Traditional Tours

Traveling for pleasure was not new in the 1820s. By the beginning of the nineteenth century, the elites of English and European society had been touring for two centuries, traveling to the great cities and the watering places, and taking the Grand Tour of the Continent—traveling for health, education, and diversion. The Oxford English Dictionary dates the first use of the word *tourist* only as far back as 1800: "A Traveller is now-a-days called a Tour-ist." But as the dictionary's definition implies, the new word described an old habit. Even in the United States, where fashions lagged behind England by as much as a generation, genteel travelers had been coming and going for years.

Curious to experience firsthand the principles of a new government, the edges of a half-civilized world, or the economic workings of a potential

Fashionable hotels distinguished themselves from homely inns
and taverns by their cupolas, piazzas, and verandas, though
perhaps no hotel boasted a "colonnade" as monumental as this
one has been made to appear. This engraving, "Colonnade of
Congress-Hall," was the work of William Bartlett, who collaborated with Nathaniel P. Willis in the production of an elegant
two-volume book of illustrations and commentary on American
scenery. From N. P. Willis, *American Scenery, or Land, Lake, and
River: Illustrations of Transatlantic Nature*, vol. 1 (London: George
Virtue, 1840). Courtesy, American Antiquarian Society.

competitor, European travelers were relatively common in the United States as early as the end of the eighteenth century. More than seventy accounts of travels in the United States written by foreigners were published in the twenty-five years following the American Revolution.[3] These curious Europeans made a unique impression on their hosts at the time, and for long afterward. Their place in the history and literature of the United States is so firmly rooted that we do not even ordinarily think of them as tourists, a word that now seems too trivial for the weighty preoccupations of Alexis de Tocqueville's *Democracy in America* and Harriet Martineau's *Society in America*.

In fact, travelers like these were acting within a clearly defined and established European touring context. The Grand Tour of Europe, as it had evolved among the English gentry during the eighteenth century, was a well-known model for touring foreign countries. Grand tourists characteristically posed weighty questions on their tours. De Tocqueville, Martineau, and many of the other European commentators on the American scene were following that pattern in their search for political and cultural insights.[4]

Not all grand tourists were equally committed or capable, of course; many expressed simple curiosity as their motive. A retired British cloth manufacturer named Henry Wansey, for example, took a tour of the United States in 1794, as he recorded, simply because he desired to learn about a country "of which we hear so much, and know so little."[5] Wansey's curiosity was characteristic, and so was his decision to write a book about his experiences. But equally typical, behind such simple curiosity grand tourists often had professional motives: Wansey planned his tour around visits to American cloth factories, hoping to discover whether American manufacturing posed a threat to his own country's trade. Other grand tourists in America hoped to find grist for their own political or economic mills in the successes or failures of American governmental experiments.[6]

With such motives, grand tourists in America naturally followed an itinerary similar to that of travelers on the Grand Tour of Europe. The Grand Tour moved from Paris through the cities of Italy, while tours of America centered in Boston, New York, and Philadelphia. (A little later, Washington, D.C., and the new western cities might be included.) Such itineraries were designed to allow as much time as possible in major towns and cities, while moving with the greatest possible speed through rural areas. Wansey's tour of America, for instance, consisted of a total of five days on the road and seven weeks in the cities of Philadelphia, New York, Hartford, Boston, and Halifax, Nova Scotia.[7] American travelers, who knew the areas more intimately, might spend more time in smaller towns, but the focus was on urban life.

The reason was clear: In cities alone would one encounter the highest and best examples of the culture of a nation. In cities, grand tourists visited the same attractions that had made up Edward Gibbon's Grand Tour itinerary of Switzerland in 1764: "Churches, arsenals, libraries, and all the most eminent persons."[8] In other words, grand tourists visited the institutions and landmarks that expressed the special characteristics and the degree of civilization of the people of the country. In Boston, for example, everyone went to see Fanueil Hall (American Southerners especially were intrigued by this revolutionary landmark), the new State House, and later the monument at Bunker Hill. Captain Basil Hall described his 1827 tour of Boston as a "round of sight-seeing" that included "Rope-works—printing-offices—houses of correction—prisons—hospitals—penitentiaries—schools—almshouses—Navy and building yards," all of which "passed in quick, but not in careless review."[9]

Church services were especially popular in cities known for their unusual (to the tourist) religious beliefs. Robert Hunter, who took an extensive tour of the United States in 1785, described one of his Sundays in Boston as a round of visits to different church services: In the morning he attended the familiar Anglican service, but in the afternoon he went to a Quaker meeting house, where he and his friend "came out no wiser than we went in"; in the evening they went to an "Anabaptist meeting," where he "heard a most curious doctrine."[10] While in Quebec, tourists attended Catholic churches; in Boston, Unitarian services were a chief attraction. By the 1820s, in fact, the sermons of Unitarian minister William Ellery Channing had become one of the best-known attractions in Boston.

No matter what the attraction, however, grand tourists like Wansey and Hunter did not venture into foreign cities alone. They relied heavily on personal connections, made with the help of letters of introduction brought from home. When Henry Wansey wanted to investigate American cloth manufacturing, for example, he and his traveling companion first dined with "Mr. Charles Vaughan, a considerable merchant, to whom we had letters of introduction." With this new acquaintance Wansey went to the Unitarian chapel on Sunday and met the minister, Mr. Freeman, who then took him on a tour of "that pleasant suburb, Charleston [sic]" and its "curious wool-card manufactory."[11]

In this circuitous way, Wansey was finally able to get what he had come for—a private tour of a factory. But even the more public parts of the tours, the visits to Bunker Hill, Fanueil Hall, Harvard or Yale, were made within the context of personal social encounters. While later tourists would visit Bunker Hill with the help of a guidebook, Wansey toured Bunker Hill with his new acquaintance Mr. Armstrong, accompanied by one Captain Greatan, "an officer on the spot at the very time," who gave them what they thought was an eyewitness account of the battle.[12] At institutions like Harvard College or the Massachusetts State Prison at Charlestown, tourists used letters or local introductions to gain access to the heads of the institutions.

Often the directors themselves conducted tours: Henry Gallaudet, founder of the American Asylum for the Deaf and Dumb in Hartford, conducted tourists through his classrooms and explained the methods used there; Kirke Boott, the manager of the Lowell mills, took tourists through the factories.[13] Visiting colleges, a favorite pursuit of many tourists, was done by means of a personal letter of introduction to the college president. One tourist described her failed attempts to tour Brown University simply as a social engagement gone awry: "I called several times at the house of the President, but never found him in."[14]

Letters of introduction were based on the assumption that the bearer was a member of the gentry. One writer reported to the *Southern Literary Messenger*, for instance, that northern city-dwellers were not inhospitable, as some people had claimed. On the contrary, they offered a cordial reception to those with the proper credentials: "strangers who bring letters of introduction, or persons whose family, education and manners are such as to entitle them to move in their circles."[15] No formal barriers kept out tourists without the proper "family, education and manners," but without letters, and without the social background letters represented, this kind of tour could be difficult to make.

Anne Royall, the author of several travel books based on her tours of the United States, frequently confronted the difficulties of making such a tour without the proper credentials. Between 1824 and 1829, she made a living by traveling and selling the accounts of her travels in books like her *Sketches of History, Life, and Manners, in the United States.* (Royall was a widow; as a young girl from a poverty-stricken family, she had married a much older and much wealthier man whose relatives had contested the legitimacy of the marriage. Her claims to gentility were further jeopardized by the fact that she supported herself by traveling alone throughout the country—and by her sometimes abrasive personality.)

Royall did not scruple to report the difficulties that plagued her:

Respecting the public library of Albany, I am unable to say any thing. The Librarian, (the greatest boor except two in Albany,) would neither let me examine the books, or show me the catalogue.[16]

Obviously, Royall had her ways of gaining access to institutions and to well-known people; she recorded interviews with the elderly John Adams, the widow of John Hancock, Noah Webster, and many others.[17] Her persistence often paid off, and she rewarded generous treatment in the pages of her books. The keeper of the Hartford poorhouse, for example, received lavish praise; he was described as "one of the most benevolent of his species," and his wife as "the most feeling, angelic, transcendently kind and charitable of females."[18] But it is apparent even from Royall's own accounts that the informal social world she hoped to write about was often closed to her.

It was this social world that constituted the heart of the American grand tour. With the proper letters, a tourist could breakfast with presidents, dine with governors, and take private tours with the heads of institutions. Wansey, like many other tourists, was able to use his letters to gain access to the most distinguished officeholders:

Had the honor of an interview with the President of the United States [Washington], to whom I was introduced by Mr. Dandridge, his secretary. He received me very politely, and after reading my letters, I was asked to breakfast.[19]

Social engagements were a crucial part of the tourist experience, and letters of introduction were the means to those engagements.

In 1827, Captain Basil Hall, a British naval officer, and his wife, Margaret Hunter Hall, together with their year-old daughter and her nurse, began a fourteen-month tour of the United States and Canada. Captain Hall subsequently published *Travels in North America*, his third travel book. Mrs. Hall also wrote extensively about the trip in the form of letters to her sister, which were not published until the twentieth century.[20] From their combined accounts, it is clear that the dinner parties, balls, and teas described mainly by Mrs. Hall were the most time-consuming—and the most productive—parts of their tour.

Arriving in Boston, for example, the Halls sent out "upwards of twenty letters of introduction to different persons in Boston . . . and sat still to watch the result."[21] The result was that they spent most of every day for over two weeks in the company of Boston's social elite, attending church in their company, visiting institutions and landmarks in Salem, Lowell, and Charlestown under their guidance, and simply socializing with them: "Our friends seemed to vie with one another, as to who should be most useful or attentive to us, by placing balls, evening parties, and morning excursions at our disposal."[22]

During these social encounters, Captain Hall did the "research" that supported his conclusions about American society and character: He discovered, for instance, that "the most striking circumstance in the American character . . . was the constant habit of praising themselves, their institutions, and their country."[23] At dinners, parties, and social occasions of all kinds, tourists were able to get the kinds of information they wanted and to make the kinds of contacts they needed. But social events were more than a means to an end; they provided both the form and the content of these tours. Social interaction with the gentry of Boston, New York, or Philadelphia was the goal of the tour, not simply a way of reaching a goal.

Traditional grand tours were integral to the life of the gentry in both Europe and the United States. Traveling for such tourists was not very different from being at home. Tourists in a strange city engaged in the same activities that they would have in their own homes. They went to church, ate dinner, visited friends and relatives, and quickly established social networks that were extensions of their native networks. They also did the kinds of work they did at home, and that "work" was often almost indistinguishable from socializing.

Timothy Dwight, president of Yale College, took a number of tours in various parts of New England and New York between the mid-1790s and 1815. On those trips he gathered statistics, looked at scenery, and visited public buildings. But he also managed to preach every Sunday in the places he was touring and to use his social encounters to strengthen a professional network of clergy and other leading gentlemen in each region.[24] Combining business and pleasure in this way would not have seemed strange to anyone involved in it. In a sense, travel *was* part of the business of such travelers. Most simply, they gathered information with which to make professional decisions: Wansey inquired about cotton manufacturing, Dwight about the state of New England's morals. Scarcely less important, though, such travel served to develop and maintain the informal kin, social and professional networks that were crucial to men and women of the gentry.

Travel arrangements thus replicated everyday social arrangements.

From the "supply side" perspective, too, travel was an integrated part of the class and economic relationships of the city. The services used by such grand tourists were subsumed within the larger economic and social networks of everyday life. Grand tourists in America were guided through social networks with local residents. While traveling, their encounters were primarily with nontravelers: They stayed at inns with local politicians and traveled in stagecoaches with merchants and shopkeepers. (Indeed, the whole premise of English tours through the United States was that the travelers were encountering typical Americans in their everyday occupations. Otherwise, their generalizations were worthless.) They were waited on by their friends' servants—people whose daily work was integrated into the local economy, who were not workers in the tourist industry but simply local chambermaids, stagecoach drivers, or cooks. In other words, many tourists had been in the United States since the late eighteenth century, but there was no American tourist industry.

The Fashionable Tour

During the 1820s, in one part of the country, a radically different touring alternative became available. Along the "fashionable," or "northern" route, tourists encountered experiences unlike any they had encountered elsewhere: gigantic scenic attractions, unheard-of transportation innovations, and crowds of people who eagerly embraced the appellation "fashionable tourist." Here, too, for the first time, tourist industries in large numbers sprang up to accommodate the needs of a new style of traveler: Fashionable tourists required fashionable hotels, attractions, and accommodations. When travelers like Captain and Mrs. Hall left the cities of the East Coast to follow the northern route to Saratoga Springs and Niagara Falls, all these new arrangements made up a touring experience far different from the rest of their American travels.

The first segment of the fashionable tour took travelers from New York City up the Hudson River to Albany. The trip up the Hudson provided a wide array of attractions. Several were worth an afternoon's stop or a day's delay. At West Point one might view the cadets drilling or picnic on the grounds of the military academy. In the Catskills the famous Pine Orchard House, a mountaintop hotel above the town of Hudson, New York, was one of the first to take advantage of the fashionable tourist's new fascination with scenery. But the heart of the experience of traveling on the Hudson was the river itself and its own scenic display; along it one would see the splendid new country houses of wealthy New Yorkers, newly built and thriving villages, and cleared farmland alternating with the wooded peaks of the nearby Catskills.

Arriving in Albany, tourists had several options. Albany offered the politically inclined tourist the opportunity to visit New York's judicial and legislative institutions: Both the state Supreme Court and the legislature met there. (The well-connected tourist might dine with the governor or some other political leader.) The city also provided a diversion in its old-fashioned Dutch architecture, so different from the newness encountered on the rest of the fashionable route. But Albany was basically a layover on the northern tour. Not far away were the well-known towns of Saratoga and Ballston Springs, resorts built around mineral springs famous both for their health-giving properties and for their wealthy and stylish clientele. Stagecoaches ran from Albany to the Springs at all hours, and the two resort towns competed with one another for thousands of summer travelers.

West of Albany lay the second segment of the fashionable tour: the journey to Niagara Falls. The trip took several days in the 1820s, but thousands ventured it. The route lay directly west across the state of New York, following the path laid out by the builders of the Erie Canal, who were pushing the canal toward completion in these years. In its first stages, the route passed through prosperous towns, but farther west the villages became smaller and newer, giving way to rough year-old settlements and finally to forest (though even that was already laid out in building lots, as many tourists remarked). Most travelers spent several days or perhaps a week at Niagara Falls before returning, either by the same route or by a longer, more adventurous trip through Canada, up the Saint Lawrence River and down through New England.

It is no accident that the first tourist industries developed along this northern route. The region of the fashionable tour was fertile ground for all kinds of industrial and commercial development in these years. Along both the Hudson River and the Erie Canal, the traveler passed through regions teeming with speculative fervor. There the resources of the countryside were being exploited to their fullest extent, cities were being built overnight, and even farming was being subjected to new methods of organization, marketing, and measurements of profit and loss. Tourist industries, too, found the ground congenial. In fact, it is almost impossible to separate the growth of tourism from the commercial and industrial development overtaking the northeastern states.

In the first place, the fashionable tour owed its existence to a series of novel transportation systems, which existed nowhere else in the United States at the time. They provided the means to reach new tourist attractions, but they were also attractions in themselves. From New York City to Albany, tourists cruised the Hudson River by steamboat, the fastest and most luxurious of all the new inventions. Travelers were impressed, even intimidated, by the speed of the steamboats: One writer described his family as "sorely shaken and bamboozled" by the speed of their Hudson River steamboat.[25] From Albany, tourists could travel west by boat on the Erie Canal—in itself a major tourist attraction—or by stagecoach on roads paralleling the canal. The stagecoaches were the most efficient in the country, running on the best roads, although the ride was still bone-shaking enough to make a canal boat a pleasant alternative. The canal boats were extremely slow (the fastest averaged only three miles an hour), but many tourists found them picturesque and relaxing. And as early as 1833, a tourist could make the trip from Albany to Saratoga by railroad, one of the first to be built in the country.[26]

Remarkable though it was, technological innovation was not the only driving force behind the tourist industry's rapid expansion in the 1820s. Even more marked were changes in the organization of businesses to fit new markets. The great speed of steamboat travel, for example, was in part the result of new technologies, but it was even more the result of competition among rival steamboat lines, which was so keen that captains sometimes even refused to come to a complete stop while passengers disembarked. The great advantage of the land routes in upstate New York was not technological but organizational: They were designed to cater to the special needs of tourists. Captain and Mrs. Hall, for example, met the same coach driver "between the Springs and Albany" and again more than a thousand miles away, "far away in the south." As Captain Hall expressed it, the driver had become a "complete bird of passage,—carrying his horses and carriages to the south in the winter; and accompanying the flock of travellers back again to the north" in the touring season. In other words, he had become a specialist, organizing his business exclusively around the tourist trade.[27]

All along the new route, similar kinds of specialization took place. Hotels, built on speculation, were erected not in the centers of villages or on turnpikes, but near the new tourist attractions: on a mountaintop in the Catskills, or beside the newly discovered Trenton Falls in the woods outside Utica. Such hotels often offered an experience that further distinguished them from the village taverns and roadside inns. Although no rigorous distinctions were made among inns, taverns, and hotels in the early nineteenth century, the word *hotel* clearly indicated that the landlord was offering (or attempting to offer) a new style of privacy and luxury that had recently become popular in the larger cities.

In an inn, for example, one would be greeted and waited on by the landlord or landlady. In a hotel, one might expect to be greeted not by members of a family but by employees, perhaps a clerk. Inns were customarily referred to by the landlord's name: "Mr. Whitney's, at the sign of the Eagle," or simply, "Mr. Putnam's house." Hotels were given high-sounding names with no personal reference: "Congress Hall" or "Cataract House." Referring to a place as a hotel also implied a specialization that would exclude many of the traditional local uses of taverns, which customarily offered meeting space for clubs, political caucuses, even town meetings. Just as the words *traveler* and *tourist* suggest different histories, the word *inn* implied uses deeply embedded in tradition, while the word *hotel* implied a new sort of market transaction.

Visually, too, modern hotels were easily distinguished from old-fashioned inns, which could be mistaken for private houses if not for their identifying signs.[28] Hotels featured wings of long corridors lined with small single rooms to ensure privacy. (At least visual privacy: Nathaniel P. Willis reported in one story that the "bachelors' wing" of Congress Hall at Saratoga Springs was "of an airiness of partition which enables the occupant to converse with his neighbor three rooms off."[29]) Hotels sported cupolas and Greek Revival porches, from which the tourist might look at the picturesque "views" and "vistas" that were becoming popular. And they were extraordinarily luxurious, at least in their public rooms. One writer had a character respond to a new hotel at West Point: "Such mirrors—such curtains—such carpets—such sofas—such chairs! I was almost afraid to sit down upon them."[30]

This kind of clear distinction between hotels and inns did not exist at the time, of course. Old habits were not easy to break, even where the new trends were clearest: Basil Hall referred to the great white hotel at Niagara Falls simply as "Forsyth's Inn" rather than by its official name, the Pavilion Hotel.[31] But the direction of change was clear, as a Saratoga Springs guidebook for 1822 reveals in a description of one such transformation. The editor noted in the text that one of the older hotels, the Union, was in need of "repair." In a footnote, he reported that those repairs had been completed as he went to press, and the hotel could now be recommended as very "elegant." In fact, his description makes it clear that the "repairs" were not to the hotel's structure but to its image: The owner had added an additional wing of rooms and a "spacious piazza" fronted by ten Greek columns three stories high. These were changes clearly designed to bring the hotel in line with the new fashions.[32]

Hotels like the Union and the Pavilion played a key role in the economic development of surrounding regions. Typically, tourist hotels formed part of an interlocking development process that combined extractive industries, farming, land speculation, manufacturing, and tourism. Through hotels and their related businesses, the tourist industry brought capitalism into the countryside in conjunction with other industries—sometimes even before any other industries. In 1803, for example, Gideon Putnam moved to Saratoga Springs to clear-cut timber on land he had leased for that purpose. With his profits from the lumber, he established a sawmill. With his profits from the sawmill, he built a tavern, located near the newly discovered Congress Springs. Putnam died in 1811 after falling from a scaffold while building a new hotel, but not before leaving his mark on the region. It was he who laid out the streets of the village and excavated, marked, and protected the mineral springs that were to be its fortune.[33] (He may also have been responsible for the many tourists' complaints that the area around Saratoga was desolate, sandy, and shadeless, since he himself had hastened the area's deforestation.)

New tourist attractions seemed almost always to be connected with manufacturing. In the Catskills, entrepreneurs turned toward tourist development in the midst of the region most heavily involved in the extraction of hemlock trees for a large-scale tanning industry.[34] Around Niagara Falls itself were clustered not only tourist hotels but also "paper manufactories, saw-mills, and numerous other raw, staring, wooden edifices."[35] Elkanah Watson reported of Glen's Falls on the Hudson River that "[m]ill races . . . water-wheels . . . and their appendages of machinery, communicate variety to the enchanting scene."[36] Not everyone agreed that such juxtapositions were attractive, but virtually everyone acknowledged that they existed.

While fashionable tourists often described the surroundings of the most popular locations as wild and wooded, or pastoral and charming, in fact tourist regions must often have looked very much like other nearby places undergoing rapid development. Saratoga Springs was described in one 1831 guidebook as composed primarily of "clusters of frail board buildings which spring up among the clumps of trees lately felled in the skirts of the pine forest," a description more reminiscent of one of the new towns along the Erie Canal than an elegant resort.[37] Another guidebook featured an engraving of Saratoga Springs that showed the stumps of recently cut trees in the streets among the fashionable hotels. The half-destroyed forests surrounding the Pine Orchard Hotel were rarely noted by tourists, but it must have been very plain that the region was being developed in more ways than one.

In addition to their connections with manufacturing and extractive industries, hotels often provided a home base for spin-off tourist industries. Parkhurst Whitney built and enlarged the Eagle Tavern (which later became the Cataract House Hotel) on the American side of Niagara Falls. In pursuit of business for his hotel, in 1818 Whitney built a stairway to the foot of the falls, allowing guides to take tourists on thrilling excursions "behind the Cataract." And Whitney also operated a ferry below the falls in cooperation with the landlord of the Pavilion Hotel (Forsyth, the entrepreneurial landlord who had built the fence around the Falls on the Canadian side).[38] And wherever there were tourists, one could count on the sort of business Basil Hall described at Trenton Falls: "a sort of shed, near the prettiest part of the falls" on which "the letters B, A, R, were written up most conspicuously." Hall reported that such "odious places . . . stared us in the face every where . . . At the Cauterskill Falls we saw two; one on each side of the cataract."[39] New businesses like these characterized the fashionable tour along its entire route.

Development was transforming the region: Clear-cutting, hotel building, roads, and mills loomed as large in the landscape as the "vast white hotel" in Willis's story. But another side to this rapid development was less apparent in the landscape. The commercialization of tourism was perhaps most evident in the booming market for guidebooks and travel literature—a field that simply did not exist as a livelihood before the 1820s.[40] Now, guidebook writers carved out a new market for themselves, substituting their wares for a service that had always been part of the tourist's personal network of acquaintances and obligations.

Gideon M. Davison's pocket-size guide, *The Fashionable Tour or, a Trip to the Springs, Niagara, Quebeck, and Boston, in the Summer of 1821*, was the first to enter the market in 1822. Other writers soon followed suit. In 1825, Theodore Dwight, Jr., published the first edition of his guidebook *The Northern Traveller; Containing the Routes to Niagara, Quebec, and the Springs*. Local guides like Abel Bowen's *Picture of Boston*, first published in 1829, also began to appear. Davison's *Fashionable Tour* went through ten editions by 1840, including two French editions, published in Paris in 1829

The
Northern Traveller,
AND
Northern Tour,
with the Routes to
THE
SPRINGS, NIAGARA, & QUEBEC,
and the
(Coal Mines of Pennsylvania,)
— also —
TOUR OF NEW ENGLAND.

Fourth   Edition.

NEW YORK.
J & J. HARPER.
1831.

By the publication of the fourth edition of Theodore Dwight's guidebook, *The Northern Traveller*, the "northern tour" had expanded to include not only "the Routes to the Springs, Niagara, and Quebec," but also "the Coal Mines of Pennsylvania" and "Tour of New England." From Theodore Dwight, *The Northern Traveller* (New York: J. and J. Harper, 1831). Courtesy, American Antiquarian Society.

and 1834. Dwight's *Northern Traveller* went through seven editions by 1841. (Sometimes it was bound together with Henry Dilworth Gilpin's *A Northern Tour*, also published in Philadelphia in several separate editions.)

For printers and writers, entering the guidebook market was a step similar to that taken by traditional innkeepers who decided to invest in modern hotels. Gideon Davison, for example, was trained as a printer: He had ascended the traditional artisanal ladder as apprentice and journeyman before moving to Saratoga in 1817 to set up his own printing shop. In Saratoga he began to print and edit the local newspaper, the *Saratoga Sentinel*—still a traditional task of a small-town printer. But Saratoga Springs was not a typical small town. It was fast becoming one of the focal points of the fashionable tour, and Davison was becoming a leading entrepreneur in that trade. Shortly after his arrival in Saratoga, Davison began to edit and print a guidebook, with a new edition coming out each year. In town, he established a reading room and bookstore. Davison also played a crucial role in the construction of the railroad between Schenectady and Saratoga in 1833, an extension of the Albany and Schenectady line built entirely for tourists. (His connections with the Democratic "Albany Regency" made him an important lobbyist for the railroad and for the town.)[41]

Davison ended his career as Gideon M. Davison, Esquire. He gave up the newspaper in 1840 and bought the modern machinery necessary to launch a career as a book publisher. Perhaps that is also when he made his move uptown: In 1821 he had lived in a building he used as a combined "Dwelling House, Library, Reading-Room and Printing-Office," but by 1861 his shop (really a small factory now) was listed in "Long Alley," far removed from his house on Broadway.[42] His three sons were launched into the region's prosperous elite as a banker, a lawyer, and a railroad president. Davison's occupation and status were completely transformed. Both he and Saratoga Springs had found a national market.

For Theodore Dwight, Jr., entering the guidebook market was perhaps even more daunting than for Davison. Dwight was no artisan but a member of an elite New England family, accustomed to holding the reins of authority. The great-grandson of Jonathan Edwards, he was also the nephew of Timothy Dwight, president of Yale. Like his uncle, whose *Travels in New-England and New-York* was published after his death, Dwight wrote extensively about his travels. Theodore Dwight's career was marked by the same didactic purposes as his uncle's. In addition to his guidebooks, he wrote on child-rearing and pedagogy, and he exhibited his filial piety with his *History of Connecticut* and a book on his uncle's policies at Yale. His writing was marked by the same decided preference for all the products of New England. Dwight's guidebooks and travel literature argued for New England's superiority in virtually every field, including the beauty of its women, the fertility of its soil, and the musical abilities of its singers. (In fact, his commitment to New England Protestantism was so fervent that he has been assigned authorship of *Awful Disclosures of Maria Monk*, the infamous and influential anti-Catholic tract said to have inspired the Ursuline Convent Riot.[43])

But uncle Timothy Dwight had remained "President Dwight" all his life. His eminence as a travel writer was due primarily to the judgment of a later generation; his status during his lifetime derived from his profession and social position. His travels took place within a traditional network of friends and professional associates scattered over New England. His was a classic grand tour, designed to cement his relationships with his peers and to defend his side of a social and political controversy. Theodore Dwight's message may have been similar, but his medium was very different. This Dwight became a professional writer and magazine editor in New York City. He was a pioneer in the genre of inexpensive pocket-size guidebooks designed specifically for the use of travelers along the fashionable tour. Whatever messages his background and ideology prompted him to include in those guides (and there were many), he could not rely on his social standing to persuade his readers. Like Davison, he found himself competing for a national and anonymous market of tourists.

Springs and Falls

Writers like Davison and Dwight and developers like Forsyth and Putnam were transformed by the work they chose. They were also agents in the transformation of the regions they advertised. In the preface to the 1830 edition of *The Fashionable Tour*, Davison acknowledged the rapid change that had overtaken his region in the past few years. The development of the northern route took three forms, as he described it. It included the "recent gigantic internal improvements" (a reference to the Erie Canal) and the "increased facilities for travelling" (steamboats, stage lines and canal boats) that were well known to all his readers. But Davison added a third factor: "the development of new and highly interesting natural scenery." What did he mean by this oddly modern reference to scenic "development"? Along the fashionable tour, scenic attractions proliferated at an astonishing rate. Hotel keepers built staircases, entrepreneurs "discovered" new waterfalls, and guidebook writers incorporated new attractions into their itineraries. Davison was in a particularly appropriate position to understand the process of developing scenery. Although he did not admit it, he was one of its chief developers.

In its earliest stages, the fashionable tour offered as many traditional attractions as it did new ones. Church services in Quebec, legislative sessions in Albany, and battlefields near Saratoga were all featured in the early guidebooks. Alexander Bliss, a young lawyer on his honeymoon journey to Niagara Falls in 1825, seemed to find it natural to stop and view the new state prison in Auburn, New York. Indeed, it was not the only prison he and his bride had toured, although it was their favorite. They had "found it much more spacious than any prison we had before seen."[44] The first edition of Davison's *Fashionable Tour* reflected these traditional touring practices. Even in his section on Niagara Falls, Davison highlighted the battlegrounds of the War of 1812, writing six paragraphs on history to one lone paragraph on the scenery of the Falls.

William Bartlett's engraving, "Sing-Sing Prison and Tappan Sea," portrays the prison as one of the Hudson River's picturesque attractions, with fashionable tourists in the lower left-hand corner—sketching, strolling, and riding through the grounds. N. P. Willis, *American Scenery, or Land, Lake, and River: Illustrations of Transatlantic Nature*, vol. 2 (London: George Virtue, 1840). Courtesy, American Antiquarian Society.

But the logic of the ever-expanding itinerary of the fashionable tour gradually detoured travelers from such old-fashioned points of interest and directed them toward new scenic attractions. Theodore Dwight's guidebook highlighted scenic attractions from the beginning, perhaps reflecting his more genteel education and background, or his own travels in Europe (and perhaps catering to a more educated clientele). Davison never became as fluent with scenic description as his competitor, but he responded to his market with vigor. In successive editions of *The Fashionable Tour*, Davison gradually changed his emphasis to reflect and encourage the new touring approach. Each new edition of *The Fashionable Tour*, grew larger, expanding to include such scenic locations as Nahant and Mount Holyoke in Massachusetts, and even the distant White Mountains, until by 1830 the guide featured page after page of "lofty cataracts," "sublime scenes," and "romantic solitudes."[45] Many of the new attractions were not on the northern route at all but branched out through New England to take in the scenery of Vermont, New Hampshire, and rural Massachusetts.

The development of scenery, as Davison aptly named it, transformed the landscape of the northern route. And more than any other attraction along the northern route, scenery would also change the experience of tourism. In pursuit of scenic attractions, tourists traveled far from the urban centers of culture and commerce into the hinterlands. Fashionable tourists of the 1820s still visited cities, but travel in the countryside grew increasingly important. Traditional tourists on the American grand tour had followed the same routes and used the same accommodations as other travelers, but travelers along the northern route increasingly found themselves in the exclusive company of other tourists. The great white tourist hotels that sprang up in out-of-the-way places—at Niagara Falls, at Pine Orchard in the Catskills, on a desolate marsh at Nahant outside Boston—were not likely to cater to business travelers, lumber speculators, or migrant farmers, as had the old inns. In such places one would find only other tourists.

Tourism thus took on an element of fantasy, and scenic touring was designed to heighten that sense of unreality. In this regard, American tourists were following a scenic path that had been well worn by European tourists a generation earlier. In Europe, romantic writers had done much to transform "savage" mountain scenes into "sublime" or "picturesque" mountain scenery during the late eighteenth and early nineteenth centuries. Wordsworth in the Lake Country of northwestern England, Byron and Shelley in Switzerland, had helped to create a new cult of romantic scenery that by the 1820s was common to both Europeans and Americans.

American tourists in the early nineteenth century followed this European scenic system as closely as they could, arranging the different categories of scenery by the emotions they inspired. Niagara, of course, was the embodiment of the sublime: Its overwhelming power inspired awe, reverence, and humility in its viewers. William Stone recorded a typical response on an 1829 visit: "Arrived at Table Rock, we were struck silent and breathless for some moments with wonder and dread and admiration of this stupendous monument of Almighty power."[46] Many of the scenes along the Hudson, in contrast, were imagined as "picturesque"—rocky, irregular, alternating light and shadow—to be discussed using the language of the visual arts. Charles Augustus Murray described one scene on the Hudson in just such terms. It was "a picture more glorious than ever mortal pencil designed," but his highest compliment was that it looked just as though a "mortal pencil" *had* designed it: "the opposite bank . . . is variegated with farms, villages, and woods, appearing as though they had been grouped by the hand of taste rather than by that of industry."[47]

Some views fell into a third category, the classically "beautiful"—pastoral, orderly, smiling and serene. For many of the more conservative fashionable tourists, these were perhaps the loveliest scenes of all. They implied not simply landscape beauty, but progress, social harmony, and order as well. Theodore Dwight's guidebook linked social and aesthetic values in his description of the view of the Connecticut River valley from atop Mount Holyoke: It was a place where "nature, animate and inanimate . . . appear[s] in unison with the Christian's Sabbath."[48]

Tourists in search of such scenic experiences traveled not only into another part of the world, but into another world altogether, where they were not grocers or lawyers but tourists, where they suffered more discomfort, but also perhaps experienced greater luxury than at home, and where they sought out intense private experiences and were expected to allow them to be overwhelming. In this new touring world, letters of introduction and social networks were no longer needed. Along the northern route, the isolation of the tourist from ordinary urban networks, combined with the proliferation of new commercial tourist industries, made it possible to take the tour without elite social credentials, outside the informal social network used by traditional tourists. In this sense, too, the new popularity of scenic attractions made the difference. One does not need an introduction to Niagara Falls, nor can the lack of social contacts prevent anyone from seeing them. But as Willis's story of Niagara Falls made clear, if social networks could not exclude anyone, fences could. Owners of scenic property would demand not letters of introduction but payment.

Viewed from one angle, the fashionable tour challenged the elitism of traditional touring, offering the experience of touring to a larger, more inclusive group of tourists, but it also guaranteed that these tourists would become customers, that is, that they would pay for the services once provided through the informal networks and social privileges of the elite. Segregated from nontourists, traveling far off the beaten track, the fashionable tourist shed other identities and became primarily a consumer.

Although the fashionable tour may have opened the boats and hotels to more people, it was anything but egalitarian. Most simply, it separated those who could pay from those who could not. But it made far subtler distinctions as well. By its very nature it served to separate the fashionable from the unfashionable, the elegant from the blundering, the wealthy from the struggling, the rising stars from the falling. All consumers, it seems, were not created equal. Virtually all the contemporary accounts of the fashionable tour suggest, openly or indirectly, that many tourists were engaged in, among other things, an expensive gamble for social status.

Tourists appeared willing and even eager to discuss the social and financial inadequacies of their fellow travelers. With emotions ranging from amusement to fury, they pointed out contrasts between their own gentility and the social pretensions of the other people on the tour. William L. Stone, a New York newspaper editor who took the tour in 1829, was outraged by the socially inferior passengers he encountered on a canal boat outside Utica. He did not specify their background, but he made it clear that poverty was not their problem: In fact, he reported that they "imagine money a substitute for manners." What made him most angry was their demand for consideration as important people—as members of the gentry: "Upstarts . . . who in the consciousness of inferiority, are overanxious to claim respect . . . are the most disagreeable travelling companions in existence."[49] That may have been true, but such upstarts must also have been the most common traveling companions in existence, if one judges from tourists' accounts.

Naturally, not many tourists assigned such a motive to their *own* tours, but the popular writing of the 1820s and 1830s implied that the fashionable tour was above all else a search for status. In addition to his story about the "great white hotel," Nathaniel Willis wrote a number of other tongue-in-cheek stories of the fashionable tour, and he was not alone in his preoccupation. In 1828, James K. Paulding published an entire mock guidebook, *The New Mirror for Travellers; and Guide to the Springs*, designed as an exposé of the tour. In Paulding's depiction, the whole point of the fashionable tour was deception: "a good portion of the pleasure of travelling consists in passing for a person of consequence." To "pass for a person of consequence," Paulding outlined a vivid and elaborate set of ploys, descending even into the details of the fashionable tourist's clothing. "Gentlemen" were advised to have plenty of *outer* clothing— "forty pairs of pantaloons and waistcoats," twelve pairs of boots, six coats—but told that they could make do with two changes of shirts, or simply with "collars, with ruffles," that is, without a shirt at all, since collars were the only visible part of the shirt.[50] Paulding's representation of the fashionable tour as essentially an exercise in fraud was extreme, but his general interpretation was not.

Most of these kinds of critiques were aimed at one end of the tour's axis: at "the Springs," where the attractions were most clearly social, and where the transformation from the old model to the new was most glaring. Saratoga Springs might appear at first to be an anomaly, a last refuge for the traditional tourist. Travel to spas had been an important part of elite social patterns for a hundred years in England. Just as Bath did for London's elite, Saratoga and Ballston Springs fulfilled traditional social needs for southern planters and for New York's and Boston's mercantile elite.[51] The Springs were a well-known marriage market, and summer visits there may have cemented commercial relationships as well: At least once in the *Saratoga Sentinel* an advertisement appeared offering to "Commercial Gentlemen from the south or east, or any of the West Indian islands" the advertiser's services as a clerk.[52] When Jeremiah Fitch and his family traveled to Saratoga Springs from Boston in 1820, they must not have been surprised to encounter "about fifty Bostonians" already there, since almost all of those Bostonians were members of wealthy commercial families who made up their social circle at home.[53]

But Saratoga Springs in the 1820s was also in the process of transformation, by modern transportation, by the proliferation of hotels, and by guidebooks. By 1822 Saratoga Springs had become the center of Gideon Davison's thriving one-man tourist development agency. By the late 1820s quite ordinary people could reach Saratoga for a visit, at least if they were from New York. One was still likely to encounter wealthy elites from northeastern cities or from the South who spent a great deal of money traveling to the Springs: Jeremiah Fitch's sixteen-day trip from Boston to Saratoga had cost $186 altogether, most of which was spent during the twelve days on the road, traveling by private stagecoach and eating and sleeping at inns along the way.[54] But one was just as likely to encounter someone who had traveled to the Springs in two days and spent only a fraction of that amount. In 1820, the steamboat from New York cost only $6, the stage from Albany to Saratoga Springs, $2.50.[55] The total travel time from New York to Saratoga Springs was about forty-eight hours. When the railroad went through in 1833, total travel time between New York and Saratoga Springs was reduced to about seventeen hours, and the total cost was cut to less than $7.[56]

Once at the Springs, the new hotels could accommodate a wide range of tastes and pocketbooks. The Congress Hotel competed with the newer United States Hotel for the wealthy and fashionable. (By the late 1820s the United States Hotel won the loyalty of Martin Van Buren, an achievement that ultimately turned the tide for it.) The Union Hotel kept out of that contest, catering to those who were equally wealthy but devout, and to those who were actually visiting the Springs for their health—the "invalid saints," as Willis described them. A number of other hotels and boardinghouses in town cost as little as one third of the price of the great barracks-like resort hotels. Price alone might determine who stayed where, but guidebooks routinely gave hints on the implications of such a decision. Dwight presented a list of the principal hotels "in the order in which they are supposed to stand on the list of gentility," and then elaborated: "Congress Hall has generally enjoyed the highest favour among the most fashionable visitors at Saratoga. . . . Union Hall is the resort of those who wish to . . . participate more moderately in the amusements of the place."[57]

In spite of all this help—indeed, precisely because of all this help—it became notoriously difficult to distinguish between the genteel and the pretenders at the Springs. All one needed was the money (or the credit, as critics pointed out) to make a show at the most stylish hotel in town. Instead of remaining a place where traditional elite alliances were cemented, Saratoga Springs quickly became a competitive arena for tourists. While the Fitches might have known exactly who and what their fellow Bostonians were, how could they determine the credentials of other visitors at the Springs? At Saratoga, tourists put forward whatever claims they thought their behavior and money could sustain, competing for the

status that might once have been granted them on the basis of family connections and letters of introduction, or simply because they were there.

Nathaniel Willis, as alert to the absurdities of Saratoga as he was to
those of Niagara, illustrated this transformation of Saratoga with a story
in which a stagecoach clerk named Mr. Brown Crash finds himself snubbed
by a local beauty in his hometown and determines to wreak vengeance
upon her by "taking the tour." At Saratoga Springs he is able to convince
everyone that he is part of high society by the "elegance and ease" of his
manners, particularly in the way he "helped the ladies out of their carriages," a skill he has learned on the job, but which the fashionable world
interprets as evidence that he has been "brought up where there were carriages and ladies." "Brown Crash" returns to his hometown as Brown
Crash, Esquire, and is then able to marry a woman even more desirable
than his original choice; his social status is transformed by his successful use of the connections he made at the Springs.[58]

What was new about the fashionable tour was not the intimate relationship between tourism and social status. For generations the traditional grand tour had depended on just such an intimate relationship. The
fashionable tour was different because instead of reinforcing traditional
hierarchies, it blurred them. On the fashionable tour, anyone could compete in an anonymous, open-market struggle for status that was the corol-
lary of the commercial tourist industry's competition for customers.
"Brown Crash, Esquire" was in a sense the product of the work of "Gideon
Davison, Esquire," who had provided tourists with the opportunity to compete for status. No one knew Brown Crash at Saratoga—and that was precisely the way this entrepreneurial tourist wanted things. In its own way,
the fashionable tour provided tourists like Brown Crash with the same opportunities it had provided its entrepreneurial inventors.

A trip to the Springs could appear as the ultimate move in a gamble for
high status. As one 1827 poem summed it up:

> For we all had been taught, by tradition and reading,
> That to gain what admits us to levels of kings,
> The gentleness, courtesy, grace of high breeding,
> The only sure way was to "visit the Springs."[59]

But probably even "visiting the Springs" was not a sure way to attain such
status. Collectively, visitors expressed more bewilderment than admiration about the social world of the Springs.

Most visitors did not confirm the exaggerated descriptions of Paulding or Willis, who imagined shopkeepers, apprentices, and bankrupts at the heart of Saratoga's fashionable society. But they did describe what seemed to them to be a very mixed assemblage. James Silk Buckingham, another of the traveling English writers, reported that, "except the small shop-keeper and mere labourer, every other class has its representatives here." As it turned out, what he meant was not as inclusive as it sounds. "Every other class" broke down into three eminently respectable categories: "[t]hose who pride themselves on their birth, connection, and breeding," who stayed at the Congress Hall; those who had nothing to pride them-selves on except their money, "rich merchants from New Orleans, and the wealthy planter from Arkansas"; and judges, clergy, and professors, who stayed at the Union Hotel.[60]

That appears to be a reasonably genteel list. But Caroline Gilman de-scribed quite a motley crew at Congress Hall: a "lovely demi-French fam-ily" with rather exotic manners and dress, a lady wearing far too much jewelry, and a man who sat across from her at dinner in a checked shirt and no vest. She concluded with palpable relief that "generally speaking," there was "an air of propriety" at Saratoga: "The manners of the ladies are discreet, their dresses modest, and the men are unassuming."[61] What was she expecting if she found it necessary to compliment these fashionable guests on their conformity with the most basic rules of society? Such con-flicting evidence suggests a simple interpretation. The tour no longer pro-vided what touring had traditionally provided—a reliable index to social status.

Even as the fashionable tour turned the traditional uses of tourism up-side down, however, it began to provide alternatives. Along the fashion-able tour, aspiring tourists would have to learn new codes that would help them to win social status and distinguish themselves from other tourists. Brown Crash's manners helped him out, but they were not the whole an-swer. Paulding rated the desirable qualities for young men in his advice to "young ladies at the Springs": "Number one of the classes of beaux . . . consists of the thrice-blessed who are accommodated with full purses." Then came fashionable display: "the fortunate proprietor of a phaeton and four" was entitled to more attention than "the second cousin of an English lord," while "Well-dressed young men" were . . . "entitled to great consideration," and "Prize-poets, players on the piano . . . all that sort of thing" brought up the rear.[62] This was parody, but it mirrored a serious en-terprise. If one could no longer trust appearances, if elegant manners, ex-pensive clothes, and the leisure to take the tour no longer meant what they had once meant, what signs could be used by the real elites to recognize one another?

Finally, the real secret of the fashionable tour was to be discovered back at the other end of the route—at Niagara Falls. Everywhere in the writings of the fashionable tour, there were clues that let careful readers know what would become the new distinguishing feature of the genteel traveler. Even in Paulding's savage indictment of the entire fashionable world there was one status symbol he did not attack. In the section of the *New Mirror* designed for the trip up the Hudson River, Paulding advised his readers bent on a showy and false display of rank not to bother to look at the scenery: "Instead of boring yourself with the scenery, read the descriptions, which will be found infinitely superior to any of the clumsy productions of nature."[63] In this reversal is a broad hint: Gentlemen and ladies who wished to be considered truly refined, educated, and distinguished would meet with Paulding's approval by paying proper attention to the scenery of the tour. Scenic attractions had transformed the experience of touring, and scenery would provide new ways of making the tourist experience meaningful. For years to come, more than any other of the gauges of status generated by entrepreneurial tourism, aspiring tourists would learn to use the not-so-secret language of romantic scenery to demonstrate their education, their gentility, and their social status.

2
THE USES OF SCENERY

Scenic Touring in the White Mountains, 1830–1860

I n September 1832, on the last leg of his northern tour, Nathaniel Hawthorne passed through the Notch of the White Mountains. He was not the only traveler to take that route. Hawthorne found the rustic inn at the Notch filled with tourists. As he later reported in a sketch of his travels for *New-England Magazine,* it was a typical group of fashionable tourists: a mineralogist, a doctor, two newlywed couples from Massachusetts on the "matrimonial jaunt," two gentlemen from Georgia, and a young man with opera glasses spouting quotations from Byron.[1] By that autumn, the White Mountains were already well on their way to becoming an important offshoot of the fashionable tour.

At first glance, the Notch must have seemed an unlikely destination for such travelers. Unlike the much-admired Hudson River valley, the White Mountain region offered few of the smiling pastoral scenes or vistas of serene grandeur to which many fashionable tourists were drawn. In contrast to the pleasant suburbs of Boston or the prosperous farm regions of the Connecticut River valley, the White Mountains presented dreary scenes of half-cleared fields and primitive shacks. And northern New Hampshire, by reputation, was only half-civilized—a place where

Thomas Jefferson Crawford's inn, the Notch House, was typical of rural inns—small, isolated settlements where landlords combined farming with innkeeping. His brother, Ethan Allen Crawford, kept another inn just up the road, at the northern entrance to the Notch. William Bartlett's sketch became one of the best-known images of the White Mountains, combining the looming grandeur of the mountains with old-fashioned comfort and cheer. From N. P. Willis, *American Scenery, or Land, Lake, and River: Illustrations of Transatlantic Nature*, vol. 2 (London: George Virtue, 1840). Courtesy, American Antiquarian Society.

southern New England's vaunted habits of literacy, piety, and order faded into frontier slovenliness and godlessness.

But Hawthorne was not alone in choosing to visit the White Mountains. Wild, inaccessible, and primitive as the region was, it also offered something that sophisticated tourists craved. To "lovers of the wild and wonderful operations of Nature," as one visitor phrased it, the White Mountains "furnish unspeakable gratification."[2] In pursuit of that "unspeakable gratification," some enthusiastic tourists were willing to brave primitive inns, bad roads, and worse food.

Such enthusiasts were still in the minority in the United States, but their numbers were growing rapidly. More than a generation earlier, wealthy English travelers had developed a similar taste for the "wild and waste" places of Europe. The Alps, the Lake District of England, and the mountains of Wales, each in their turn had been transformed in the eyes of English tourists from "savage" mountains into "sublime" or "picturesque" mountain scenery.[3] Educated at Niagara Falls and along the Hudson, increasing numbers of American tourists were prepared to approach the mountains of New Hampshire with a new perspective, seeing in them not the rough roads and half-cleared forests of a frontier region but the sublime peaks and picturesque valleys of a romantic landscape. That new perspective was not the result of chance but of hard work.

Producing Scenery

Tourists in pursuit of romantic scenery at Niagara Falls or along the fashionable tour had been assisted by clusters of entrepreneurs who cleared land, built taverns, and published guidebooks. In the White Mountains, a similar business grew out of the efforts of the pioneering Crawford family. The Crawfords had moved to the White Mountains at the beginning of the century, attracted both by the cheap land and by the possibilities of opening the region to trade. In one sense, the Crawfords were typical backwoods pioneers, clearing land, planting crops, and fighting off the ravages of blizzards, floods, and wild animals. But their location in the Notch of the White Mountains, however isolated, was strategic. The Notch was cold, forbidding, and remote, but it was also the most direct trade route between the city of Portland, Maine, and the hinterlands of northern New Hampshire and Vermont.

The Notch was usually impassable to heavy commercial traffic, but the packed snows of midwinter often made it possible for wagon trains to get through the pass, providing an opportunity for trade that was seized by Portland merchants. Abel Crawford and his sons Ethan Allen and Thomas Jefferson Crawford did everything they could to encourage the growth of that trade. In 1803, the state of New Hampshire granted a turnpike contract to a group of subscribers from Portland, and Ethan Allen Crawford went to work building and maintaining the road through the Notch. In the next few years, the family built three inns along the road to accommodate the wagon drivers and lumberjacks who used the Notch in winter.

Gradually, the Crawfords noticed a new sort of customer in the Notch. A few curious travelers were beginning to make their way through the Notch to climb Mount Washington, then reputed to be the highest mountain on the continent. The Crawfords were quick to grasp the potential of this new trade. During the 1820s, they took control of it and created central roles for themselves as guides, innkeepers, road builders, and promoters of the region. Ethan Allen Crawford in particular took the initiative in developing the tourist trade. In 1819, he cleared the first footpath up Mount Washington. In 1827, he began to improve that path to make it usable for horseback riders. Working almost alone, year after year, Crawford labored to extend the path farther up the mountainside. At the same time, he advertised his family's inns and the surrounding attractions in regional newspapers.

When Nathaniel Hawthorne decided to write a sketch of his White Mountain tour, it was no accident that he described not the summit or even the scenery, but his night in Ethan Allen Crawford's old-fashioned inn. Crawford was the inventor, the organizer and the driving force of the White Mountain tour. In addition to his inn's food and shelter, he provided an endless variety of other services. As the guide for travelers ascending Mount Washington, he led them on the proper paths, pointed out the views (when they were visible), and told tales of his life in the mountains. One tourist described an 1832 ascent of Mount Washington led by Ethan Allen Crawford, in which all eight tourists were riding horses he had somehow managed to locate, while Crawford himself walked beside them. Three of the eight tourists were even wearing Crawford's clothes, one Bowdoin student "in a huge woollen coat of Crawford's, hanging about him like a meal-sack over an iron bar."[4]

A keen sense of the value of his landholdings as scenery fueled Crawford's work. He understood that his visitors were intrigued by the "savage" and "romantic" scenery that surrounded his home, and he was adept at accentuating the "wild" elements he knew would please his clients. Like the guides of the Swiss Alps, who would fire a cannon to set off avalanches for the benefit of tourists, Crawford greeted stagecoaches at his inn by firing a shotgun or blowing a tin horn from his doorstep to produce the haunting echoes that would impress tourists with the grandeur of the surrounding mountains. He kept a bear in a cage near his door and maintained a deer park and tame wolves at the inn.[5]

The Crawfords got their first big break in 1826, when it seemed as if the mountains themselves were cooperating by providing a brush with wilderness even more thrilling than Ethan Allen Crawford's bears and wolves. In the summer of 1826, one of the few neighboring families in the Notch was completely destroyed by a tremendous rockslide following days of heavy rain. The tragedy of the Willey family made national news that year, and the publicity it generated created a national reputation for the White Mountains' wild scenery. The Willeys' story was fascinating to would-be tourists in the 1820s, not only because of the sensational and violent way the family died, but also because the catastrophe appeared to be the result of the direct intervention of God through the power of nature: Even though the family had had time to escape their house, they had run directly into the path of the landslide. The house, which remained standing just as they had left it—ashes in the fireplace, beds unmade—became a tourist attraction overnight.[6]

Ever on the lookout for publicity, Crawford noted that this "great and wonderful catastrophe" had "caused a great many this fall to visit the place."[7] He made sure that the site of the tragedy was appropriately marked. Travelers through the Notch could experience for themselves the lonely isolation of the family's home beneath the towering mountain. They could tour the house, place a stone on the spot where some of the bodies had been recovered, and imagine the terror of the family who "fled . . . from the house to seek their safety, but thus threw themselves in the way of destruction."[8]

For Ethan Allen Crawford, the Willey family's tragedy provided a much-needed increase in business, but it could do no more than hold at bay his own family tragedy. Like many pioneering entrepreneurs, Crawford lived to see the tourist trade he had founded carried on by rivals. Illness, competition, and debt drove him out of the mountains in 1837, though his father and brother remained in the Notch.[9] By that time, the scenic tourist trade Crawford had worked so hard to encourage was well established and growing fast in the hands of rival developers.

By that time, too, local developers were beginning to receive help from a very different source. After the Willey landslide made national news, the Notch began to attract large numbers of visitors. And these were not just any fashionable tourists. Between 1827 and 1839, the list of visitors recorded in the Crawford guestbooks reads like an early nineteenth-century Who's Who. Thomas Cole, Daniel Webster, Washington Irving, Ralph Waldo Emerson, Nathaniel Hawthorne, James Russell Lowell, Charles Sumner, and Henry David Thoreau all recorded their visits to the Notch in these years, along with dozens of other eminent scientists, teachers, and writers.[10]

Among these distinguished or soon-to-be distinguished visitors was a cluster of ambitious young writers and painters who hoped to use the scenery of the mountains to further their own goals. Nathaniel Hawthorne, for example, was not making the northern tour simply to avoid cholera in the summer of 1832. As he explained only half-jokingly in a letter to his friend Franklin Pierce, he made the "northern tour . . . on account of a

book by which I intend to acquire an (undoubtedly) immense literary reputation."[11] And Hawthorne was not alone. When Thomas Cole visited the
White Mountains in the summer of 1827, he went on the advice of his patron, Daniel Wadsworth, in search of scenery to paint that would make
him famous. Cole wrote to Wadsworth from the mountains that "in such
sublime scenes . . . man sees his own nothingness."[12] But he must also
have seen the possibilities of his own greatness. His paintings of the bet-
ter-known Catskills had already brought him his first public recognition
and his first patrons.[13]

Cole and Hawthorne, along with dozens of other would-be professional
writers and painters, used the Willey tragedy for all it was worth. Both
Cole, in his 1839 painting "The Notch of the White Mountains" (reproduced
for a large audience in Willis and Bartlett's *American Scenery*) and
Hawthorne, in his 1835 story "The Ambitious Guest," took advantage of
the national interest in the Willeys to draw attention to their own work.
In the meantime, both works added immeasurably to the fame of the White
Mountains. The "ambitious guest" featured in Hawthorne's short story
was actually traveling in the White Mountains with the vague hope of finding some way to achieve undying fame. In real life, too, ambitious young
men and women were turning to American scenery for help in carving out
careers.

One such young woman, Sarah Josepha Hale, clearly spelled out the opportunity that scenery offered to artists. She echoed a popular critique
of "the barrenness" and "vacancy" of American scenery, which, as she put
it, arose from "the want of intellectual and poetic associations within the
scenery." European scenes were admired because they called forth a wide
variety of feelings, memories, and attachments—"associations" that
would draw the observer into an emotional relationship with the object,
that would give the observer an "interest" in the scene. What American
scenery needed, then, was associations, or as Hale put it, the "light of song
poured over our wide land, and its lonely and waste places 'peopled with
the affections.' "[14]

Hale suggested that writers and artists could take on the task of endowing American scenes with "interesting associations," of giving to them
the meaning and cultural significance of older, historically richer European
scenes—in short, of *developing* American scenery. (That is precisely what
Wordsworth and Byron had done in Europe, but by the 1830s the process
had worked so well that its consequences seemed a natural part of the
landscape of the Alps and the Lake District.) Romantic artists and romantic

scenery would thus depend on one another. Scenery would become more popular, and artists (including Hale herself, who followed up her prescription with a romantic story of her own, set at Lake Winnipesaukee) would be invested with an important and exalted—even patriotic—occupation.

Hale's prescription would have seemed a natural one in the 1830s: Scenery and artists were already closely linked in the minds of many Americans by then. When Ralph Waldo Emerson published his famous essay on "Nature" in 1836 (four years after his trip to the White Mountains), he articulated a similar vision of the relationship between scenery and artists. At the very beginning of the essay, Emerson made a crucial distinction between two ways of seeing the land. He distinguished the "stick of timber of the woodcutter from the tree of the poet"—in other words, the mundane uses of *land* from the poetic uses of *landscape*. "The charming landscape which I saw this morning is indubitably made up of some twenty or thirty farms. Miller owns this field, Locke that, and Manning the woodland beyond." But none of these farmers owned "the landscape." That was a new sort of property—"a property in the horizon," as Emerson called it—"which no man has but he whose eye can integrate all the parts, that is, the poet."[15] Farmers owned the productive land, but only a romantic artist could "own" the landscape. Only a "poet," with all the powerful connotations of that word, could truly understand and interpret landscape.

What Hale and Emerson both knew but chose not to comment on was that scenery was fast becoming, not only a field for artists, but also a marketable commodity. Emerson was arguing that the "poet's" sort of property was not for sale. But he was wrong: By the 1830s, "property in the horizon" was fit to be exploited by any Miller, Locke, or Manning with the imagination and the capital to develop it.[16] And, although Emerson tried to segregate the domain of romantic artists and romantic scenery from the world of market transactions, the poet's uses of the landscape had property value in the market, too.

From this perspective, touring artists like Hawthorne or Cole were simply another kind of scenic entrepreneur. They hoped to create careers for themselves out of their mediation between the landscape and its viewers. But White Mountain scenery offered them something more than it offered the Crawfords: not only work but a vocation, the exalted profession of Emerson's poet. In that sense, they had little in common with the hardworking innkeepers of the Notch, who had to divide their energies among clearing roads, harvesting crops and guiding tourists up Mount Washington. (And, of course, the careers of artists did not depend on the successful promotion of a single place. *Any* landscape could serve as grist for their mills.)

Still, the two groups did share a common enterprise: the creation of a national market for scenery. Crawford's back-breaking work clearing paths and roads was complemented by the work of painters like Thomas Cole, who transformed White Mountain scenery into art, and by writers like Hawthorne and Hale, who developed the literary associations that made its scenery attractive. In the largest sense, even Emerson shared in this enterprise. His groundbreaking essay not only described but encouraged the growth of the cult of scenery in the United States. His elevation of scenery into a romantic experience was almost an advertisement for scenic touring, promising that a person who valued and understood the landscape could expect to be considered especially gifted (a poet, in fact). That was a very tempting promise for tourists in the early nineteenth century.

Mass-producing Scenery

All these pioneering scenic enthusiasts, from the trailbreakers to the painters and poets, shaped the American understanding of White Mountain scenery in the 1830s. But their monopoly was short-lived. Between 1840 and 1860, the White Mountains became one of the most popular scenic regions in the country, and the White Mountain tourist industry grew explosively. Face-to-face, small-scale transactions between promoters and tourists were rapidly replaced by large-scale tourist industries with higher technological and capital requirements. During the 1830s, a visit to Crawford's had been synonymous with the White Mountain experience. By the 1840s, the rustic Crawford inns were being replaced by a whole network of grander and more luxurious accommodations. And by the 1840s, too, the trickle of paintings, essays, and stories created by a handful of individual artists were in danger of being overwhelmed in an increasingly voluminous outpouring of prints, travel literature, and guidebooks.

One of the clearest signs that a new commercial era was beginning was the takeover of Ethan Allen Crawford's inn by a merchant from Maine named Horace Fabyan. Unlike the developers who were to follow him in the White Mountain hotel business, Fabyan was not a large-scale corporate investor. But he was no mountain man, either.[17] A provisions dealer and unsuccessful land speculator, Fabyan invested in White Mountain hotels in anticipation of the completion of the Atlantic and Saint Lawrence Railway, which was to pass through the White Mountains only eight miles from Mount Washington on the east. When Ethan Allen Crawford was forced out of business by debt, Fabyan took over the Crawford House in 1837 and the Willey House in 1845.

The Crawford House, which Fabyan renamed the Mount Washington House, accommodated over a hundred guests by 1845 and the newly rebuilt Willey House over fifty. The humble accommodations of the Crawford inns, where a tourist might expect to share a bed with a stranger, or even to be offered a blanket on the floor in the attic, were gradually replaced by the luxuries and comforts of urban hotels.

Fabyan, too, eventually suffered the common fate of tourism entrepreneurs in this period: Outmaneuvered on several fronts, when his Mount Washington House burned down in 1853, he was unable to rebuild because of legal battles over the land on which it stood.[18] But by now the region's tourist industry no longer depended on a single entrepreneur. As Fabyan established his two modern hotels in what was now becoming known as the Crawford Notch, other areas also began to bill themselves as part of the White Mountain tour. In the Franconia Notch to the west, the Lafayette House opened in 1835, followed by the Flume House in 1848. By 1853, when the Atlantic and Saint Lawrence Railway was completed, two new hotels had been built on the eastern side of Mount Washington, an area previously little known to tourists. One of these hotels, the Alpine House in Gorham, had been built by the railway itself. The manager of this hotel also ran the Summit and Tip-Top houses, two small hotels built on the top of Mount Washington in 1852 and 1853.[19] By the end of this railroad-inspired building boom in the mid-1850s, there were nine hotels in the interior White Mountain region. These hotels, added to those in North Conway and the other surrounding villages, could accommodate as many as two thousand tourists at a time.[20]

Railroads began to reach toward the White Mountains in the mid-1840s, not initially as accommodations for tourists but as commercial conduits between the port cities and the northern hinterlands. In spite of that, railroads had an immediate impact on the White Mountain tourist industry. Between 1850 and 1855 the railroads reached the foothills of the mountains as close as Littleton on the west, Lake Winnipesaukee to the south, and Gorham on the east, bringing travelers within eight miles of Mount Washington.

The Lafayette House in the Franconia Notch was not as large and luxurious as its successors would be, but it was more modern than the Crawfords' inns: It had a porch, an elegant name, and rows of private rooms. It was built in the Franconia Notch, to the west of the Crawfords' notch, in 1835. In 1853, a new owner would replace it with a much more elaborate hotel and rename it the Profile House, in honor of the Franconia Notch's greatest attraction. William Oakes, "The Franconia Notch with the Lafayette House," plate 8, in *Scenery of the White Mountains* (Boston: Little and Brown, 1848). Courtesy, American Antiquarian Society.

Within the region, a unique social environment began to take shape. Frederika Bremer wrote in 1849 that although "the whole of this mountain district is very wild, and there is scarcely a dwelling to be seen excepting the hotels for travelers," the place was

overflowing with noisy, unquiet company . . . and . . . all kinds of noisy pleasures. . . . Champagne corks fly about at the hotels, gentlemen sit and play cards in the middle of the day, ladies talk about dress-makers and fashions.[21]

By 1862, Anthony Trollope was able to report (with only a little exaggeration) that the White Mountains were "dotted with huge hotels, almost as thickly as they lie in Switzerland."[22]

On the cultural front, too, the industry grew rapidly. Lucy Crawford's *History of the White Mountains from the First Settlement,* published in 1845, marked the beginning of a new generation of White Mountain publications, devoted to publicizing the region for a mass market. Lucy Crawford was Ethan Allen Crawford's wife; the couple wrote the book together in the hope of financing their return to the White Mountains. (Once again, others reaped the reward for their work. Crawford did manage to live the last few years of his life near his old home in the Notch, but the book's fascinating tales of the pioneering adventures of its authors fueled an interest in White Mountain legends that paid off primarily for other developers.)

Mass-produced visual images of the White Mountains were becoming increasingly available to would-be tourists. Twelve White Mountain scenes were included in the handsome two-volume series *American Scenery,* an 1840 collaboration between William Barrett, a well-known English engraver, and Nathaniel P. Willis, who wrote the accompanying text. The botanist William Oakes published his collection of lithographs and essays, *Scenery of the White Mountains,* in 1848. It was followed by the first accurate map of the region, published by George P. Bond in 1853 together with five lithographs taken from Benjamin Champney drawings.

In the 1850s, a flurry of White Mountain guidebooks appeared: Benjamin Willey's *Incidents in White Mountain History;* John Spaulding's *Historical Relics of the White Mountains;* Samuel C. Eastman's *Guide to the White Mountains;* and finally, the definitive guidebook for the period, Thomas Starr King's *The White Hills.* Most guidebooks were locally produced, by writers with close ties to the region and its tourist industries: Benjamin Willey was the brother of the famous Samuel Willey, whose family's tragic deaths had created one of the prime tourist attractions of the mountains; John Spaulding was the manager of the Tip-Top House on Mount Washington; Samuel C. Eastman and his brother wrote and published books in Concord, New Hampshire. Along with hotel keepers like Horace Fabyan, they were the new professionals in the mountains.

During the 1850s, the White Mountains also began to receive more extensive notice in regional and national guidebooks. Portland's *Guide Book of the Atlantic and Saint Lawrence Railroads,* published in 1853, was designed primarily as a travel guide to the White Mountains (although its main emphasis was on the trains themselves, which it said combined the elegance of parlors with the "rapidity of thought"[23]). Appleton's first edition of the *American Guidebook* (1846) had featured two pages on the White Mountains as part of a tour of New England. By the 1857 edition (with the new title *Appleton's Illustrated Handbook of American Travel*), the White Mountain tour had taken a leading position in the national travel circuit. It was one of five itineraries set out as "package tours" for New York travelers.[24]

The definitive guidebook for the period, Thomas Starr King's *The White Hills,* came out in 1859, marking the high point of this formative period in White Mountain tourism. Starr King was not a local promoter but a Unitarian minister from Boston who had made scenery his second profession. He made a name for himself by promoting the area in the Boston *Transcript* and in his guidebook. (Starr King later moved to San Francisco and performed the same services for the Yosemite region.) *The White Hills* scarcely fit the guidebook category at all: Too large to carry around on a tour, the book was bursting with literary references, sketches, and inspired prose. Along with the new hotels and trains, Starr King's elegant "coffee-table" volume epitomized the success the White Mountain trade had achieved by 1860. From its local, small-scale origins, the industry had evolved into an enterprise of mass-produced elegance, speed and luxury.

Consuming Scenery

The history of the production of White Mountain scenery—what might be called its supply side—is a dramatic story in its own right. But what about its "demand side"? What was it that brought all those tourists to the White Mountains, by the dozens at first, by the thousands in the 1850s? At first glance, this question may not seem difficult to answer. We might assume that nineteenth-century tourists went to the White Mountains in search of what late-twentieth-century tourists find there: perhaps a back-to-nature experience, solitary hiking trails, or superb views. But that was not quite the case.

For one thing, the most common activity of early scenic tourists appears to have been not hiking or riding but writing. Scenic touring was more than anything else the work of words. Not only ambitious writers but also tourists with no ambition to become published authors wrote extensively about their scenic experiences, in their private journals and even in hotel guestbooks. When they were not writing, they spoke to one another about scenery, quoting poetry or extemporizing. Harriet Martineau's 1827 White Mountain tour included "sketching, reciting, and watching" in the Franconia Notch and a drive through the Crawford Notch that ended with her group "deep in the mutual recitation of poetry."[25] Hawthorne's group of tourists in the Notch included a "well-dressed young man" who appeared to be quoting "some of Byron's rhapsodies on mountain scenery." If not involved in "mutual recitation," tourists might write poetry of their own in the guestbooks of their inns, as Hawthorne's Byronic young man did at Crawford's.

The heart of the early tourist experience was the expectation that tourists, like professional artists, would generate poetic associations with the landscape they encountered. Nor would just any associations do. There were conventions for this process—conventions that had been devised in Europe—and they were usually followed with some care. Such scenic conventions were already established when a Boston editor recorded his responses to a trip through the Notch in 1826:

No words can tell the emotions of the soul, as it looks upward and views the almost perpendicular precipices which line the narrow space between them; while the senses ache with terror and astonishment, as one sees himself hedged in from all the world besides.[26]

Here is the conventional language of the "sublime," so often employed in the Notch: Terror, astonishment, and dizziness were the usual responses called forth by craggy peaks, abysses, and narrow passageways.[27] A tourist might also encounter the "picturesque," a term used to designate wild, irregular, but charming landscapes. The "beautiful" referred specifically to scenes of symmetry, serenity, and grace, and was usually encountered only at lake scenes in the mountains. In general, the sublime held sway throughout the White Mountains.

Sublime scenery was in some sense overwhelming. It inspired the viewer with awe, reverence, perhaps even fear.[28] Towering mountains, a massive waterfall, an overhanging cliff, could all serve as reminders of one's own insignificance and weakness in the face of larger forces. In an encounter with the sublime, the observer would be deeply moved by the overwhelming power of the sight. Hence the most common convention of all, the denial of the power of words to express the experience. In the Boston editor's words, "no words can tell the emotions of the soul."

Not everyone put a great deal of effort into applying these conventions. Some travelers were satisfied with a phrase tossed off in the midst of a detailed account of inns and meals: "We reached Bartlett . . . at 9 oclk [sic] & had an excellent breakfast. . . . And soon after leaving this house, the scenery began to assume a grand & sublime appearance."[29] Others made only the gesture of avowing their inadequacy to the task: "It is impossible for a person who has such a weak mind as mine to describe the view that we there had of the beauties of nature."[30] But few travelers before mid-century wrote of their scenic journeys without at least a perfunctory gesture toward the language of scenery: "I should advise everyone who wishes to see the sublime and beautiful to come to the White Mountains."[31]

And many did work hard to express their experiences properly. Samuel Johnson was a young Harvard graduate about to enter divinity school when he took his White Mountain trip in 1842. He wrote a lengthy private travel journal devoted almost entirely to scenic description. In a typical passage, Johnson gave an account of the sublime scenery of the Flume (a narrow river gorge in the Franconia Notch): "Nothing can be grander than this mighty work. . . . [T]his tremendous abyss . . . made us dizzy when we looked over into the whirling stream." The Flume made Johnson acutely aware of the power of God—"At Creation or by some terrible convulsion was it cleft down to the mountain's heart, as by a sword"—and nature—"the winds have made havoc, wild & terrific, with the woods that overhang the steep."[32]

Some scenic tourists seemed chiefly aware of the power of their own emotions. Caroline Barrett began to keep a diary as a young schoolteacher in southern New Hampshire. Like Hawthorne's character with the opera glasses, she quoted extensively from Byron, copying page after page of "Childe Harold" into her diary. Often, her descriptions focused on her own emotional state in regard to the scenery: "the . . . sweet picture . . . haunts me like some strain of music whose melody falls with strange power upon the enraptured ear." Descriptions were often interrupted by emotional exclamations: "Yesterday I rode through a wild and beautiful part of the surrounding country—Oh! nature how beautiful—how sublime are thy scenes!" Even a familiar view of Mount Monadnock evoked a passionate response: "Never before did I gaze upon the sublime picture with such rapture."[33]

In retrospect, such language sometimes seems pretentious and overwrought. It is certainly easy to mock. The late-Victorian British writer Samuel Butler, for one, wrote a wickedly accurate parody of such sentiments, in which he had his mock traveler record in his diary, "I was so overcome by my feelings that I was almost bereft of my faculties, and I would not for worlds have spoken after my first exclamation till I found some relief in a gush of tears."[34] Even at the height of its popularity, scenic language was subjected to ridicule. The much-quoted Byron himself, as early as 1821 interrupted his own elaborate description of the Oriental splendors of an Ottoman court to mock the fashionable appetite for travel and scenic descriptions:

> I won't describe; description is my forte,
> But every fool describes in these bright days
> His wondrous journey to some foreign court
> And spawns his quarto and demands your praise.
> Death to his publisher, to him 'tis sport,
> While Nature, tortured twenty thousand ways,
> Resigns herself with exemplary patience
> To guidebooks, rhymes, tours, sketches, illustrations.[35]

But if Byron mocked the scenic sensibility, he was nevertheless acutely aware that "description was his forte," and that it was his yearning evocations of romantic nature that had made him the early nineteenth-century equivalent of a rock star. As he well knew, scenery and the emotions it engendered were of tremendous importance to the travelers and would-be travelers who modeled their writing on his poems.

What was it that inspired scenic tourists to the flights of rhetoric displayed even in their private writing? George Templeton Strong recorded a charming and revealing passage in his diary during an 1843 trip to the Catskills. He began quite solemnly and conventionally, by comparing the hills that formed the background of his view to the "emblems of everything that's true and unchangeable, of the Awful Realities below and amid which the little noisy Stream of Life goes fretting onward and disappears." But he concluded rather less solemnly, with a parenthetical reflection on his own cleverness: "(Rather fine, that last sentence?)"[36]

Most scenic tourists did not display this sort of ironic self-knowledge, though they probably worked as hard on their "fine sentences" as Strong had. Perhaps his humor was related to another feature of the cult of scenery. Strong was already married and well established in his career in 1843, and the cult of scenery may have been connected with the crisis of young adulthood. Its most fervent practitioners tended to be young, perhaps traveling after graduation from college, or immediately before or after marriage. Caroline Barrett and her fiancé Francis Adams White, for example, seem to have used the language of scenery as a way of communicating their emotions about one another. In 1849, Caroline Barrett recorded in her journal that she had received a letter from "her friend" in Europe that revealed to her his deepest feelings: "His soul seems on fire as he attempts to convey an idea to me of the emotions awakened within him on visiting some of the shrines and ruins."[37] After Caroline Barrett became Mrs. White she continued to write extensively about her travels and about scenery, but the pitch of picturesque emotion diminished. Scenic language like this was popular for over twenty years, but it is hard to imagine any single individual sustaining such an emotional high over all that time.

Strong's humor may have been unusual, but his self-consciousness was not. Scenic tourists were eager to experience the proper responses to scenery and anxious to express them properly. They were painstakingly attentive not only to their own reactions but to other people's as well. Some took comfort in comparing their own responses to those of their fellow travelers, which often appear in their accounts as woefully inadequate. William Stone, the New York editor whose anger toward socially inferior fashionable tourists was described in Chapter 1, was also concerned with the *inner* responses of his fellow travelers. He recorded that he and his friends had experienced the correct emotions at Niagara Falls; they had been properly filled with "wonder and dread and admiration of this stupendous monument of Almighty power." He also recorded what he imagined the other tourists were experiencing: "[their] feelings and perceptions are no more awakened by the prospect, than were those of the tailor, whose notions of the sublime were indicated by the significant exclamation, 'Oh, what a fine place to sponge a coat!' "[38]

Nathaniel Hawthorne's travel sketches focus similarly on his characters' pretensions. In his story of the Notch, he made fun of the Byronic young man's effusions about the White Mountains. The young man had a well-known name in magazines and annuals, and had contributed a poem to the guestbook at the Crawfords' inn, but he offended the story's narrator by his insincerity, his "coldness": "The lines were elegant and full of fancy, but too remote . . . and cold."[39] In his Niagara Falls travel sketch, "My Visit to Niagara," Hawthorne had his narrator engage in an extended analysis of his difficulties in responding properly to a scene that did not live up to his expectations. He had come there "haunted with a vision of foam and fury, and dizzy cliffs, and an ocean tumbling down out of the sky," a vision impossible to be fulfilled. He was forced to confess to himself that "a wretched sense of disappointment weighed me down." In time he came to appreciate the scene, but much of the rest of the story is occupied with descriptions of others who did not: an English lady "so intent on the safety of her little boy that she did not even glance at Niagara"; the lady's child, who "gave himself wholly to the enjoyment of a stick of candy"; a tourist with a copy of "Captain Hall's tour" in hand, who "labored earnestly to adjust Niagara to the captain's description"; and a sketching tourist who criticized the visual arrangement of the falls.[40] In comparison to these, the narrator's responses were not so inadequate after all.

The question of whether such travelers and their companions experienced the proper relationships with romantic scenery may seem trivial, but it was not. The experience of scenery was bound up with political and social controversies that early nineteenth-century Americans took seriously indeed. For one thing, the cult of scenery had been closely associated since its origins with the tastes and values of the English aristocracy. If only for that reason, scenery raised touchy issues of national pride, and perhaps more important, of social class.[41]

For contemporary American observers, the cult of romantic scenery seemed inextricably linked with its elite English consumers. So close did this relationship appear that some early nineteenth-century American writers wondered whether the United States could be said to possess real scenery at all, or whether scenery was something that could exist only in Europe, among the picturesque ruins of old societies, and with the patronage of long-established elite classes. Nathaniel P. Willis, for example, argued in 1837 that landscapes in England had a social, even financial meaning that American scenery could not possess, because they had literally been *created* for some wealthy landowner. "Trees in England . . . are statistics, as it were—so many trees, *ergo* so many owners so rich." American scenery, in contrast, was socially insignificant: "Trees grow and waters run, as the stars shine, quite unmeaningly." However beautiful, this was not scenery because it did not testify to the wealth and taste of any owner: "There may be ten thousand princely elms, and not a man within a hundred miles worth five pounds five."[42] (Willis was referring to the carefully shaped landscapes of gentry estates, but his remarks applied as well to the "wild" landscape of romantic scenery. Without an elite consumer, as he saw it, there was no real landscape.[43])

Not many early nineteenth-century writers put it so bluntly, but many did share Willis's view that there was something deficient in American scenery—or in American consumers. Sarah Josepha Hale had put the matter in its most optimistic light, arguing that the deficiency was in American scenery's lack of associations, and that it was easily remedied by the appropriate artistic intervention. Emerson had simply suggested an alternative patron for scenery: For Willis's elite English aristocrat he substituted an equally elite visionary poet with the necessary perception to appreciate the landscape.

Basil Hall, one of those English travel writers whose books generated so much controversy in the 1830s, shared Willis's perspective. But his critique focused even more sharply on the inadequacies of American institutions and class arrangements. In two lengthy passages in his much discussed critique of American institutions, Captain Hall echoed the private judgments of his wife, who had written scathingly of American pretensions: "There is no want of talking . . . about sensibility and romantic scenery and being passionately fond of this thing and having a passion for that . . . but it is all 'words, words, words,' and there is plainly a want of sentiment."[44] The Halls highlighted this inadequacy because it bolstered one of their favorite arguments: Democracy destroyed culture. As Captain Hall argued, "where the fine arts are not steadily cultivated . . . there cannot possibly be much hearty admiration of the beauties of nature."[45] For the Halls this was not only an aesthetic criticism, it was also a political judgment. Without a leisured class, which they believed did not exist in the United States, there could be no proper appreciation of scenery.

And the Halls were partly correct. The cult of scenery *was* an indicator of social class, in the United States as elsewhere. In England, Wordsworth argued passionately against the extension of a railroad into Windermere in the Lake District, which would have brought people of more modest means into the scenic areas. In a letter to a newspaper in 1844, Wordsworth wrote that "the perception of what has acquired the name of picturesque and romantic scenery is so far from being intuitive that it can be produced only by a slow and gradual process of culture"—that is, by a process available only to the gentry.[46] As Mrs. Hall put it, mere "words, words, words" would not suffice.

Proper appreciation of scenery was a sign of gentility on both sides of the Atlantic. That fact alone goes far toward explaining the fearful significance of scenic experiences for many American travelers. But during the 1830s and 1840s the politics of scenery were especially acute in the United States. Many social conservatives became scenic enthusiasts in the 1830s as part of a larger political struggle. Old Federalists like Theodore Dwight and William Stone held fast to scenery as a means of distinguishing the culture of the gentry from that of the Jacksonian rabble. Some scenic advocates took a more aggressive stance. They wanted to short-circuit the "slow and gradual process of culture" provided for the elite, hoping to train a new, properly educated gentry more or less overnight. Thomas Cole's patrons, for example, were drawn from a circle of New York and Connecticut Federalist families who were moving toward a Whig affiliation. They hoped to use their influence over American culture to counterbalance what they saw as the excessive political democracy and unstable economic climate of the Jacksonian years.[47]

When Thomas Cole addressed the Catskills Lyceum in 1835 on the subject of American scenery, he expressed a hope that people who had recently acquired wealth and status could be trained to the appreciation of romantic scenery. He spoke of the "advantages of cultivating a taste for scenery" in transforming "those whose days are consumed in the low pursuit of avarice, or the gaudy frivolities of fashion." Cole hoped, in fact, that the cultivation of good taste, especially in scenery, would be a powerful defense against the "meager utilitarianism" and "sordid tendencies of modern civilization."[48] In other words, scenery could transform nouveaux riches into gentry and give such newly wealthy people the social values of the already established gentry.

In this context, it is easier to see what ordinary people intended to gain from their diligently reported emotional responses to scenery. When George Templeton Strong applauded his carefully wrought scenic analogy, when Caroline Barrett filled page after page of her diary with lyrical accounts of the beauties of nature, they were making statements about themselves and their own capacity for expression and experience. Since the 1820s, fashionable tourists had used their travels to stake a claim to status. But scenic touring made the most powerful claim of all: not about money, but about gentility.

In that sense, the cult of scenery was indeed a kind of "conspicuous aesthetic consumption," as Raymond Williams termed it. But it went even deeper than that. The scenic tour offered many things to many tourists: the promise of a successful career to a traveler like Thomas Cole, of upward social mobility to a young schoolteacher like Caroline Barrett, and perhaps even, to political conservatives like Theodore Dwight, of a defense against Jacksonian aggressions in politics and the marketplace.[49] But its most powerful offer was internal: the assurance that one truly deserved the social authority awarded to the "refined and cultivated" classes.

Mass-consuming Scenery

Unfortunately for these "refined and cultivated" tourists, they, along with the rustic innkeepers and genteel artists who interpreted their experiences for them, were in danger of being overwhelmed in the deluge of White Mountain tourists by the 1850s. As the tourist industry expanded, the experience of scenic touring became available to all sorts of people who either did not have the means to pursue such a genteel experience or who simply did not have the inclination.

White Mountain tourists by mid-century had become a surprisingly diverse group. Well-to-do merchants and professionals from Boston and other large northeastern cities made up the majority, as one would expect. But as Peter Bulkley discovered by analyzing the only known White Mountain guest register for the 1850s (from the Tip Top House atop Mount Washington for 1853 and 1854), many other White Mountain tourists did not fit the usual description of travelers as well-educated, affluent, and urban. Nearly thirteen percent were lower-level white-collar workers, a surprising twenty percent were identifiable as laborers, and ten percent as farmers.

These clerical workers and "laborers"—usually carpenters and skilled workers like engravers, printers, and machinists—came mostly from nearby small cities and had perhaps two or three days to spare. Farmers generally came from neighboring towns.[50] It is unlikely that all these tourists shared the special sensibility required to tour the White Mountains in the approved way. Even among the more affluent tourists from Boston and New York, the new rapid trains and luxury hotels of the 1850s were beginning to offer attractions to visitors with only a casual interest in romantic scenery.

In the long run, neither the diversity of the new tourist population nor its lack of training (or perhaps even interest) in scenic conventions slowed the growth of the scenery industry. By the 1850s, an infrastructure was in place to prod, cajole, and threaten such tourists into the proper scenic experience of the White Mountains, whether they had been trained for it or not. Developing the tourist industry also "developed" tourists: It transformed masses of people into scenic consumers, while it simultaneously made the scenic experience available to them on easy terms. After that had happened, almost anyone could tour the White Mountains without fear of losing the way, either geographically or socially.

Early tourists had expected to generate their own associations out of their store of memorized poetry and experiences with literature and painting. By mid-century, tourists increasingly found they could buy these mass-marketed associations "off the rack." The guidebook writers of the 1850s played a key role in making scenic touring easier. They defined the sights worth seeing. They developed the associations necessary for scenic touring and made them available more or less on the spot. They continually expanded the number of attractions and views it was important to experience, drawing larger and larger geographic areas into the traveler's itinerary. And by the same processes they drew in larger audiences. For less sophisticated travelers (or lazier ones), guidebooks were the key to experiencing scenery properly.

Some guidebook writers had their own motives for offering such help, openly proclaiming their hope of training people to the right appreciation of scenery and, by extension, to the proper social values. Starr King was the most openly didactic of the guidebook writers, as befitted his position as Unitarian minister: "The object of this volume is to help persons appreciate landscape more adequately; and to associate with the principal scenes poetic passages."[51] King, like Thomas Cole before him, hoped that training in the experience of scenery would have far-reaching effects on overall artistic taste (and thus on morality): "The effect of White Mountain journeys should be seen in our homes, in a purer delight in art, and an intelligent patronage of it."[52]

In pursuit of these goals, King and other travel writers were careful to explain to their readers how best to experience the scenery they viewed, giving instructions on where to stand, what time of day to visit, and even how to react: "The surprise to the senses in first looking upon a noble landscape, ought to show itself in childlike animation. . . . perpetual surprise and enthusiasm are signs of healthy and tutored taste."[53] Of course, this was manifestly an impossible prescription, and it reveals a little of the difficulty involved in teaching scenery, or any other romantic sensibility.[54] The proper scenic response was spontaneous, heartfelt, unstudied. But it was also the product of intensive cultivation—of memorized poetry, of studies of landscape painting, and of extensive travel.

Most guidebook writers assumed with King that their audience did not have such a background, but not all of them offered King's elaborate training in the aesthetics of gentility. Most offered something more like a crash course: a chance for tourists to fulfill their own expectations of themselves as scenic consumers with minimal effort. If all else failed, one could follow Samuel Eastman's injunction for use on the top of Mount Washington, perhaps the most fail-safe (and least demanding) of all strategies: "Words fail to give adequate expression to the feeling that has come over you and you stand in mute silence before this awe-inspiring scene."[55]

Shaping the Landscape

Guidebooks were not the only new aid available to scenic tourists in the White Mountains. The land itself was being shaped by the needs of its new consumers. The "pretourist" White Mountain region, like most of New England, had been organized by town. Its population was concentrated in the river valleys and lowlands. In a sense, tourism turned the region inside out, making the most remote and unlivable parts of the interior—the notches and the peaks—appear to be the center of the region. From mid-century on, town centers began to show up as increasingly vague entities on the edges of maps, while hotels and attractions located deep in the mountains appeared at the centers.

Railroad routes contributed to the new shape of the land. Trains brought tourists to the edges of the scenic areas; from there, stagecoaches carried them "inside" to hotels close by the chief scenic attractions. The White Mountain region thus acquired very clear borders: The towns where the railroads ended (Littleton, Gorham, Center Harbour, and Plymouth) formed a rough circle around the central attractions and functioned as gateways. Inside that circle scenery began.

A clear pattern of travel emerged within that circle as well. Most tourists took the train from Boston or New York to the outskirts of the region and spent a night or more in a hotel in one of these towns, taking walks, climbs, and drives to the clustered points of interest in the area. Then they traveled by coach in a circular route through the mountains in carefully timed stages, stopping at each of the important sites. Inside the region, stagecoach rides were the key to the scenic experience, since so many of the best views were seen from the road. Enthusiastic tourists tried to get seats on the roof for the most celebrated parts of the drive. Schedules were often timed for the coaches to arrive at the scenic areas when the best light illuminated the scene.

When Caroline Barrett White and her husband visited the White Mountains in 1854, they managed to hit all the highlights of the tour in four days. They took the approved route in the usual direction. On September 6 the Whites traveled up Crawford Notch from North Conway to the Old Crawford House. From this direction, the scenery of the Notch was said to be more dramatic. On the following day they climbed Mount Washington on horseback. On the third day they traveled to Littleton, where they climbed Mount Willard, probably intending to get one of the recommended views of the Presidential Range from the west. The end of that day found them in the Franconia Notch, at the White Mountain House—a good hotel, Caroline recorded, with good food and service and "a splendid Chickering piano." The Whites had their own horses and buggy and could have arranged their travel any way they wished. In spite of that, their circular itinerary was much the same as everyone else's.[56] By the 1850s, it was increasingly difficult to imagine the tour in any other way.

Naming the Land

On the most basic level, the transformation of the White Mountain landscape can be read in the struggle over its names. Names of geographic features were the first interpretation of the landscape that tourists encountered. The naming of unnamed places and things was crucial to making the region scenic: The more named things, the more places for tourists to visit, and the more orderly and differentiated the landscape became. But some names were clearly better than others for this purpose.

Local inhabitants had named places either for the people who lived there or for the places they had left behind. Israel River, for instance, was named for Israel Glines, a hunter who had camped there. Berlin Falls was named for the town of Berlin, Connecticut, from which local settlers had migrated. Scientific explorers were responsible for the many names of political figures in the region. In 1820, for example, a party of scientists and local officials ascended Mount Washington and officially began the process of naming the peaks—Mount Adams, Mount Madison, and the others—that are known as the Presidential Range.

But scenic enthusiasts wanted local names to be poetic evocations of the legendary and literary associations needed to make a landscape scenic. By the 1840s, these concerns had begun to have an impact on White Mountain names. Some tourist names memorialized earlier explorers, hotel keepers, and popularizers: The Notch became Crawford Notch, in memory of the by-then legendary first innkeepers; Tuckerman Ravine and Oakes Gulf were named for two well-known botanists who were enthusiastic explorers of the region. Increasingly, though, new names were not those of "founding fathers," whether of the nation or of local hotels. Instead, romantic names—Silver Cascade, Giant's Stairs and Sleeper's Ledge—began to crowd out earlier, simpler names like the Flume, the Pool, and the Basin.

Romantic names, such as Diana's Baths, could evoke general romantic associations or more particular regional associations: Mount Chocorua was named for the Indian hero of a legend associated with the region.[57] Perhaps even more important, the names served a negative function, to make clear that the White Mountains were not simply the backwoods. The names given by the original settlers were worse than useless, not only because they were unromantic but because they were associated with the prosaic concerns of the residents of the region. Poetic names disassociated the region from its connections with the merely mundane considerations of crops, lumber, and local or even national politics. On this principle, new names crowded out old: Cow Brook, which flowed near the site of the landslide that had destroyed the Willey family, was renamed Avalanche Brook, replacing a name with the most mundane of all possible associations with one that evoked the experiences of the fated Willeys.[58]

Samuel Johnson approved of the romantic names he encountered on his tour. They had a charm, he wrote, that demonstrated that the inhabitants were "none of your Utilitarian goaheaders [sic], but people fit to live where Indians have left their fishing and hunting grounds untouched by engineers or mill builders."[59] The hotel keepers of the White Mountains were not very different from nearby mill builders, but it was now important that they not *seem* to be carrying on utilitarian operations. In this business, romance was required.

Some promoters came to see the remaining prosaic names in the region as a great handicap to its development. Starr King was most outspoken in his opposition to the names of the White Mountains region, referring to the names of the Presidential Range as "absurd" and "a wretched jumble," and calling for a renaming of the peaks.[60] Most writers did not openly attack local names, especially those of the Presidential Range, which possessed at least some meaning for mid-nineteenth-century tourists, but instead opted for a kind of parallel unofficial naming system, based on real or imagined Indian names for places. Many guidebooks opened their first chapters with a discussion of the "original" names of the region and their meanings. It was a convenient way of attaching romantic Indian associations to the region, since the writer was free to embellish the interpretation of such Algonquin terms as "Waumbek," which means "white rocks" but could be interpreted as something like "Mountains of the Snowy Foreheads."[61]

These shadow names had become so conventionalized by mid-century that Henry David Thoreau could make an inside joke of them. His book on Cape Cod, like many other pieces of scenic writing, began by tracing the origins of a local name. In Thoreau's hands, it was pure parody:

> I suppose that the word Cape is from the French *cap;* which is from the Latin *caput,* a head; which is, perhaps, from the verb *capere,* to take,—that being the part by which we take hold of a thing. . . . And as for Cod, that was derived directly from that 'great store of cod-fish' which Captain Bartholomew Gosnold caught there in 1602; which fish appears to have been so called from the Saxon word *codde,* 'a case in which seeds are lodged' whence also, perhaps, codling . . . and coddle—to cook green like peas.[62]

Thoreau had not always mocked such scenic conventions. At one time, he had actually anticipated a career like Hawthorne's or Cole's, making a living interpreting scenery to readers. Thoreau wrote extensively about his travels and, at least at first, he too attempted to attach romantic associations to the landscape.[63] But by the middle of his traveling career, he had come to see scenery very differently.

After his 1846 trip to Mount Katahdin, Thoreau turned against the patching of human associations onto the landscape. He began to portray the places he visited as examples of nature untoured: "vast and drear and inhuman," like Mount Katahdin; "inhumanly sincere, wasting no thought on man," like the deserted beaches of Cape Cod.[64] He traveled as far away as he could get from genteel tourist regions, and his writing took the form of antiscenery tracts. But Thoreau's mocking discussion of the origins of the name Cape Cod ended on a serious note, with his famous description of the Cape as the "bare and bended arm of Massachusetts." Even for Thoreau, writing about scenery led to the irresistible temptation to create serious associations.

Manufacturing Associations

For promoters, by the 1850s the creation of associations had become a full-time business. Naming and unnaming the features of the landscape was only the beginning of this enterprise. From the 1840s on, associations were being mass-produced for the White Mountains by promoters who were happy to enlist any material they could find—American, European or Indian—in their campaign to interest tourists in the landscape.

The most general of all associations were those grafted onto the White Mountains as a reflection of European landscapes and ideas. They included simple references to "the Switzerland of America," or phrases like, "On the left he will see realized his conceptions of Italian scenery."[65] They also included the popular image of "mountain freedom," which associated historical or legendary events that had occurred in other mountain areas with the White Mountains. The Notch, for instance, was a mountain pass, "like those in the old world where often a few brave men, defending their liberties and native soil, have driven back or destroyed invading armies."[66] The fact that nothing like this had ever happened in the Notch was not as significant as the area's ostensible resemblance to European sites where such things had occurred.

The equation of mountains and freedom was characteristic of European image-making. Wordsworth had described the Lake District before tourism as "a perfect Republic of Shepherds and Agriculturists . . . whose constitution had been imposed and regulated by the mountains which protected it."[67] And Switzerland's mountain republics had been immortalized in Schiller's *William Tell.* But in the White Mountains, this association became naturalized so that it seemed to reflect the image of the region, and even contemporary politics. One 1856 guidebook made a connection between scenery and the self-image of a region on the verge of civil war:

No oppression . . . can ever exist around the White Mountains. . . . No slave can ever live on them, or near them. They are consecrated to freedom. They are suited to produce a race of vigorous freemen.[68]

The White Mountains were "consecrated to freedom," in stark contrast with other places unnamed, where oppression and slavery made their home. It is not hard to imagine what places this Yankee writer had in mind in 1856. But it is not entirely clear who he had in mind when he used the expression, "a race of vigorous freemen." He may have been thinking of the early white settlers of the region, or he may have meant the native people the settlers had driven out.

Writers frequently made use of "Indian legends" to create romantic associations. Mount Chocorua, for instance, was associated with the legend of "Chocorua's curse," which describes an Indian chief driven to the brink of a cliff by white pursuers and finally forced to jump to his death. In the early days of tourism, the legend appeared in Thomas Cole's 1830 painting and in Lydia Maria Child's short-story version in *The Token*. By the 1850s, all kinds of versions were cropping up in guidebooks and collections, often with crucially different plots. (Some versions placed the blame on the white men who killed Chocorua, while other blamed Chocorua himself.) But guidebook writers frequently lamented the dearth of Indian associations in the region. Where "noble savages" had not left enough influence on the landscape, promoters could turn to the equally noble (and perhaps equally "savage") first white settlers of the region.

By the 1850s, the Crawfords themselves were being featured prominently in these sorts of tales, often as heroic figures—picturesque peasants, noble savages, and hardy yeomen rolled into one. In Starr King's description of his first trip to the mountains in 1849, he recalled a stage load of people looking at a bear chained to a pole, but "equally interested in seeing a specimen of the first settlers and of the aboriginal tenants of the wilderness."[69] King wrote of Abel Crawford that "during the last ten years of his life he was a noble object of interest to thousands of visitors from all parts of the United States."[70] And John Spaulding described Crawford's early life as a time when "he dressed in the tanned skins of the moose, and became in the chase a perfect Nimrod."[71] (Not surprisingly, no guidebook ever made use of the struggles of Ethan Allen and Lucy Crawford. Debtor's prison, debilitating illness, and bankruptcy were not the stuff of romantic legend.)

Local artists proved to be even more usable than the Crawfords. Samuel Thompson of North Conway, an innkeeper and owner of a stagecoach company, struck an interesting bargain with the artists who had begun to visit North Conway during the 1840s. He agreed to board them for the low price of $3.50 per week and to send their lunches out to their "sketching-grounds." In return they agreed to "date all their mountain sketches from North Conway"—a simple, but ultimately very successful, advertisement for local scenery.[72] By the mid-1850s, North Conway had become a well-known artist's colony, attracting some forty established artists each summer, and of course many other tourists who wished to see (or to be identified with) them.

The most successful scenic attractions were the work of many different promoters, and usually combined a number of different associations in one more-or-less harmonious whole. The so-called Profile in the Franconia Notch (also known as the Old Man of the Mountains) was the product of just such a complex transformation, one that is worth exploring in some detail. The Profile has proved to be the most lasting symbol to come out of the White Mountains. To this day it is featured on the highway signs of New Hampshire. It was considered such an important part of the state's heritage that when the face showed signs of crumbling in the late 1920s, the state of New Hampshire had its rocks bolted and chained in place.[73]

But while the ascent of Mount Washington and the Willey House in the Crawford Notch had been well-known since the 1820s, the Profile emerged as an attraction only gradually. It seems to have been noticed by road workers as early as 1805, but early guidebooks referred to the Profile during the 1830s as only one of several mildly interesting natural curiosities.[74] Theodore Dwight's 1830 guidebook *The Northern Traveller* described Franconia (the town nearby) as a place "where are iron works, and a curious profile on a mountain, called the Old Man of the Mountain."[75] Harriet Martineau remembered it from her 1827 trip but was not impressed: "The sharp rock certainly resembles a human face; but what then? There is neither wonder nor beauty in it."[76] She even located it in the wrong notch.

During the 1840s and 1850s, the Profile was transformed from a local curiosity into a nationally recognized symbol of the White Mountains, and indeed of New England as a whole. William Oakes, in his important collection of lithographs, *Scenery of the White Mountains,* featured a series of sketches that portrayed the Profile from various vantage points, with a text describing the changing faces and their characteristics, ending with a description of a "toothless old woman in a mob cap."[77] In 1850, Hawthorne's story "The Great Stone Face" was published. In 1853, the new owner of the Lafayette House changed its name to the Profile House, both recognizing and contributing to the Profile's new fame. Eastman's 1859 guidebook described the route to the Profile from the Profile House: A road from the hotel led to a "rude bench by the wayside" and a "guideboard inscribed with the single, simple word, 'Profile.'" Starr King went so far as to prescribe the best time of day for viewing it—"about four in the afternoon of a summer day."[78]

Although the Profile clearly benefited from Hawthorne's story, the most enduring associations with the Profile came from an entirely different source. At the foot of the mountain where one views the Profile today, a sign records an anecdote attributed to Daniel Webster. This same anecdote showed up in guidebooks as early as 1856. In Willey's *Incidents in White Mountain History,* it is told this way:

William Oakes, a respected botanist and White Mountain enthusiast, provided a key
to interpreting the Profile's physiognomy: "The expression is severe and somewhat
melancholy, and although there is a little feebleness about the mouth . . . the face of
the 'Old Man of the Mountain' is set, and his countenance fixed and firm." Oakes
carefully illustrated the Profile's character from various points to the right and left of
the best location, pointing out that from the left the Profile's character changes to a
"toothless old woman in a mob cap," before the illusion is lost. From William Oakes,
"The Profile Rock," plate 10, in *Scenery of the White Mountains* (Boston: Little and
Brown, 1848). Courtesy, American Antiquarian Society.

Said an eccentric speaker, at a celebration a few years since in Fryeburg,
"Men put out signs representing their different trades; jewellers hang out a
monster watch; shoemakers, a huge boot; and, up in Franconia, God
Almighty has hung out a sign that in New England he makes men."[79]

In slightly different forms, this remark was quoted by Eastman in 1860 and
in almost all later guidebooks. Somewhere along the way the "eccentric
speaker" became Daniel Webster, and the story gained a specific relation to
the state of New Hampshire rather than simply Franconia or "these regions."
In this enduring image of the Profile, the granite face came to represent the
Granite State, its people, and their political beliefs. By the 1860s their long-
standing resistance to slavery appeared to be an outgrowth of "granite"
principles, intrinsic to the region, rooted in the very hills and stones.

By 1860, the Profile had become one of the best-known images of New England, and one of the most famous scenic tourist attractions in the country. The surrounding area became a backdrop for the Profile. Tourists stayed in the Profile House, climbed Profile Mountain, and rowed in Profile Lake. Spin-off attractions in other parts of the mountains made use of the Profile's new fame: the Old Maid of the Mountain, the Infant, the Imp, and the Young Man of the Mountain were discovered on other rocky mountainsides.[80]

By then, the White Mountains had become a booming tourist region, with as many as ten thousand visitors every summer.[81] The region had also become quite densely populated with imaginary figures, romantic stories, names, and associations. In contrast to earlier years, writers after 1860 considered the chief attraction of the White Mountains to be their wealth of associations. Tourists drove and walked through mountain scenery about whose every peak and waterfall they had read stories and poems; stayed in hotels with romantic names; and viewed scenes they had often seen already, in gift books, guidebooks, prints, and paintings.

The End of Scenery

Finally, though, both the White Mountain region and the cult of scenery were transformed by their own success. The more accessible the wilderness of the mountains became, the more comfortable tourists could feel with it. Caroline Barrett White's 1854 journey already pointed the way to such a culmination. She responded with emotion to the grandeur and wildness of the mountain scenery she saw, but she also felt comfortable with the region in a way that would have been unimaginable for a tourist in the days before good hotels and railroads. She recorded two days after her visit to the summit of Mount Washington that she had not thought of anything "save *the mountains* since my ascent of Mount Washington." But the emotion they inspired was not awe: "I often feel like exclaiming 'dear old mountains.'"[82] And when she and her husband climbed Pleasant Mountain outside Fryeburg, they spent a leisurely afternoon on the top, looking at the view, having "an excellent dinner with four gentlemen," and playing ten pins—a very pleasant day, but hardly a thrilling experience.

Mid-century tourists encountered a region transformed by its own popularity. By 1859, more than five thousand people ascended Mount Washington each summer.[83] A fairly arduous climb in the company of a few fellow adventurers and a rustic guide was replaced by a horseback ride

By 1875, the Profile was a popular attraction. Like the other attractions of the White Mountains, however, it had lost much of its mystique. These tourists clambering over the Profile betray little of the earlier visitors' romantic perspective, nor do they appear to be interested in a transcendent emotional experience. From George L. Keyes, *Keyes' Handbook of Northern Pleasure Travel* (Boston, 1873). Courtesy, American Antiquarian Society.

up to a hotel, from which one could look at the view in the company of perhaps a hundred other tourists, eat dinner, buy a souvenir, and return back to one's lodgings in the same manner. By the 1860s, the ascent of Mount Washington had become so popular that tourists who were interested in communing with God or nature were obliged to avoid the beaten track. The "commonly travelled routes to the summit" no longer supplied the "loneliness and wildness . . . and . . . adventure" they had formerly promised.[84]

Sometimes no alternate route could compensate for the changes that crowds brought with them. The Willey site, such an awe-inspiring experience during the 1830s, had been irrevocably changed by 1855, when a "commodious two-story" hotel was built near the house. By 1859, guidebook writers were beginning to express irritation over its commercialization. Samuel Eastman's guidebook pointed out that the Willey house was both too crowded and too commercial for serious scenic tourists. Although "of late years it has become important as a showplace, twelve and a half cents being charged for showing each person through the house," he believed that there was "nothing within the ruinous edifice of sufficient interest to warrant even this trifling expenditure." And he made it clear that tourists in the know would avoid the Willey house, which he dismissed as "sight-seeing . . . made easy for beginners."[85]

Some places were clearly too crowded, but a more important change was at work in the mountains, too. The experience of scenery itself had been transformed by its popularity. The process of mass-marketing the attractions of the region—making scenic touring "easier for beginners"—by its very nature interfered with the informal poetry recitation, conversation, writing, and sketching that had been the heart of scenic touring and with the very goals that had made it attractive in the 1830s and 1840s. While genteel scenic touring *could* take place (and probably always had) in an atmosphere of competitive jostling for attention, it could not take place to advantage in a crowd of people of varied social classes, all equally (if superficially) versed in guidebook-acquired scenic conventions. The more widespread scenic conventions became, the less effectively they could carry the special weight attached to them.

A few brave souls rejected the crowded scenic regions in favor of a more isolated wilderness experience. Thoreau remained a caustic critic of popular scenic touring. Boston Congregationalist minister William "Adirondack" Murray began in 1869 to encourage urban professionals to find salvation by plunging into the wilderness rather than simply looking at it.[86] But most tourists went in the opposite direction. They continued to travel to the White Mountains, but they simply lost interest in the scenery. The intensity and conviction with which tourists had used scenic language in the 1840s had all but disappeared by the 1860s. By the 1880s, expressions of emotion in response to scenery were considered in bad taste. Instead of the rather time-consuming and labor-intensive work of scenic touring, affluent tourists were increasingly content with easier forms of conspicuous consumption, for which the great hotels provided ample op-

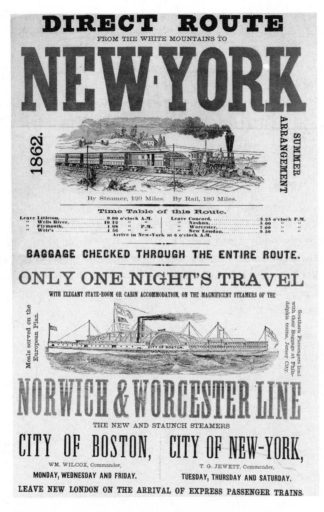

DIRECT ROUTE

FROM THE WHITE MOUNTAINS TO

NEW·YORK

1862.

SUMMER ARRANGEMENT

By Steamer, 120 Miles. By Rail, 180 Miles.

Time Table of this Route.

Leave Littleton,	9.00 o'clock A.M.	Leave Concord,	3.25 o'clock P.M.
" Wells River,	10.12 "	" Nashua,	5.00 " "
" Plymouth,	1.08 " P.M.	" Worcester,	7.00 " "
" Weir's	1.56 "	" New London,	9.50 " "
		Arrive in New-York at 6 o'clock A.M.	

BAGGAGE CHECKED THROUGH THE ENTIRE ROUTE.

ONLY ONE NIGHT'S TRAVEL

WITH ELEGANT STATE-ROOM OR CABIN ACCOMMODATION, ON THE MAGNIFICENT STEAMERS OF THE

Meals served on the European Plan.

Southern Passengers land with their Baggage at Philadelphia trains, Jersey City.

CITY OF BOSTON

NORWICH & WORCESTER LINE

THE NEW AND STAUNCH STEAMERS

CITY OF BOSTON,   CITY OF NEW-YORK,

WM. WILCOX, Commander,   T. G. JEWETT, Commander,

MONDAY, WEDNESDAY AND FRIDAY.   **TUESDAY, THURSDAY AND SATURDAY.**

LEAVE NEW LONDON ON THE ARRIVAL OF EXPRESS PASSENGER TRAINS.

By the 1860s, the White Mountains had become primarily a high-priced resort offering luxurious hotels and convenient connections with northeastern cities. This 1862 handbill advertised the Norwich and Worcester Railroad's "summer arrangements" for travelers between New York and the White Mountains. The handbill directs special information to "Southern Passengers," who could take the steamboat as far south as Jersey City and travel from there—at least, if their journey was not interrupted by the movements of the Union and Confederate troops encamped around Washington, D.C., in the summer of 1862! Graphics Collection, American Antiquarian Society. Courtesy, American Antiquarian Society.

portunity. Perhaps the expression of scenic sentiments lost currency as it "trickled down." Or perhaps scenic conventions had simply served their purpose.

The great hotels and rapid trains embodied the promoters' success, not only in marketing scenery but also in persuading tourists that the proper appreciation of scenery was the sign of a cultivated taste, ample leisure, and elite sensibilities. But that very success brought change. Between 1820 and 1840, the White Mountain region had been transformed from a half-settled agricultural backwater to a scenic wonderland. Between 1840 and 1860, the region was transformed again, this time from a scenic wonderland to a fashionable summer place, a resort for the increasing numbers of well-to-do people who found it necessary and desirable to "go away" for part of the summer. Instead of reading about such places in scenic albums, poetry, and short stories, most people in the 1860s read about them in the society pages of city newspapers. The White Mountains were still scenic, but their scenery was now part of a package deal that included, as Thoreau put it, "a ten-pin alley, or a circular railway, or an ocean of mint julep."[87]

3
COTTAGE HEAVEN
Creating Consumers on Martha's Vineyard, 1860–1876

By the 1860s, summer travel had become an established part of life for wealthy northeastern city dwellers. City newspapers carried reports of the social scene at fashionable resorts in Saratoga, Newport, the White Mountains, and the Catskills. Wealthy urban neighborhoods were almost empty in July and August. Special "summer arrangements" of railroad schedules were designed to accommodate these well-to-do crowds, and elegant hotels in the scenic regions were crowded with guests from New York and Boston. These tourists were a select group; most ordinary citizens would probably never reach such high-priced destinations. But increasingly other places, closer to home, offered vacations to those with less time and money to spend.

Just outside many northeastern cities, the business of providing for tourists was expanding into rural and coastal areas previously unnoticed by travelers. And it was expanding to include vacationers with backgrounds far removed from those of the genteel travelers of the White Mountains and Newport. A growing number of Americans of limited means were finding ways to take a week or two away from the cares of their city lives: boarding at farms or lodging houses in rural areas, or erecting "tent

This illustration from B. W. Gorham's *Camp Meeting Manual* probably depicts
Wesleyan Grove in an early stage of its development. The society tents circling the
preacher's stand are labeled with the names of Methodist church congregations; "4
St.," second from the left, is probably the Fourth Street Methodist Church in New
Bedford (after which Fourth Street Avenue in Wesleyan Grove was later named).
From B. W. Gorham, *Camp Meeting Manual* (Boston, 1855), frontispiece. Courtesy,
American Antiquarian Society.

cities" or cottage colonies along the coast. These tourists, and the people
who catered to them, created entirely new tourist industries, characteristically inexpensive, but also designed to fulfill social needs and aspirations
distinctly different from those of the tourists who filled the hotels of
Saratoga or the White Mountains. At the same time, these vacation industries brought more and more people into the leisure marketplace.

Wesleyan Grove

In the summer of 1865, the *New York Times* featured its usual summer
travel columns. Reporters sent in descriptions of "the season" in the White
Mountains, Saratoga Springs, and the Catskills, well-known destinations
for wealthy city dwellers in the 1860s. But this August, the *Times* also ran
its first report from a place the reporter assumed would be new to most
of his readers—Wesleyan Grove, on the island of Martha's Vineyard.

Wesleyan Grove was not exactly a resort. In fact, it was a Methodist camp meeting ground, where yearly summer religious revivals took place. But it was undergoing a remarkable transformation, and in the process attracting curious observers from all over the Northeast.

Martha's Vineyard had been a thriving whaling center in the early nineteenth century. At the height of its prosperity, the island's major port, Edgartown, had been devoted almost entirely to that profitable venture. In 1835, a visitor estimated that out of an island population of about three thousand, five or six hundred were at sea for most of their lives.[1] But by the 1840s the whaling industry was badly damaged by competition, and during the Civil War the island's whaling fleet was almost entirely destroyed. Martha's Vineyard was not as dependent on whaling as nearby Nantucket, but the 1860s and 1870s were a period of depression and retrenchment for both islands. Local investors, searching for alternatives to whaling, found one in the unlikely form of the camp meeting at Wesleyan Grove.

The camp meeting had been founded in 1835, during a wave of Methodist revivalism that swept over southeastern New England, converting thousands of people to its emotional, fervent brand of Christianity. Local Methodists gave the name Wesleyan Grove to a piece of barren ground they leased to hold their revivals. The camp meeting, so characteristic of Methodist revivalism in all parts of the United States, took deep root in Wesleyan Grove. It grew dramatically over the following two decades, acquiring a national reputation as one of the most successful and institutionally stable of the Methodist camp meetings. Its week-long revivals took place in August and often gathered thousands of worshipers from the islands, from Cape Cod, and from the nearby mainland cities of New Bedford, Fall River, and Providence. Worshipers stayed in communal "society tents" set up by their home churches, ate in communal boarding tents, and slept on straw.

In 1859, Wesleyan Grove's success reached a pinnacle. That year twelve thousand people attended the Sunday preaching, and four hundred tents graced the grounds. But 1859 was also the last year in which Wesleyan Grove's supporters could look at its growth with unmixed satisfaction. During the 1850s, while Wesleyan Grove grew, it also began to exhibit some strange symptoms. Gradually, many families began to stake out their own pieces of ground and to set up *private* tents in place of the communal society tents of local church groups. In 1855, 150 such private family tents were set up on the grounds. By 1859, other signs of change appeared as well. The first local newspaper correspondents showed up from the mainland that summer, and an artist from New Bedford took stereoscopic views of the grounds during camp meeting week. Perhaps most significantly of all, the first permanent residence was built on the grounds: A young Providence architect named Perez Mason designed a cottage for his family and another family to share.[2]

Over the next ten years, the transformation of Wesleyan Grove continued at a bewildering pace. Hebron Vincent, the secretary of the newly formed Martha's Vineyard Camp Meeting Association, recorded the yearly changes with a mixture of delight, confusion, and trepidation. Looking back in 1867, he wondered whether he had been imagining the whole transformation. Family cottages built with "taste and elegance" were replacing the collective tents in increasing numbers. In 1864, there were forty cottages in the Grove (scattered among more than 450 private tents); by 1869, there were more than 200 cottages (and more than 600 tents and cottages together). At the same time, the grounds had expanded to cover thirty-four acres, with several new neighborhoods of cottages and tents surrounding small parks of their own.[3] Finally, the Martha's Vineyard Camp Meeting Association purchased Wesleyan Grove in 1865, after having taken up a collection among the holders of tent and cottage lots that summer. Where once had been a few hundred "poor, humble, followers of the Master," as Vincent remembered it, he now saw thousands of well-dressed and respectable visitors promenading the grounds.

These new visitors were also behaving differently. In the 1860s, families began to come to the grounds *before* the week of camp meeting, to "rusticate." By 1864, the correspondent for the *Providence Journal* was on the grounds two weeks before the beginning of the meeting, reporting that "a week or two here with a circle of friends, in advance of the great concourse, is in many respects pleasanter than the week of the meeting."[4] Croquet, sea-bathing, and walks occupied more and more of the time once devoted to prayer meetings and services. Steamboats at the rate of four or five a day brought crowds of day-trippers. Perhaps most significant, Hebron Vincent stopped recording the number of conversions at each camp meeting, preferring after 1863 to refer only to "some," "a few," or "several" people whose hearts had been changed.

By the mid-1860s, visitors from near and far were remarking the changes at Wesleyan Grove. From the summer travel section of the *New York Times* to the editorial pages of Boston's Methodist weekly, *Zion's Herald*, reporters and editors covered the situation at Wesleyan Grove from widely different angles. The national Methodist weekly, the *Christian Advocate*, commented severely in 1865 that, after having received "glowing accounts of the beautiful situation, fine opportunities for sea bathing, and luxurious private dwellings" at Wesleyan Grove, after hearing that "the singing was . . . superb, the preaching superior, the congregations immense," it had been appalled by Vincent's announcement that only one person had been converted there that year: "A good many fishers of men to drive so little business!"[5]

Close to home, the editor of the *Vineyard Gazette* in Edgartown added his voice to the complaints in 1866, when he wrote that "instead of . . . the work of grace and goodness, we hear the merry jest and see the rallying around the croquet ground."[6] But the *Times* correspondent for that summer defended the camp meeting: "The atmosphere is a religious and moral one, and while this shall be its pervading character . . . it can never fail to possess a healthy moral tone, that must be beneficial to all who attend it."[7] And an anonymous writer to the *Vineyard Gazette* agreed, arguing that "the world should not be made sad, but as much like heaven as possible."[8]

Christian Leisure

Probably not many issues were being debated simultaneously in the editorial pages and the summer travel sections in the mid-1860s, but this was a special case. Vacationing was a controversial topic. In 1867, an *Atlantic Monthly* article reported that "even our farmers are beginning to have their little after-harvest trips to the sea-shore, the Hudson, Niagara or the west."[9] Closer to Wesleyan Grove, the editor of the *Providence Journal* in August 1865 described and applauded the tremendous growth in the summer vacation habit among those he called the "brain-workers" of the city—the bank cashiers, clerks, and bookkeepers—and applauded that habit. The editor (who also happened to own a cottage at Wesleyan Grove) attributed this new habit to the increasingly crowded and frantic city environment, and he argued that vacations had become essential to the health of (white-collar) city dwellers.[10]

Supporters of the vacation habit usually pointed out the physical and mental benefits of vacationing: the healing powers of sea or mountain air, the escape from the overstimulation of work and social life (what would now be termed stress), from the "rush and whirl and anxious haste" of the city. But if the content of the argument was primarily medical, the terms of debate were often religious. While most Protestant ministers of the Northeast still played their traditional role in cautioning their parishioners against idleness and its temptations, some of them now began to take a new approach to the question of leisure. These religious leaders argued that relaxation and certain kinds of leisure activities, when used properly (and by the right kinds of people), were not dangerous to the character but good for the soul. Many of the people who took their first summer vacations during these years may have done so not on the advice of their doctors but on the advice of their ministers.

Ministers had a variety of motives for promoting vacations. Boston Unitarian minister Thomas Starr King made a name for himself in the 1850s with his glowing descriptions of White Mountain scenery and equally glowing accounts of the moral benefits of scenic tourism. His purposes were not quite the same as those of Henry Ward Beecher, who wrote extensively from his pulpit in Brooklyn Heights during the same years on the moral and religious uses of vacationing. Starr King was preoccupied with the development of taste, gentility, and a refined religious sensibility among those with sufficient leisure to support those characteristics; his projected audience was affluent, educated, and aspiring. To such an audience he wrote, "The effect of White Mountain journeys should be seen in our homes, in a purer delight in art, and an intelligent patronage of it."[11] Scenic touring could be presented almost as a moral obligation—a part of one's duty to promote culture and refinement in a money-grubbing world.

Other sorts of vacationers required different justifications. Henry Ward Beecher's arguments, for example, were carefully tailored to his young, ambitious parishioners' needs. For professional men and their families, he counseled, a month in the country was not really self-indulgence. It was somewhere between therapy and a religious retreat, allowing the lawyer or minister to "forget the city and lay aside its excitements" and giving him time for "the most earnest reflection, and for the most solemn resolutions for the future." Beecher's role here, as in many other areas, was to reassure his upwardly mobile professional congregation that the pursuit of their own gratification—in the form of beautiful houses, artwork, or a month in the Berkshires—was not incompatible with the self-denying religion they had inherited from their ancestors.[12] Vacationing, in Beecher's capable hands, became another sort of religious obligation. As he put it, "God says some things to the soul in the open field, along the sea-shore, or in the twilight forests, which he never speaks through books or men."[13]

These same kinds of arguments were also being made at Wesleyan Grove. But the campground was an especially difficult battlefield for such ideas. Even more than other Protestant Americans, mid–nineteenth-century Methodists were wary of the moral effects of leisure, conspicuous consumption, and amusement. Wesleyan Grove's campers bore little resemblance, socially or doctrinally, to Starr King's genteel Boston Unitarians or to Henry Ward Beecher's upwardly mobile Brooklyn Heights congregation. They were by tradition and by choice wedded to a "producer's ethic" of self-denial, frugality, and hard work. It would be a difficult business to convert such people to the gospel of consumerism and relaxation. At Wesleyan Grove, the new vacationing habits were infiltrating into enemy territory, into the heart of what might be called hard-core Christianity—and they were quite literally confronting it on its own consecrated ground.[14] Not surprisingly, there was a battle.

In the heat of the struggle, Hebron Vincent, the secretary of the camp meeting, took on the antivacationers in his yearly chronicles. Vincent wrote his fullest defense of Wesleyan Grove in 1864, when he warned of the danger of other, nonreligious resorts: "Many without scruple go to Saratoga, Niagara Falls, or some similar resort, from which they return with depleted wallets and with, to say the least, no more religious principles and enjoyment than they went with." Going to Wesleyan Grove would at least be better than that. And besides, Vincent argued, using both medical and ethical weapons, there is no fundamental conflict between vacationing and Christianity. Vacationing was essential to the preservation of health and, he concluded, "Is not health a blessing, which, as Christians, we are bound to preserve and promote?"[15]

Hebron Vincent devoted large sections of his yearly chronicles for 1863, 1864, and 1865 to a defense of Wesleyan Grove's growing secularization. But these arguments were published in the Martha's Vineyard Camp Meeting Association's yearly reports, for an intended audience that was presumably already half-converted. When Vincent argued that "relaxation from business cares" was "consistent with the Christian character," that it was in fact a Christian duty, he was not simply offering a justification to the outside world. He was presenting an argument to the cottagers of Wesleyan Grove, a group of people who, like Vincent himself, were perhaps more accustomed to the idea that one's Christian duty was unremitting labor. He was offering, in effect, to take their moral uncertainty about leisure and vacationing off their hands—promising that at Wesleyan Grove, if nowhere else, vacationing was "consistent with the Christian character."

Vincent was able to convince his fellow Wesleyan Grove Methodists that the transformation of their campground was harmless or even beneficial, in part because Methodist opposition to leisure was already being insidiously undermined from within, and by one of the church's most distinctive institutions: the camp meeting itself. A camp meeting manual published in 1854 made it clear that camp meetings thrived in part because they provided a kind of vacation from the world: "Do you not need, just now, a protracted season of rest from worldly care?" the enthusiast questions the skeptic. And afterwards, "Did you find any great difficulty in leaving your home and your secular business to attend the meeting?" No, replies the former skeptic, "I found I could easily arrange my engagements so as to leave."[16] Methodists at Wesleyan Grove were already accustomed to leaving home for two weeks in August; they would not find it too difficult to make the switch to vacationing.

A Shopkeeper's Vacation

Still, such potential vacationers did confront special obstacles. While many Americans in these years were uncertain about the proper uses of leisure and uncomfortable with the idea of vacationing, that discomfort was especially intense for the vacationers who were becoming Wesleyan Grove's special constituency. Wealthy, well-educated people were accustomed to summer leisure and travel. And at the other end of the spectrum, poor and working-class city dwellers were not likely to grudge themselves a hard-won Sunday afternoon at the beach. But Wesleyan Grove's visitors were neither the genteel, highly educated travelers who toured the White Mountains nor the struggling factory workers, servants, and day laborers who constituted the majority of those left behind in the city during the summer. (With a price tag of around $400, a cottage at Wesleyan Grove would have cost the entire year's wages of a typical industrial worker during the 1860s.)[17]

Were they, then, "middle class"? The majority of those who built cottages between 1862 and 1872 fell into two occupational categories: artisans and shopkeepers. Out of 101 cottage owners whose occupations were identified in city directories, twenty-eight were described as artisans— coopers, blacksmiths, tanners, and watchmakers.[18] Another quarter (twenty-four) were shopkeepers of varying degrees of wealth and status— Fall River grocers, Hartford milliners, and New Bedford "merchant tailors." Ten held white-collar jobs ("brain workers," as the Providence editor had it) as agents for factories, bookkeepers, and clerks.

Cottage owners probably made up the *upper* levels of Wesleyan Grove society, as compared with the many family and communal tent dwellers who still occupied the grounds in the 1860s. But only a handful were clearly of the professional status which could command substantial summer leisure.[19] Ten of the cottagers were listed in the city directories as "manufacturers." Some of these were clearly wealthier than their neighbors: James Davis and Henry T. Stone, partners in a Providence box-manufacturing business, for instance, were loyal supporters of Wesleyan Grove. Both were on the finance committee for several years, and they contributed a total of $150 to the collection to buy the grounds of Wesleyan Grove in 1865. (Most cottagers gave only $5 or $10 to the cause.) But between these manufacturers and their artisanal brethren, there may have been less social distance than first appears.

For one thing, the occupational labels used by the city directories were sometimes misleading. This was especially true for the kinds of work done by Wesleyan Grove's cottagers. As Stuart Blumin has pointed out, the boundaries between old-style artisans and newly-minted "manufacturers" and "retailers" were very porous.[20] Cottage owner Henry Dean of New Bedford was listed as a blacksmith in 1865, but in 1875 he appeared as an "iron work manufacturer." Edmund Chase the "tanner" may have been on the verge of becoming a boot manufacturer, and Henry T. Stone the "manufacturer" probably began life as an artisan's apprentice.

Furthermore, individuals in both categories shared a common background. Wesleyan Grove cottagers were a remarkably homogeneous group. Whether manufacturers, artisans, or shopkeepers, they were deeply rooted in their urban communities. They lived lives bound by family, neighborhood, and church ties, in close proximity to their work and the work of others in their communities. Henry Dean, for example, was transformed in the directory from a blacksmith into a manufacturer, but that change probably affected his life comparatively little. He remained at the same address in downtown New Bedford during the twenty years that witnessed his climb. Dean's neighbor George F. W. Gammons inherited his father's business as a teamster and resided throughout his life at his business address, surrounded by family members listed as "teamers" and "truckmen." Two New Bedford dentists, Frank and David Ward, were brothers who lived next door to each other and to their offices on Union Street. (They had another brother who worked as a dentist in Falmouth.) Their relative, Benjamin Ward, lived on Elm Street for over twenty years, very near the County Street Methodist Church, for which he was a steward. (At Wesleyan Grove, the family had several cottages on County Park, named for their New Bedford neighborhood.)[21]

As a group, these cottagers could perhaps be most accurately described as poised at the edge of the middle class. They belonged to a class in transition. They were relatively economically secure, paid taxes, and (evidently) had money to spend on summer cottages. But for many of these cottagers and their families, that was a new state of affairs, achieved only at the height of their productive years. They worked in jobs that were practical, even grubby—not far removed, if at all, from hard physical labor. Almost none of them held occupations that could be described as "genteel," or that required substantial education. Out of 101 identifiable cottagers, for example, not one was a lawyer or a teacher. Few could have grown up with the amenities associated with middle-class life, although their children were becoming accustomed to pianos, upholstery, and books. In their experience, long hours of work, years of patient saving, and habitual self-denial had been absolutely necessary to reach the modest success they had attained.

Their religious and social training had been designed to encourage them in that disciplined behavior. Perhaps that was why many of them had become Methodists in the first place. (Most of the cottage owners were either first- or second-generation Methodists.) Methodism, with its emphasis on hard work and its rigid personal moral requirements, was a reflection of their own needs and aspirations. Many Methodists believed that their sect was especially adept at raising the poor and humble to new heights of respectability and prosperity; they thought this was because Methodists embodied "industry, sobriety, intelligence, the love of order, and purity of life" and that such traits led to wealth, or at least to security.[22]

Perhaps Methodism also offered something more substantial than that. The Horatio Alger–style biographies of the rise of wealthy Methodists often reveal that the impoverished young man on his way up was given generous financial assistance by his church community.[23] More often, the church offered a degree of security to many who might otherwise have dropped away from even the very margins of respectability. The careers of the Methodist clergymen who appeared in the Wesleyan Grove list illustrate how close to that margin many Methodists were. (Clergymen were the least stable category of cottage owners.) Out of the six clergymen listed, one had been described in 1856 as a "mariner," another moonlighted as a homeopathic physician, and a third was listed at various times as a fruit dealer and even as a "laborer."[24]

A fourth was Hebron Vincent, the chronicler of the Martha's Vineyard Camp Meeting Association. Vincent's background was typical: The child of an impoverished Martha's Vineyard farm family, he was originally apprenticed to a shoemaker, then worked his way through a very sketchy education in order to prepare for the ministry. Vincent never became wealthy, but he did become a pillar of his community, as Methodist minister, secretary for the Martha's Vineyard Camp Meeting Association, and advocate of educational reform. And he attained a measure of security through a handful of Edgartown town offices, which he held for most of his adult life.[25] Vincent's entire career was devoted to strengthening the community of Methodists at Wesleyan Grove and the ties that bound together these cottagers in a self-conscious shared understanding of the world and their place in it.

Not Newport

The resort that these industrious and sober citizens made from their camp meeting grounds reveals a vacationing sensibility far different from that of the educated and fashionable at Newport, Saratoga, and the White Mountains. Its image was necessarily a complex one, offering aesthetic and sensual pleasures to those who were not fully convinced they ought to have them. Even when they had the money and leisure to take part in the life at the fashionable resorts, such vacationers would not have been comfortable there, either with the high-flown rhetoric of scenery or with the carriage-riding, card-playing, dancing, and champagne-drinking that set apart the fashionable from the plain. Wesleyan Grove was able to offer to such plain people a vacation shorn of its dangerous associations with high living and immorality.

Cottagers found Wesleyan Grove attractive precisely because it was not an elite resort. Far from hoping to climb socially by imitating their social "betters," these vacationers rejected the recreations and amusements of the elite. One Hartford resident reported, for instance, that he had decided to buy a cottage in Wesleyan Grove in 1865 because he believed that "what Saratoga, Newport, and other places of like character are to the gay and festive, this would be to the moral and religious."[26] Again and again, promoters and visitors emphasized the qualities of Wesleyan Grove by comparing it to what it was not: It was not a fashionable watering place; it was not Saratoga. Above all, everyone agreed, it was not Newport.[27]

Newport by the 1860s was the most socially exclusive and fashionable American resort. Its rise to prominence mirrored that of the White Mountains in almost every detail, from the "discovery" of its scenery in the 1840s to its "discovery" by the wealthiest New Yorkers in the 1860s. Its social and financial requirements were becoming more rigorous than those of any of the other resorts of New England. Although it was not yet exclusively the home of millionaires that it was to become by the 1880s and 1890s, its name was already synonymous with money and high society. And for many of those living in the nearby cities of southern New England, the name Newport was also synonymous with the vice and idleness of the rich.

Chief among those vices was alcohol. Southern New England's Methodists had, in common with many of the respectable shopkeepers and artisans of their cities, an intense hostility to the traditional forms of leisure—"Sabbath-breaking," holiday rowdiness, gambling, and especially drinking—that were indulged in by both poor and rich. John S. Gilkeson has found that, in Providence, artisans and shopkeepers waged a successful campaign against the customary rowdy recreations of the poor *and* the dissipations of the rich in the 1850s.[28] Newport was a thorn in the side of such reformers. It was well known for its defiance of Rhode Island's liquor laws: "persistent Newport visitors, who have grown old with their sherry and their port," simply flouted state laws by bringing along their stores of liquor rather than buying from their hotel keepers.[29]

The contrast between Wesleyan Grove and Newport reflected such urban contests between the entertainments of respectable working people and those of the idle and profligate rich. That was the first and clearest meaning of "not Newport." But perhaps equally important, "not Newport" implied low prices. Not many of the vacationers at Wesleyan Grove could have afforded a visit to Newport even if they had found it to their taste. Most of the cottages at Wesleyan Grove were hardly more than tents themselves (and indeed were built to mimic the tents they replaced); but the expense of constructing one of these cottages involved a substantial commitment for people of modest means. In the mid-1860s, the cottages cost an average of $400 to build, an expense that seems often to have been shared among families and groups of friends. More than one family often occupied, and perhaps helped to pay for, these tiny cottages. Moreover, the other expenses after building the cottage were small. The rent for the ground was only a few dollars a year, and food was prepared in kitchen shacks or tents to the rear of the cottages.

In one (not entirely typical) case, we can trace in detail the building of a cottage at Wesleyan Grove. David Clark was not a Methodist, but his introduction to Wesleyan Grove came about through his acquaintance with the Reverend Moses L. Scudder, the minister of Hartford's Methodist church and a neighbor of Clark's. Clark was clearly a wealthy man, although his occupation was listed as "farmer" in the Hartford directory; Moses Scudder was to achieve a modest celebrity in the next few years through his publication of a popular history called *American Methodism*. Clark visited Wesleyan Grove in the summer of 1865 on Scudder's recommendation that "many who are not Methodists" found the place charming as a summer resort.

While he was there David Clark took a step that many other visitors also decided on that year. He and fifty other people ordered cottages to be built for the next summer. Clark's cottage cost $500 and was slightly larger and more ornate than many of the new cottages. It was designed to accommodate both Clark's family of four and the Reverend Scudder's family of five. (The typical cottage contained two small rooms on the ground floor, divided by partitions or curtains, and sleeping quarters under the steeply pitched roof. Cooking was done in a tent or shed behind the cottage. Clark's cottage followed this pattern but was a little larger than usual.) According to Clark, the original plan was to combine both families' housing in two adjoining lots. Scudder's two sons would live in a tent next to the cottage. That was probably a common arrangement. Pictures of the cottages and their occupants in the 1860s and 1870s reveal a startlingly large number of people in each cottage, and estimates of the population and number of tents and cottages indicate that six or seven people per cottage—and perhaps more—must have been normal during camp meeting week.[30]

Most of the early cottage owners had more connections on the campground—familial, business, or religious—than David Clark did, connections that might have made the expense seem reasonable. Many were devout Methodists and church officers in their home communities, as was Clark's fellow Hartford resident Galusha Owen, a milliner whose connection with Wesleyan Grove sprang from his long-term family commitment to the Methodist church at home, where both he and his father were trustees. Some had business partners or connections among the cottagers: Joseph Buckminster and William Macy were partners in a drygoods store back home in New Bedford.

And many had direct business ties to the island. Both Warren Ladd and Andrew G. Pierce of New Bedford played supporting roles in the development of Wesleyan Grove. When the elders of the camp meeting decided in 1865 to buy the land on which it was held, Ladd and Pierce each gave $50 to the cause. Both of them stood to gain, indirectly, from Wesleyan Grove's development. Ladd was superintendent of the New Bedford and Taunton Railroad, the principal means by which travelers from southern New England reached the steamboat for Martha's Vineyard. And Pierce was the treasurer of the New Bedford and Martha's Vineyard Steamboat Company.

Many of the cottagers who lived on Martha's Vineyard year-round had even closer financial ties to Wesleyan Grove. Sirson P. Coffin of Edgartown, the superintendent of the campgrounds for many years, was also a lumber dealer and builder. Several island families were cottage builders as well as cottage owners. Charles Worth, who became quite a well-known cottage builder and real estate broker, lived year-round on the campground. (Worth's life illustrates an aspect of Wesleyan Grove's transformation that is actually part of another story—the work it brought to the island when it was in a serious economic and population decline. Worth had left the island for California twice already, and returned for good only in 1861 with the beginning of the cottage boom.[31])

These connections may often have reduced the expense of vacationing at Wesleyan Grove. At the same time, they constituted one of its chief attractions. Many cottagers found there a virtual "home away from home," populated with acquaintances from their city neighborhoods and relatives from other nearby cities. They followed a social schedule much like that at home and lived in cottages that seemed more like their own urban parlors than anything else. However alien the *idea* of vacationing might have been, the world of Wesleyan Grove must have seemed reassuringly familiar.

For the men, there was the familiar world of business, often intertwined with family and religious connections. For the women, Wesleyan Grove continued the mixture of social calls and domestic work familiar to them at home. The *New York Times* reporter for 1867 observed "children . . . playing in the walks; ladies sitting sewing or reading or chatting in the doorways," and "the hum of the sewing-machine" in the background. In Wesleyan Grove, though, women's work was often much more visible than at home. Many observers reported seeing women cooking dinner, laying tables, and making beds through the open doors and windows, "the processes of cooking, ironing, and other household duties, performed by the mothers or daughters themselves, with graceful unconsciousness or indifference to outside eyes."[32]

Glimpses of scenes like this one intrigued journalists, who found the "graceful unconsciousness" of women campers at their chores startlingly revealing. From the journalists' standpoint, watching respectable women cook was a little like watching them dress or undress. "Cooking," from "Camp-Meeting at Martha's Vineyard," *Harper's Weekly*, 12 September 1868.

Visitors to Wesleyan Grove were most impressed by this peculiar openness. The cottages, like the tents they replaced, seemed to offer an extremely public existence. They stood very close together, with wide windows and doors usually left open, and much of family life taking place in plain sight of neighbors and tourists. Gazing into private family space, and especially seeing women at what was obviously considered private work, was disconcerting to some observers: "It seems to be a point of etiquette to show as much of the interiors as possible, and one can learn something of cooking and bed-making and mending, and the art of doing up the back hair."[33] But many observers found this appealing: The "graceful unconsciousness" of the women while they worked seemed to reveal "a veritable age of innocence, like Eve's before she bit the fatal apple."[34] The *New York Times* reporter for 1866 felt as if he had somehow "got into" Eden, where "beautiful and charming young ladies . . . sit on the piazzas in light and airy attire."[35]

In fact, the extraordinary openness of life in the cottages did not strike observers as an extremely public existence, but as a peculiar kind of privacy. Wesleyan Grove's living arrangements were not particularly "public" when compared with those in the great resort hotels, where people occupied public space for virtually every activity except sleeping—eating, playing, and socializing in vast halls and dining rooms. But in the great hotels public space was formal. People dressed to be seen, and the preparation was kept in the background. Wesleyan Grove, by contrast, seemed informal, domestic, and intimate.[36] This "Eden" was a paradise where even reporters who were strolling through the lanes peering into other people's kitchens and bedrooms had a sense of shared privacy. They were looking, not at a public presentation, but at an intimately private world.

Even the word *cottage* bore similar associations with informality, domesticity, and family intimacy. Although Wesleyan Grove's cottages did not conform to the style set out in Andrew Jackson Downing's influential patterns of the 1840s and 1850s, they shared the connotations of simplicity and rural informality that were attached to the medieval and rustic styles of Downing's cottages. To these associations they added their own clear references to Gothic religious themes and to the tents that preceded them. Like the "cottages" of Newport, and like many others that bore no resemblance whatever to the Downing style, Wesleyan Grove's cottages laid claim to a social meaning of simplicity and artlessness rather than to a specific architectural style.

The cottages, moreover, were eminently domestic—"best suited to families"—since they both "embodied economy" and "insure[d] the privacy of home life."[37] In the great hotels, there was little place for children. Part of the appeal of the new cottage and tent vacation communities was the ease with which children could be included. At Wesleyan Grove, that atmosphere was exaggerated into an almost idyllic sense of safety. The informality of life, the inexpensiveness, and the moral safety all contributed to the sense that children were welcome there.[38] More than one observer described small children wandering unsupervised through the "rustic lanes" of Wesleyan Grove with labels attached to their backs detailing the cottage or tent to which they should be returned, "as safely as the lambs in Paradise before Eve listened to the serpent."[39]

The physical design of Wesleyan Grove contributed to the sense of shared domesticity. In contrast to the long straight avenues of Newport or the rows of hotels at Saratoga, Wesleyan Grove's curved, narrow streets and closely packed cottages gave outside observers the sense of walking through a private world. Whole neighborhoods turned inward around their own private parks, where the children could play under the eyes of one or another of the cottagers. This sense of privacy was no doubt enhanced by the fact that such small neighborhoods were often composed of cottagers from the same cities, even the same neighborhoods, on the mainland. Of the forty-four cottages at Wesleyan Grove

Visitors reported that Wesleyan Grove residents used their front porches and yards as extended "parlor" space. These cottagers have decorated their front porch with chairs, a rug, and a bird cage hanging in front of the door. The cottage, typical of Wesleyan Grove's tiny Gothic cottages, probably had two connected rooms downstairs and one room upstairs, perhaps partitioned by a curtain. These six people were probably living there. Graphics collection, American Antiquarian Society. Courtesy, American Antiquarian Society.

owned by residents of New Bedford, twenty were in the circle named County Park. (Many of these cottage owners lived on County *Street* in New Bedford.)

That connection between home and Wesleyan Grove was not accidental. In some ways life at Wesleyan Grove was, more than anything else, like life at home in the city. The cottages were decorated in parlor fashion, "with pictures, books, pianos, melodeons, shell ornaments, and other devices for ensnaring."[40] The interior parlors spilled out onto the verandas and lawns around the cottages. Inhabitants hung their bird cages and parlor decorations from tree branches and received guests on the grass in front of their doors. The cottages were often referred to as "parlorlike," and indeed they looked in some cases as if they were nothing *but* parlors, with all the style and function of those rooms in the 1860s. The informality and domesticity emphasized at Wesleyan Grove conformed to the most popular domestic advice of the period. Homemade decorations, an abundance of plants, comfort over formality, were all part of the scheme of creating an attractive, inexpensive style of living suited to urban families of limited means.[41] And, of course, having a parlor—a room where no work took place, used for quiet entertainments and socializing—was perhaps the single most infallible sign of having achieved middle-class status.

Filled with the acquaintances and routines of home, Wesleyan Grove was reassuringly familiar. It was not Newport—not expensive, not elite, not formal, not fashionable. And it was safe, too, from the dangers at the other end of the class ladder, or so its enthusiasts claimed. As Vincent put it, the residents of Wesleyan Grove were "bent on excluding from their midst whatever defiles or degrades humanity"—principally "bad characters" and "intoxicating drinks."[42] As the cottages went up, however, the need to protect Wesleyan Grove from such dangers seemed more urgent. The campground's own *Camp Meeting Herald* of the summer of 1866 saw fit to publish a "WORD OF ADVICE" to all "light-fingered gentry, and rowdies generally, to keep clear of Wesleyan Grove, for they are sure to be caught if they attempt to carry on their evil practices."[43]

There was a great deal of talk about protecting Wesleyan Grove from "evil practices," but in spite of the concern, it *was* a safe place to vacation. From time to time, Vincent's chronicle or the *Vineyard Gazette* would report a minor skirmish with evildoers—a cache of liquor found and destroyed, a "worthless vagrant" arrested—but the handful of incidents that were reported only emphasize the relative safety of the community, particularly in comparison with the cities where most cottagers lived. Even the local *Vineyard Gazette* tended to make a joke of these incidents. In August 1869, when five men were caught gambling on the bluffs above the camp meeting, the *Gazette* took full advantage of the opportunity to make puns about "bluffing"—which was also Wesleyan Grove's term for flirting.[44]

"Not knowing, however," as Vincent put it, "what wicked men might be tempted to do," Wesleyan Grove took pains to protect itself. It was not, after all, only crime which threatened the cottagers. Apparently in the same category as "rowdies and rogues" and "worthless vagrants" were destitute beggars. In 1867 Hebron Vincent reported that a committee had been drawn up to discourage "private charity" on the campground, since so many people in need had been appearing during camp meeting week.[45] "Poor humble followers of the Lord" were all very well, but Wesleyan Grove could no longer afford the threat to its communal safety that seemed to arise from such obvious destitution.

Wesleyan Grove seemed "safe" because it protected its vacationers not simply from pickpockets and toughs, but also from daily encounters with people far above or below them on the social scale, and particularly those with different values—from Newport sherry-drinkers to underworld gamblers, from the idle rich to the idle poor. In this one important matter, of course, Wesleyan Grove was nothing at all like Fall River or New Bedford. Most of Wesleyan Grove's cottagers did not live in class-stratified neighborhoods at home. Although in mid-century the wealthiest residents of many cities were beginning to isolate themselves in segregated neighborhoods or in the new suburbs, most of the cottagers of Wesleyan Grove were not able (or did not choose) to make that kind of move.

Out of the forty-four cottagers from New Bedford, for example, only one appears to have moved to the suburbs in the years between 1856 and 1875.[46] All the other forty-three cottagers stayed at home in their tightly knit, mixed-use neighborhoods, where manufacturers, merchants and grocers shared living quarters with their factories, shops, and churches. Wesleyan Grove may even have functioned as an alternative to suburbanization. Several cottagers with money to invest chose to buy cottage lots on Martha's Vineyard, when in theory they might have invested in suburban house lots. For those lacking that extra money, Wesleyan Grove nevertheless offered a small-scale, temporary suburban experience: an opportunity to surround themselves with people of similar experiences and values, and to keep out the diversity of the industrial city.[47]

Camp Meeting Wars

Ultimately, Wesleyan Grove seemed safe because it protected vacationers from themselves, from the new temptations of wealth and leisure, and from their fears of falling backward into poverty. But that sense of safety was not achieved without struggle. In the formative period of the 1860s, outsiders often described Wesleyan Grove as if it were in a state of open conflict. A correspondent for the *Providence Journal* asserted in 1868 that there were two completely different kinds of visitors on the campground: Methodists, and "a great many other people whose Methodism consists mainly in some *method* of getting to Wesleyan Grove every summer."[48]

The *New York Times* correspondent in the summer of 1867 described the difference in terms of social class. He wrote that the cottage residents—respectable and prosperous "families from the mainland" who were spending "the season" at Wesleyan Grove—rarely went to the religious meetings "except to wander around in idle curiosity." As for the visitors who were there for the camp meeting, the *Times* correspondent lampooned such primitive Methodists for the "vehemence" of their religious expression, their bad table manners, and their lowly origins.[49]

The cottages, and the new uses of Wesleyan Grove they represented, did intensify conflicts on the campgrounds, and some of them were clearly rooted in class differences. Hebron Vincent reported, for instance, that in 1865 a number of tent dwellers were displaced to make way for new cottage lots. As Vincent put it, "some of the old settlers" were rather upset about the procedure because they "had the misfortune to be removed from their endeared spots to others less enjoyable." This was unavoidable progress, as Vincent saw it, but however inevitable the progress that doomed one's "house of cloth . . . to be superseded by one of wood," it was not a process that inspired unity or trust.[50] For the most part, though, the discord within Wesleyan Grove did not have such clear origins. The *New York Times* reporter saw an unambiguous conflict between prosperous, secular cottage owners and penniless Methodist enthusiasts. But the real conflict went deeper.

One controversy over a cottage illustrates some of the origins of that disharmony. David Clark had built a cottage on the campground for his family and the family of the Reverend Moses Scudder to share, and the two families *had* managed to share the cottage for the season of 1868. Soon after that, however, the Reverend Moses Scudder was telling his friends that Clark had bought the cottage as a gift for *him*, and Clark was claiming it as his own. The conflict became public in 1869 when the two men began to exchange accusations in the *Hartford Courant*. Clark even had a pamphlet published, entitled *How the Reverend M. L. Scudder Got His Cottage*, in which he told his side of the story.

Most cottagers did not end up hiring lawyers and exchanging insults in the newspapers as Clark and Scudder eventually did, but many of them must have encountered similar difficulties. For one thing, the tiny cottage was occupied by seven adults during August 1868 (and sometimes more—at one point Clark invited some relatives to spend the night). Opportunities for conflict arose almost daily. Scudder's daughter apparently insulted Mrs. Clark, and Clark's grown son complained to him that the Reverend Scudder's tantrums got on his nerves: "I would not stay here with that fussy man, Scudder, for one hundred dollars a day."[51]

One of the most obvious sources of tension between the two families was the disagreement over who was to pay for the groceries. Clark believed that Scudder always contrived to bring him along whenever anything needed to be paid for: "I soon saw that he possessed a spongy nature, and concluded not to accompany him any more; but from the bakers, fruit dealers, and poultry-men, I continued to supply the table as long as we remained."[52] Scudder in turn accused Clark and his family of living off him while they were on Martha's Vineyard.

Here was exactly the state of affairs camp-meeting advocates must have seen in their worst nightmares: petty quarrels over money replacing communal generosity; an open rift between a distinguished minister and a wealthy supporter; the good name of the campground and of the Methodist church dragged into the public press. The new pursuit of vacation pleasure could interfere with Wesleyan Grove's pursuit of Christian community in ways that were both comical and deeply serious.

There *was* a fundamental conflict between the traditional detachment from worldly things the camp meeting had always hoped to encourage and the new excitement over the cottages and the vacation experience. Cottage owners were no less pious than their tent-dwelling brothers and sisters, but even a fairly unenthusiastic worshiper might summon up enough generosity and patience to get through a week-long, intensely emotional religious meeting. And even an ardent and committed Christian might *not* be quite so generous and self-denying on a vacation that lasted a full month, particularly if that vacation had raised expectations of leisure and enjoyment one might not have brought along to a traditional camp meeting.

And, as the story of the Clarks and the Scudders makes clear, these conflicts were not only about religion and leisure. They were also about something potentially even more divisive: money.

A Gentile Suburb

In 1867, Hebron Vincent's chronicle announced, with resignation, that
"[w]herever, in this land of the Pilgrims, there is any special gathering
of the people . . . there will be the indomitable Yankee, with . . . his plans
of some kind for turning up the dollar." More to the point, "there, too, will
be gentlemen, all ready . . . for a profitable investment."[53] In that year, gentlemen investors had formed a company with local resident Captain
Shubael Norton, the owner of a large piece of land bordering Wesleyan
Grove which the company hoped to turn into a resort community. The
Oak Bluffs Land and Wharf Company, as they called their corporation, laid
out plans for a wharf and a hotel and began selling cottage lots that very
summer. That year, the creation of a frankly secular resort at the edges of
Wesleyan Grove brought into a startlingly clear light all the submerged
conflicts on the campground. The pursuit of profit, even more than the
pursuit of pleasure, seemed to threaten the purposes of Wesleyan Grove.

At first Wesleyan Grove's leaders looked for ways of blocking out whatever secular influences Oak Bluffs might turn out to harbor. In 1866, the
Vineyard Gazette joked about the "Camp Meeting war" and warned of a
plan to build a "Chinese wall" around Wesleyan Grove.[54] And in 1869,
Wesleyan Grove cottagers actually did just that. A fence was constructed
around the campgrounds, and the gate was closed nightly at 10 P.M. But
more frequently, Wesleyan Grove's efforts to protect itself from the influences of Oak Bluffs were marked with some ambivalence.

As the Oak Bluffs Company transformed the area adjacent to Wesleyan
Grove, the leaders of Wesleyan Grove went into business on their own behalf in 1870 with another nearby piece of land across a lake (or "over
Jordan," as it came to be called). As an "escape route" in case the camp
meeting was forced to move, they formed the Vineyard Grove Company,
and they, too, began selling lots for cottages at Vineyard Highlands. By
1872, the two companies together had sold over six hundred cottage lots
and had completely transformed the area. Promoters began to speak of a
"Cottage City" encompassing all three locations. But for all that, the leaders of Wesleyan Grove continued to be wary of the influence of Oak Bluffs
and saw their own speculative ventures not as collaboration with the
enemy but as a defensive maneuver.

Though the leaders of Wesleyan Grove drew a circle to keep Oak Bluffs out, Oak Bluffs did not respond in kind. Rather than setting itself up in opposition to Wesleyan Grove, Oak Bluffs embraced it. The Oak Bluffs company directors took pains to enforce Methodist moral requirements in their development. No steamboats landed at their wharf on Sundays. No liquor was to be sold (openly) at their fashionable hotel. Oak Bluffs land deeds bound buyers to the rules of the Martha's Vineyard Camp Meeting Association. Oak Bluffs' directors seemed to recognize the extent to which the appeal of their location depended on the special mix of religion and pleasure that constituted the world of Wesleyan Grove. So they acted to widen but not destroy the boundaries of safety and comfort established at Wesleyan Grove.

Oak Bluffs' developers followed Wesleyan Grove's social styles as closely as possible. Their pitch emphasized the "non-Newport" attributes that had made Wesleyan Grove attractive. Oak Bluffs was explicitly advertised as cheaper than aristocratic Newport or Saratoga, designed for those who desired the "benefits of the sea air and out of door exercise without the discomforts of a fashionable and crowded watering place."[55] Although Oak Bluffs cottages were often considerably larger, more ornate, and more expensive than those at Wesleyan Grove, they were still more like Wesleyan Grove cottages than like the ornate "cottages" being built at Newport. As Ellen Weiss has pointed out, some of the professionally designed cottages of Oak Bluffs intentionally mirrored the cottage styles of Newport, but in the smaller scale that brought them back down to actual "cottage" size— yet another way of demonstrating that Cottage City was "not Newport."[56]

At Oak Bluffs, as at Wesleyan Grove, a "social home life" was the biggest attraction. Oak Bluffs, too, offered "comfort and benefit consistent with the average purse," and its moral and class safety were the key to its popularity. To businessmen who left their families on vacation and commuted back and forth to work, Oak Bluffs advertisements offered complete assurance: "Your wife and daughter can mingle with the multitude and hear no word to offend and your little boy and girl can go and come at their pleasure without fear of trouble or harm."[57] Oak Bluffs was not on sacred ground, but it was near enough to partake of many of its blessings. It was, as one observer phrased it, a "gentile suburb" of Wesleyan Grove.[58]

Ultimately, Oak Bluffs presented a mix of business, pleasure, and religion quite different from that on the campgrounds, but the boundaries between the two were often blurry. On the campgrounds, for instance, the land was safeguarded by the Martha's Vineyard Camp Meeting

Association: It could not be bought or sold. At Oak Bluffs (and at Vineyard Highlands) speculation was uncontrolled. By the 1870s, land prices had quadrupled. But the speculators were not all outsiders with no ties to the camp meeting. Some of the most devoted supporters of Wesleyan Grove made money (or tried to) by speculating in cottage lots at Oak Bluffs or Vineyard Highlands.

Wells Baker, a dry-goods merchant from New Bedford, had given $20 in 1865 to help the Martha's Vineyard Camp Meeting Association purchase the grounds of Wesleyan Grove. Between the summer of 1871 and the summer of 1872 he also made a substantial profit on two Oak Bluffs lots, which he bought for $225 and sold for $1,300. He kept a third lot for his own use. Physically, sacred ground and speculative ground were not very far apart. Pequot Avenue at Oak Bluffs, where Baker's lots were located, is directly across the street from one of the entrances to Wesleyan Grove, no more than a few hundred feet from the gate. The same profits could be made "over Jordan," at Vineyard Highlands. The Reverend Moses Scudder bought the first lot sold by the Vineyard Grove Company in 1870 for $100 and sold it two years later for $400.[59]

Oak Bluffs took the picturesque elements of Wesleyan Grove's life and gave them full play. At Oak Bluffs, cottages sprouted turrets and towers and boasted ocean views. Sometimes whole cottages were removed from the campgrounds and put together to make larger ones at Oak Bluffs. Street names were frankly fanciful, referring more to other fashionable scenic resorts than to the campground's religious underpinnings: Narragansett, Penacook, and Samoset were intended to evoke the Indian associations of the White Mountains and Newport rather than the campground, where the streets bore the more somber names of Siloam, Commonwealth, and Trinity.

Oak Bluffs was laid out by Robert Morris Copeland, a popular landscape architect who had made his name designing fashionable cemeteries. Copeland took the circular motif of Wesleyan Grove and expanded it into an elaborately curved, studiedly informal design—mirroring the intimacy of scale at Wesleyan Grove but maintaining more normal spatial arrangements. Deeds to Oak Bluffs land specified the distances allowed between cottage and street and between the cottages, and they explicitly prohibited the erection of tents there. In short, Oak Bluffs was made to look like Wesleyan Grove without any of its visual ties to the camp meeting—almost as picturesque, but without the inconvenience and primitive conditions of Wesleyan Grove.

A few Oak Bluffs residents were far wealthier than Wesleyan Grove cottagers, but even they shared the background and commitments of their less wealthy brethren on the campground. Two of Oak Bluffs' wealthiest cottagers, William A. Claflin and Isaac Rich, were millionaires as well as fervent Methodists. Claflin was the governor of Massachusetts but also the son of manufacturer Lee Claflin, who had started life in desperate poverty. Isaac Rich had risen from childhood poverty to millionaire status in the 1870s and had gone on to become the principal founder (with Lee Claflin) of Methodist Boston University. Both Lee Claflin and Isaac Rich had achieved great wealth by a route that had been at least partly traveled by many of their neighbors. Lee Claflin, for example, began life as an orphan, apprenticed to a tanner. With the help of substantial loans from fellow Methodists, he turned his small tannery into a boot manufacturing complex that formed the basis of his investment ventures. Here, too, Oak Bluffs stretched the boundaries of Wesleyan Grove, but remained rooted in the familiar.

In fact, the ornate cottages and higher style of Oak Bluffs reflected a new current in Methodism in the second half of the nineteenth century. In earlier times, leaders of the church had prided themselves on their great appeal to poor and hard-working Christians and feared the results of prosperity. In the second half of the nineteenth century, the entire church was being forced to come to terms with the new prosperity of its members, in their discipline, in the style and opulence of their churches, and in their uses of leisure.[60] Oak Bluffs offered an important bridge for such a gap. Rich Methodists would never feel at home among the elite at Newport, but increasingly, they saw no reason why they could not bring a little "Newport" to Oak Bluffs.

Cottage City

The creation of Oak Bluffs eased the tension within Wesleyan Grove, since it made its conflicts in part geographical rather than internal. And it also acted to broaden the appeal of the two places taken together, by expanding the ways in which they could include the secular and the sacred, the profit-making and the pleasure-seeking, in one place. By the end of the 1860s, the development of Oak Bluffs had substantially changed the nature of what was now being referred to as Cottage City, not by eliminating or directly competing with the religious atmosphere at Wesleyan Grove, but by expanding the range of possibilities while maintaining the sense of religious safety.

Eventually a continuum of acceptable entertainments evolved, ranging from the camp meeting itself to the more worldly pleasures of billiards, dancing, and roller skating. Visitors arriving at the Oak Bluffs wharf were greeted by a brass band, while more conservative vacationers landed at the Highlands wharf and stepped ashore in dignified silence. At Oak Bluffs, "harmless" leisure pursuits could go on full-scale without colliding directly with prayer meetings. This was especially important for croquet players, who had overrun the campgrounds in the late 1860s, occupying every open piece of lawn, even around the preacher's stand. (The Camp Meeting Association had been forced to take drastic measures: In 1867 they prohibited the game during the week of the meeting.)

At Oak Bluffs, a fashionable hotel could be erected without fear of disrupting the homelike neighborhoods of the grove—and croquet could proceed without fear of disruption from religious services. Not that Oak Bluffs transformed the piety of Wesleyan Grove into a front for secular entertainments: Both forms of entertainment coexisted. Even when Oak Bluffs sponsored the first of its immensely popular "illumination nights" in 1869, a number of people still preferred to go to one of the two "largely attended" prayer meetings on the campgrounds.[61]

Illumination Night was one of the most successful entertainments sponsored by the Oak Bluffs Company, and it also revealed the extent to which the new entity of Cottage City both assimilated and transformed the meanings of Wesleyan Grove. On Illumination Night cottage dwellers in all the communities—Wesleyan Grove, Oak Bluffs, and Vineyard Highlands—strung Japanese lanterns everywhere and decorated their cottages with banners. The slogans on the banners reveal an intense awareness of the campground's history, referring back to the camp meeting in an assortment of puns and jokes designed to connect religious and vacationing themes: "The Vineyard is Our Resting-Place, Heaven is Our Home" or "We Trust in Providence, Rhode Island."

Perhaps the most evocative of all was the slogan, "We'll Camp Awhile in the Wilderness, and Then We're Going Home." It seems to be a straightforward reference to vacationing but is actually lifted from an early Methodist hymn that would have been familiar to everyone there, if only as a relic of the primitive past. In the revival song, home was heaven, and earthly life was the wilderness. In the Illumination Night version, Cottage City was now the "wilderness" (shorn of all its former associations with hardship and danger); and after "camping in the wilderness," the cottagers were returning to their true "home"—not heaven, but their daily lives in

Fall River or New Bedford. The summer sojourn on Martha's Vineyard no longer reflected an image of a future heavenly "home"; it was now both a respite and a continuation of "home" in the city.

Cottage Cities

By the time Wesleyan Grove had become Cottage City, it had been joined by an entire army of oceanfront resorts up and down the coast of New England, from Newport to Bar Harbor, "an almost continued chain of

This stereograph was taken during an illumination in honor of the visit of President Ulysses S. Grant in 1876. The domelike banner in the center of the picture says "Welcome President"; to the right is a banner with the slogan, "The Vineyard is Our Resting Place—Heaven is Our Home." In the upper left-hand corner, barely visible on the cottage balcony, is a banner reading, "We'll Camp Awhile in the Wilderness." Graphics collection, American Antiquarian Society. Courtesy, American Antiquarian Society.

hotels and summer cottages," as an 1886 *Harper's* article described it. "When one is on the coast in July or August it seems as if the whole fifty millions of people had come down to lie on the rocks, wade in the sand, and dip into the sea."[62] And Cottage City had become a prototype for these new resorts. The Oak Bluffs Land and Wharf Company invested thousands of dollars to make Cottage City popular with all kinds of visitors. As many as twenty boats a day landed at the Oak Bluffs wharf during August, bringing thousands of day-trippers from New Bedford or Fall River, as well as cottage and hotel visitors. The Sea View Hotel was a model resort hotel, with all the latest improvements in style and comfort, including a billiards room, barbershop, gas lighting, and steam heat.

None of the new seaside resorts would have been complete without a hotel like the Sea View, if only for the sake of its function as a visual and geographic center. The hotels' impressive size, their ornate architectural style, their huge public rooms, and their technological innovations made them landmarks rather than simply living quarters. Hotels like the Sea View became powerful symbols of the resort experience. Even today, seventy-five years after most of them burned down, the "great hotels" remain foremost in our imagination of nineteenth-century vacationing. Linked to the cities by the increasingly extensive railroad connections of the last quarter of the nineteenth century, such resort hotels commanded ever larger potential markets. The Oak Bluffs Company, for example, succeeded in bringing the Old Colony Railroad down to Woods Hole (where the steamboats set off from Cape Cod), thus adding a direct link with Boston to their superb connections with the cities of southern New England.

Corporate development became typical of coastal resorts during the last quarter of the century. On Martha's Vineyard alone, there were several other attempts to imitate Oak Bluffs' success. Along the shores of Katama near Edgartown, and in several other parts of the island, speculators divided up land into cottage lots and planned to build hotels and wharves. Most of these ventures went nowhere, and like the Oak Bluffs Company itself, most investors went bankrupt in the 1874 credit crisis. But all along the northeastern shore, corporations continued to invest in railroad lines, build wharves and hotels, and divide lots for sale in the same way.

Other resorts tapped into the special features of Wesleyan Grove, promising the same informality, privacy, and domesticity, "the entire absence of conventionalities or conditions which require the sojourner to continue irksome society customs or relations."[63] This style became popular even at resorts catering to a much higher social class than Oak Bluffs did. William Dean Howells remarked about his wealthy summer community in York, Maine, years later, that "a visitor from the world outside" had "burst out with the reproach, 'Oh, you make a fetish of your informality!'"[64]

Cottage City was also characteristic in its carefully wrought appeal to a clearly defined clientele. The northeastern shore trade was rigidly divided by class, one town specializing in the elite trade with fashionable hotels and private houses, the next building up a middling trade with boardinghouses and inexpensive cottages, the next offering services to day-trippers from the lower echelons of nearby cities. Howells described the stratification of York's vacation community with precision: "Beyond our colony, which calls itself the Port, there is a far more populous watering-place . . . known as the Beach, which is the resort of people several grades of gentility lower than ours." This next beach was "lined with rows of the humbler sort of summer cottages . . . supposed to be taken by inland people of little social importance." Down even farther were the beaches for excursionists, who came to the beach by trolley and spent "long afternoons splashing among the waves, or in lolling groups of men, women and children on the sand."[65]

Wesleyan Grove and its offshoots took part in all the experiences that were transforming the northeastern coast: the economic speculation, the shift in vacation styles, and the segregation of tourist towns along class lines. Cottage City came to provide options for people of various classes: It had its day-trippers and its fashionable sightseers. But it remained preeminently the summer home of the "inland people of little social importance" whom William Dean Howells had heard of, but never met. Someone he *had* met, Charles Dudley Warner, described Cottage City with amused ambivalence in an 1886 serial story for *Harper's*. Like everyone else, he contrasted it with Newport: "On the New Bedford boat for Martha's Vineyard our little party of tourists sailed quite away from Newport life."[66]

To Warner's eyes, the vacationers were a peculiar sort: "Most of the faces are of a grave, severe type, plain and good, of the sort of people ready to die for a notion." Wesleyan Grove offered those "grave, severe" people an opportunity to experience leisure in their own way: "These people abandon themselves soberly to the pleasures of the sea and of this packed, gregarious life, and get solid enjoyment out of their recreation."[67] It was still a "sober" sort of pleasure, but they had irrevocably

The artist who took this stereograph of the crowd under the preacher's tent may not have been able to focus on every face equally clearly, but enough faces are in focus to reveal that they are indeed of the "grave, severe type, plain and good" that Charles Dudley Warner encountered at Wesleyan Grove. Graphics collection, American Antiquarian Society. Courtesy, American Antiquarian Society.

"abandoned themselves" to it, and to a new world of leisure and consumption. For better or worse, Cottage City offered its own special package vacation to its own people: inexpensive pleasures, domestic informality, and the opportunity to practice a new Christian duty—the duty of relaxation.

4
"MANUFACTURED FOR THE TRADE"
Nostalgia on Nantucket, 1870–1890

ottage City was one of the most popular of New England's resorts in the last quarter of the twentieth century, but some tourists sailed right past it without any interest—and on to the island of Nantucket. One such enthusiast on an 1881 visit judged that four-fifths of her fellow steamboat passengers got off at Oak Bluffs, that "paradise of the commonplace," while only a discriminating few went on with her to Nantucket. In this tourist's view, Cottage City was far from heaven. On the contrary, it seemed to her to be a punishment out of Dante's "Inferno": to be "condemned through infinite ages to live in a small wooden house open in front, rear, and on both sides to the eyes, ears, and tongues of the good and happy grocer and his family." Fortunately, there was Nantucket, where the grocer and his family were not apt to be encountered. As this traveler saw it, "some of us love the dust of centuries, some of us love the almighty dollar; and as only twenty miles of water lie between Nantucket and Oak Bluffs, we may all be satisfied almost simultaneously."[1]

What was it that made Nantucket so different from Martha's Vineyard in this tourist's eyes? And what distinguished those who loved the "dust of centuries" from the "good and happy grocers" of Cottage City? At first

By the end of the nineteenth century, Nantucket's image—and its appeal to visitors—was closely linked to its old buildings, which had come to signify the island's romantic past. This gentleman is pursuing pipe dreams of the landmarks of Nantucket: the Oldest House, the Old Mill, and other well-known old buildings. A popular sentimental song, "How Dear to My Heart Are the Scenes of My Childhood," suggests the nostalgic underpinnings of the appeal of these buildings. From William Macy, *The Story of Old Nantucket* (Boston: Houghton Mifflin & Co., 1915).

glance, Nantucket might not appear to offer a vacation experience so very different from that found on its neighboring island. Nantucket was farther out to sea, but steamboats connected both islands with direct railroad lines to Boston and New York. And Nantucket's charms as a seaside resort were much the same as those of Martha's Vineyard. Both islands promised the same cool breezes, the same healthy air, the same opportunities for sea-bathing.

But according to increasing numbers of tourists and promoters, Nantucket had one asset quite unlike anything at Oak Bluffs: The "dust of centuries" seemed to be settling on it. Its quiet and solitude seemed lifetimes away from the bustling, crowded wharves of Oak Bluffs. Only a few years earlier, tourists had shunned such backwaters, but now travelers were developing a taste for them, finding something attractive in the "grey old wharves of Newburyport, of Salem, of Plymouth," and "many another quaint bygone place."[2]

Several cultural currents were making such "quaint bygone places" newly attractive to tourists in the last quarter of the nineteenth century.

In the past, tourist industries had occasionally catered to tourists' interest in historical landmarks: Revolutionary War battlegrounds like Bunker Hill had been popular since the beginning of organized commercial touring in the 1820s. Some Civil War battlegrounds became tourist attractions almost before the fighting stopped. And the preoccupation with romantic scenery had produced its own industry of legends and associations with landscape. But this interest in "grey old wharves" was something different.[3]

It was part of the fascination some Americans were developing in these years for all that was not modern, urban, and industrialized: for handcrafted works and "primitive cultures"; for the history and artifacts of the "colonial" period in American history; and for the "old days" vaguely associated with preindustrial farm and village life. This fascination took firm root among the wealthy old stock of the great eastern cities (and also among leading families of what was now becoming known as the Old South), but it was not confined to the highest spheres of birth and position. In one form or another, the fascination was widespread in the upper reaches of the middle class.[4] Such impulses among people with disposable income naturally created a wide array of new industries, from historical novels to "colonial revival" reproductions of furniture and silverware. In the tourist industry, they fueled a veritable revolution. Whole regions that had been traveled through—and ignored—for generations now seemed ripe for the development of their newly valuable "quaint" assets.

Nostalgic touring was not necessarily backed by a coherent ideology. It was more often a mixed bag of unexamined impulses and emotions that motivated nostalgic tourists. Travelers who felt stifled in their parlors and libraries might hope to experience some of the dangers and difficulties once faced by hardy pioneers. Those who were uncomfortable with the industrial order's mechanization and regimentation were drawn to places where independent farmers and artisans performed traditional tasks with simplicity and dignity. Those beset by alien faces and languages in their home cities might search for a place where "Anglo-Saxon" purity still prevailed. This bundle of impulses often shaped highly specialized tourist trades in different areas. Those who cherished fond memories of a simple, virtuous farm childhood they had abandoned in the search for wealth or success might "return," if only in fantasy, to the motherly hills of rural Vermont (the subject of Chapter 5). "Colonial revival" travelers sought out the imagined serenity and grace of a more stable class order in the faded maritime cities of Portsmouth, New Hampshire, and York, Maine (Chapter 6 will explore that phenomenon). And those with a taste for the exotically quaint discovered Nantucket.

The island of Nantucket might seem to have little in common with the hills or coastal towns of northern New England. But tourists in search of nostalgic experiences increasingly imagined their destination in regional terms, as "New England" rather than as "the seaside," for example, or the town of one's birth. And all such places were imagined as the repositories of a common New England heritage, as the natural homes of those long-lost values of stability, virtue—and Yankee bloodlines. The notion of New England as a distinctive region until now had figured only casually in tourist promotion. The scenic tourist trade of the White Mountains in the 1830s and 1840s, for example, had relied heavily on a sense of place and landscape, but the mountains were rarely referred to as "New England" mountains. (Promoters generally interpreted them as anything *but* New England: Switzerland and Italy were more common reference points.) Beach resorts up and down the northeastern coast depended on developing a vivid sense of place to distinguish themselves from their competitors, but the promoters of the coastal towns of Maine, New Hampshire, and Massachusetts had not claimed distinctive "New England" qualities for their beaches. Now, being part of the New England region offered rural and isolated parts of the six states a new way to market their assets.[5]

Earlier tourists had imagined the region of New England, when they thought of it at all, as the home of the most modern social and technological innovations of their day—a hive of factories, schools, sharp bargainers, and reforming agitators. When early nineteenth-century tourists had expressed an interest in seeing the distinctive features of New England, they had in mind the imposing educational edifices at Harvard and Yale, the technological and social innovations of Lowell, perhaps even the notoriously radical theologians, political theorists, and reformers around Boston. Now there was widespread nostalgia for another sort of New England, a place that was understood to exist chiefly in the rural and remote villages of the region, where railroads, banks, and the latest fashions had not penetrated. Travel books, nostalgic literature, and advertisements portrayed the entire region as a living museum, a storehouse for cherished ways of life that no longer seemed to exist in the cities (even the New England cities) where tourists lived.

Tourists in search of that new "Old New England" were looking for an imagined experience of the past—virtuous simplicity, rural independence, class harmony. Not coincidentally, the visual images that signified Old New England were also signs of isolation and economic failure. Rotting wharves and grass-grown streets, old buildings and outdated fashions, could now be read as something other than poverty and failure. Inland "colonial villages" like Deerfield, Massachusetts, and Litchfield, Connecticut, had been passed by in the scramble for railroads; their quiet and isolation came to represent the serenity and dignity of the old days. Few immigrants were attracted to places with few jobs, so rural and northern New England had preserved its racial "purity." In old port towns like Newburyport, Salem, and Portsmouth, "Yankee" customs, quaint clothing, and uncouth accents suggested an adherence to the "simple habits and old-time virtues" that could provide an antidote to "the anxiety and restlessness that so greatly cloud so many lives."[6] When visitors began to turn toward Nantucket in the 1870s and 1880s, they were attracted by just such signs—by the empty streets, rotting wharves, and isolation that Nantucket had only recently acquired.

Neither Nantucket's history nor its situation in 1870 made the island especially susceptible to this sort of romanticization. (Perhaps few of the towns that underwent this reinvention were especially fitted to the task.) Far from being a pristine New England village with ties to the colonial past, Nantucket was a commercial town in decline. In the midst of a newfound enthusiasm for New England rural and agricultural life, Nantucket presented an almost entirely entrepreneurial and even urban history. Nantucket natives were neither rustic nor naive. On the contrary, they had always enjoyed a reputation for being widely traveled, urbane, and shrewd. Instead of a communal and harmonious past, Nantucket presented an unusually fragmented and disorderly one. Racial and class tensions abounded, and traditional loyalties were weak or nonexistent. Not even religious homogeneity tied this community together. Nantucket had been settled by Quakers, but they had lost their predominance in the free-wheeling days of the early nineteenth century. Neutral in everything but the pursuit of profit, Nantucket boasted none of the Revolutionary War heroes who were becoming such an important part of the imagined New England past.[7]

Just as New England as a whole had made its mark in the early nineteenth century largely on the basis of its economic and technological modernity, Nantucket had made a name for itself as a leader in one of the most lucrative, but also one of the most volatile, of early nineteenth-century businesses: the whaling industry. Nantucket's whaling industry had prospered whenever it was unhindered by war, but the trade had reached its peak during the 1830s and 1840s, when the island's renowned whaling captains had dominated the high-risk, high-profit Pacific whale fishery, "like so many Alexanders; parceling out among them the Atlantic, Pacific, and Indian oceans," as Herman Melville described them in *Moby Dick*.[8] During those years, island families rolled up immense fortunes and used them to transform downtown Nantucket into a small but elegant and modern city, complete with elm-lined streets, brick commercial buildings, and their own stylish Greek Revival mansions. Scores of whale-related industries, including no fewer than thirty-nine candle and oil factories, employed hundreds of people and added to the prosperity—and to the urban landscape—of the island.

But by the late 1840s, Nantucket was already beginning to feel the pinch of its heavy reliance on a single industry. Whale products had always been subject to extreme fluctuations in price, and the industry itself was now in trouble, threatened by the growing scarcity of sperm whales and the growing abundance of substitutes for whale lighting oil. In the end, Nantucket's decline was precipitated by all these factors and by its inability to compete with the deeper harbors of newer ports like New Bedford. During the best years of the whale fishery, as many as eighty-five Nantucket vessels at a time were at sea; in 1853, only fifteen sailed from port.[9]

The island's wealthiest families began to withdraw their investments from whaling industries and to look for outside sources of income. Many of Nantucket's ordinary citizens made similar decisions. They continued to sail out of Nantucket, but they often decided not to sail back. In 1849, one Nantucket ship lost its entire crew to the gold rush when the ship stopped in San Francisco. But even without that special incentive, people were leaving the island. The population of Nantucket was already in decline by the end of the 1840s; it continued to decline precipitously, from a peak of almost ten thousand to a low point of about 3,500 by 1880. The last whaling ship left Nantucket in 1869, but by then visitors were already remarking on the town's rotting wharves and empty streets.

Making Something of Nantucket

The story of the rise and fall of Nantucket's whaling industry can be read in any of the dozens of popular histories and guides to Nantucket written from the 1870s through the 1980s. But the story of the island's vacation industry is a little more difficult to recover. How exactly did New England's new nostalgic tourist trade replace whaling as the primary means of livelihood on Nantucket? Most accounts have described the transformation from older trades to tourism as largely accidental. Nantucket's chronicler put it this way: "If it had not happened that just about that time the American people began to acquire the vacation habit, the probabilities are that our old town would soon have been almost entirely depopulated."[10]

In reality, of course, tourism did not become Nantucket's primary industry by accident, any more than New Bedford *accidentally* replaced its own declining whaling industry with textile mills. As early as the 1860s, while nearby Wesleyan Grove blossomed into a summer resort, it had become clear to many islanders that the "summer business" might be an effective alternative to whaling. In 1865 the editors of the *Nantucket Inquirer and Mirror*, Henry D. Robinson and Roland B. Hussey, printed a three-page pamphlet designed to capture the Boston summer trade with a description of the "Beautiful Island of Nantucket," its unsurpassed "Pure Sea Air," and its hospitable inhabitants. In editorials of the mid-1860s, the editors encouraged islanders to invest in the summer trade, and to think of it as a business proposition: "We have something to sell; that something is health, comfort, and pleasure."[11]

The editors of the *Nantucket Inquirer* made it clear that they hoped for better things. They were not alone. Edward Godfrey, a guidebook writer and tourist promoter himself, reflected both the hope and the sense of desperation of many islanders when he pleaded with his fellow citizens, "Make [Nantucket] a watering-place, make her a manufacturing town, make her an agricultural town, make her all three, but in heaven's name make her all three, but in heaven's name make her something!"[12] Many islanders would have preferred to have followed the New Bedford route from whaling to factories (even though so many twentieth-century tourist promoters and preservationists have been grateful for Nantucket's "salvation" from industrialization). In an editorial entitled "Our Future," the *Inquirer* encouraged its readers to "have a higher ambition than to make Nantucket only a watering place." New Bedford, they pointed out, "has two shoe factories. . . . She has a tanning establishment, blue works, a petroleum factory, and two flour mills."[13] Nantucket, too, could aspire to this level of industrial prosperity, if a few difficulties could be overcome.

The editors put forth several reasons for Nantucket's lack of success in new enterprises. They blamed in part the island's "more than Turkish apathy"—the druglike torpor that had settled on its inhabitants in the wake of commercial disaster. But the editors also knew that at least one potential industry, the cod fishery, was not stagnating for lack of energetic workers but for lack of capital. Editorials pleaded with investors to put money into the cod business, the "small fishery" that was making money for Gloucester, Newburyport, and Provincetown: "Men of moderate means, we call on you! . . . put a part of your well-earned means in a fishing vessel, and . . . benefit not only yourself alone, but also your island home."[14] (They had apparently already given up on men of great means.) The *Inquirer's* editors believed that fish were more reliable than tourists. Rather than "catering to the wants and tastes of a capricious city folk, and the chance of making anything only given to a few," Nantucket might be able to take "first rank among the fishing towns in Massachusetts."[15]

Where *was* the capital that could have "made something" of Nantucket? Some of the great fortune holders had simply left the island. Jared Coffin, who had built one of the great brick houses in downtown Nantucket in 1846, sold it the very next year and moved to Boston. But other island resources were being invested elsewhere. If no capital was forthcoming to invest in the "small fishery" of cod, there was more than enough to invest in railroads and real estate speculation on the island. During the 1870s, a handful of residents and former residents of Nantucket invested heavily in the island's development as a resort. In a pattern typical of the period (very much like the development of Oak Bluffs, for example), these investors planned interlocking projects—several "cottage cities," a luxury hotel, and a railroad to run between the resort center and the old town. Corporations were formed to sell shares in these enterprises; lots were surveyed and divided; advertisements were placed in city newspapers and local guides.

Much of this development was based on a few families' extensive landholdings. The Nantucket Surfside Land Company, for example, was incorporated in 1873 with Henry Coffin as its president. Its investors intended to set up a resort community on the south shore on land that belonged to Charles and Henry Coffin. The Coffin brothers were heirs to one of the greatest of the island whaling fortunes, which had included in the 1850s a fleet of seven whaleships, half a million dollars in inventory, warehouses, shipping supplies, a number of candle and oil factories, and a substantial amount of real estate on the island.[16] Their land, like much of the undeveloped land on Nantucket, was held as shares of commons, a remnant of the original proprietors' settlement.

Until the early nineteenth century, most of Nantucket's land had been held in common by the families of its original settlers, and most islanders could claim a proprietary interest, if only a tiny fraction of a share. Shareholders had customarily petitioned the proprietors to "set off" their share of commons when they wished to build a house or settle a farm. By the early 1820s, the common holdings had been greatly reduced in a lawsuit brought before the state supreme court by a group of prominent island merchants, who challenged the entire system's legality.[17] But even in the 1860s and 1870s, large stretches of barren land and shore were still held in common, simply because nobody had wanted them before. In the 1870s, investors found a use for this land: Barren seashore had become beachfront property. From that time on, there were increasing numbers of petitions to "set off" pieces of land on the shore for development, land which had virtually no value unless and until it became resort property.

Most local investment was in the form of landholdings like these, but Nantucket developers could also bring in outside capital through extended family networks. The Nantucket Railroad, for example, was capitalized at $100,000, most of which was raised in Boston at $100 a share. But the railroad was primarily the creation of islanders. The idea had come from Philip Folger, a Boston resident who was the grandson of a wealthy Nantucket whaling merchant. Folger was instrumental in organizing Boston capital to invest in the Nantucket Railroad; his island connections allowed him to do business there, too. In 1881 he was paid $8,500 by the railroad corporation for a piece of land that had been "set off" to him twenty years earlier.[18]

As was typical of such resort enterprises, Nantucket's railroad and land development schemes were closely linked. The Nantucket Railroad's general manager was Charles F. Coffin, the son of Henry Coffin, and its treasurer was John Norton, who was also a principal investor in Surfside. The railroad depot became the real estate office of the Surfside Land Company. In fact, it was the only building on the south shore for several years, until in 1883 the company finally managed to erect the Surfside Hotel, a structure they had bought in Rhode Island and moved to its new location. The hotel provided a destination for excursions from town and hosted summer entertainments for vacationers and natives.

Together with the railroad that ran to its door, such a hotel might have provided the nucleus for a thriving cottage city as the Sea View Hotel had done on neighboring Martha's Vineyard, but the Surfside Hotel and the Nantucket Railroad were all that came of this development. No cottages were built on the south shore of the island. On the basis of newspaper accounts, one would have thought that the Surfside Company was having remarkably good success selling real estate: In July and August of 1882 the *Nantucket Inquirer* reported that the company had sold almost 180 lots. But that success was an illusion. A grand total of only seven people had bought lots at Surfside between 1872 and 1881, for which they had paid $20 or $30—at a time when a normal price for such a lot would have been at least $100, and when many Oak Bluffs lots were going for $400. It is technically true that 136 lots were sold in 1882, but these transactions involved fewer than twenty people, who paid $1 for anywhere from one to fifteen lots at a time. Some of the buyers were local people involved in the tourist trade. Joseph Barney, who "bought" thirty-six lots from the Surfside Land Company in 1882, was the agent of the Nantucket and Cape Cod Steamboat Company. The Mowry family, which opened the Sherburne Hotel in 1877, took possession of thirty lots in 1882. Perhaps the cottage lots were being given away along with stock in the company, or as part of some other kind of incentive program. At any rate, no cottages were built on these lots. The success of the development was entirely on paper, a fact that was made clear in 1887 when nine hundred acres were sold at auction to cover debts.[19]

And the Surfside Land Company was not the only failure. Joseph and Winchester Veazie, former islanders who had sold some of their "set-off" land to the railroad, also planned to sell seventeen hundred lots in a vast development to be called Nauticon. In 1876, another group of investors laid out Sherburne Bluffs on the north shore. The Coffins, a few other islanders, and some wealthy off-islanders, including the well-known painter Eastman Johnson, were involved in the scheme. Sherburne Bluffs was to have had 150 house lots but apparently foundered over a disagreement between wealthy would-be cottagers and island investors over a road to be built between the cottages and the sea.[20] Sunset Heights, near the village of Siasconset, was marketed by another local team in the 1870s. In all these cases, lots were laid out and marketed; ambitious land plans were registered with the registry of deeds. But by 1881 only a few scattered cottages had been built in any of these developments.

This speculative disaster was not unique to Nantucket. Resort-development ventures had high failure rates everywhere during the 1870s and 1880s. Even the eminently successful Oak Bluffs Land Company on Martha's Vineyard was forced out of business in 1882 after selling its remaining lots and the Sea View Hotel to pay its debts.[21] But Nantucket's failures occurred just at the point when tourists were flocking to the island in larger numbers each year. The hotels of Nantucket were full every summer, and each summer they were expanded to accommodate more guests. The Nantucket Railroad and the Surfside Hotel were in fact very popular with those increasing numbers of guests, playing a key role in the life of the summer community by hosting dances, clambakes, skating parties, and picnics.

A clue to understanding this paradox is that a variety of small-scale tourist businesses were thriving alongside the failed large developments. An 1882 guidebook listed nine hotels and more than twenty boarding-houses on the island. And visitors did build their own summer houses— not in the planned developments, but on individual lots overlooking the bay near town and in the village of Siasconset (pronounced Sconset) on the southeast corner of the island, where fishing shacks were refurbished as vacation homes. Other tourist businesses were also profiting from the new trade. Isaac Folger's 1874 *Handbook of Nantucket* featured an advertisement on every right-hand page: Bathing-machines and ice-cream parlors, yachts for pleasure cruises, and a "fashionable tailor," all attested to the buying power of the summer visitor.

Nantucket *was* becoming a summer resort in the 1870s, whether or not its largest investors were making money. But in spite of the hopeful letter to the *Nantucket Journal* in 1879 arguing that a projected railroad might "have the effect of dotting the plains with . . . cottage cities", Nantucket was not going to be another Oak Bluffs.[22] It was not simply that the efforts of investors were failures but that they misjudged Nantucket's developing clientele, who seem to have been interested neither in the "crowded haunts" of elite watering places nor the gregarious closeness of a Cottage City. Those visitors who sailed past Cottage City to Nantucket preferred the privacy of boarding at a small hotel or with a family. As the *Nantucket Inquirer* put it, they "do not care for such a variety [of people] as they expect to find at hotels."[23] The *Providence Journal* pegged the summer people of Nantucket as the sort who "value good breeding more than fashion," which was perhaps to say that they could not afford the "fashionable display" of Newport, but that Cottage City–like familiarity was beneath them.[24]

Nantucket's visitors were far more cosmopolitan than the cottagers of Martha's Vineyard. The registers of the Sherburne Hotel (one of the largest on the island) for the summers of 1879 through 1881 reveal a much wider range of geographical backgrounds among Nantucket's tourists than those at Oak Bluffs. Visitors from cities as far away as Cincinnati and Baltimore

were quite common. Most were from New England or New York, but almost a third lived outside the region, in the mid-Atlantic, the Midwest, and
even a handful in the Southeast.[25] Most were from substantial cities.

Both the hotel registers and anecdotal evidence suggest that Nantucket
summer visitors were far different from the "happy grocers" of Martha's
Vineyard. The pages of the hotel registers were liberally sprinkled with
the signatures of attorneys and college professors. (None of these professionals were to be found at Wesleyan Grove in the 1860s and 1870s.)
Miss Florence Crawford of Topeka, Kansas, for example, was the daughter of a politically active lawyer and one-time governor of the state of
Kansas. Among the acquaintances she made on Nantucket during the summer of 1891 were the daughter of a Professor Francis H. Snow, from
Lawrence, Kansas, and a "fearfully intelligent . . . maiden lady" named Miss
Willis, who taught three languages at a Massachusetts school for women.[26]
Another account of summer life in the island village of Siasconset reported
a mostly professional crowd: "literary men and women," artists, college
professors and "weary women, teachers of seminaries," as well as "men
of affairs," who brought their families to the island for the summer and returned themselves for a shorter stay.[27]

These tourists were looking for a special kind of resort experience on
Nantucket. Accounts of visits to Nantucket indicate that tourists were as
intrigued by the quaintness and romance of Nantucket's history as they
were by its cool breezes and surf. Indeed, even if they were *not* initially intrigued by history and quaintness, they might soon be driven to take an
interest from sheer boredom. After a day spent playing cards, Florence
Crawford resolved to "get books written about the island and read all the
legends I can find," in spite of the fact that she had already heard more
legends and stories than she cared to record: "Every new person you meet
tells the same things until they grow rather tiresome."[28]

But most visitors to Nantucket knew what to expect. Few sought out
the island for its modern conveniences or fashionable hotel social life. At
the very moment when Nantucket's promoters were straining to provide
the typical resort entertainments and luxuries for their visitors, those visitors were looking for something quite different. Novelist Edward Bellamy
visited Nantucket one summer in the 1870s. In a thinly veiled autobiographical account of his visit, published in the form of a novel, Bellamy
made it clear he did not expect to find a typical resort there. His doctor
ordered him to spend some time on Nantucket precisely because it was
an "out-of-the-way, switched-off sort of place"—or as the overworked jour-

nalist characterized it, a "ridiculous little dead-alive down-east sandbank."
But the doctor prevailed, holding out the promise of an intriguing experience: "You've no idea how much you will enjoy studying the queer society and customs of the place."[29] And Bellamy would not be the only
tourist-turned-anthropologist on Nantucket.

Quaint Islanders

According to off-island enthusiasts, visiting Nantucket was something like
a trip to a living history museum. Since the 1860s, visitors had been writing descriptions of Nantucket that highlighted its whaling past. As with
Rome, the ancient glory of Nantucket had faded, but its heritage remained.
As a *Harper's* article put it, "the fame of Nantucket is historic, and the glory
of having given birth to the boldest and most enterprising mariners that
ever furrowed the seas is hers, imperishable and forever." The article went
on to draw a connection between Nantucket's main product—whale oil
for lighting—and the experience of the "good old days" that Nantucket
now represented. Between the ages of "lusty barbarism" (lighted by tal-
low) on the one side and "overstrained and diseased civilization" (lighted
by kerosene) on the other, stood Nantucket and the "golden age of reason"—lighted by whale oil.[30] Samuel Adams Drake, whose books did much
to romanticize the coast of New England, followed a similar train of
thought: "In coal oil there is no poetry; Shakspeare [*sic*] and Milton did
not study, nor Ben Jonson rhyme, by it."[31]

Nantucketers, too, were proud of their history and considered relics of
the past an important feature of the island. In 1869, local Episcopal minister Frank C. Ewer drew up a map of the island which became perhaps
the most popular image of Nantucket for the rest of the century. At first
glance the map looks similar to ones drawn up for Martha's Vineyard
tourists; but unlike Martha's Vineyard maps, almost half its space is covered by an elaborate historical time-line. The map highlighted historical
locations— "Site of Old Indian Meeting House" and "Site of the Old Sheep
Pens"—as the most important landmarks of the island.

But outsiders were often not so much interested in historical landmarks
as they were in the *people* of the island, whom they often imagined as historical relics themselves. In his 1868 *Book of Summer Resorts*, Charles
Sweetser, like Edward Bellamy's doctor, urged travelers to "go to Nantucket
and see the islanders."[32] Nantucket's people were portrayed as the last representatives of a sturdy race whose boldness and vigor had surpassed all

other nations. According to the guidebooks, the "frank, hearty, high-toned elements which have always characterized [Nantucket's] population" were all still to be seen there in the 1870s. Nantucketers were enterprising, vigorous, frank, hospitable, honest, and temperate. These characteristics reflected both their unique maritime experiences, which had formed their heroic characters, and their ethnic purity—the island's "population [was] not increased, nor has it ever been, by . . . discordant elements from varying climes and nationalities."[33]

That was not literally true, but it carried the germ of an important argument. Nantucket was *not* ethnically "pure," any more than the whaling industry had been conducted solely by "Anglo-Saxons." Both the island's Native American population and large numbers of Portuguese, South Sea Island, and African American sailors had worked on Nantucket whaling ships in their heyday.[34] But the notion that Nantucket's people were its most important "natural resource" worked nicely as a rationalization for its decline: Such a vigorous, restless "race" could not be confined at home, but instead must spread its admirable qualities all over the country. Many other parts of New England were busy constructing similar justifications for their own loss of economic and demographic power during the late nineteenth century, and Nantucket fit right in to the general argument that "New England's most important product was its men."[35]

Admiration for the heroic character of native Nantucketers, moreover, often barely masked another attitude. Off-island enthusiasts were not always precise about what kind of "character" one would find on Nantucket. Sometimes, contemporary islanders were portrayed as the last remnants of New England's heroic and enterprising manhood, "the boldest and most enterprising mariners that ever furrowed the seas." (This worked better for Nantucket *men*, of course, but the respectful attitude could be extended on occasion to the heroic wives who waited and worked while the men journeyed for years in search of whales.) Sometimes, though, Nantucketers appeared less as representatives of native *character* than as native *characters*, quaint "old salts" with accents and expressions amusingly reminiscent of former days.

Guidebooks and travel accounts of the 1870s and 1880s were filled with stories of Nantucket eccentrics, whose charming oddities were recounted tirelessly. A typical article in *Scribner's* included seventeen illustrations, five of which were portraits: "The Town Crier," "The Old Fish Dealer," "Abraham Quady, the Last Indian," "Portrait of Admiral Coffin," and "The Hermit of Quidnit."[36] Of these, only the portrait of Admiral Coffin could be said to possess any heroic qualities of the sort that were ostensibly being admired in Nantucketers. The portrait of Abraham Quady, the "Last Indian," certainly possessed dignity, but that came through in spite of his portrayal as a local curiosity.[37] (Martha's Vineyard also had a "Last Indian," Dorcas Honorable, who was presented as one of the local attractions of *her* island.) The "Hermit of Quidnit," whose name was Fred Parker, was a similar figure, noted chiefly for his peculiarities. These characters were usually presented in guidebooks as parts of a tour, to be visited along with the Oldest House and the Old Mill—focal points of a drive through the countryside.

The most popular character on Nantucket was the man featured in *Scribner's* as the "Town Crier," whose name was Billy Clark. Billy Clark was a central attraction in every nineteenth-century guidebook and in twentieth-century guides for generations after his death.[38] Clark had constituted himself the town crier, which meant he announced the arrival of steamboats and the most recent news from on and off the island. Some accounts suggested that Clark had lost his mind in the Civil War; some gave no reason for his peculiar conduct but suggested it was somehow typical of Nantucket quaintness. (Again, there is a close analogue on Martha's Vineyard in the figure of Nancy Pease, who lived alone with a large number of chickens for whom she wrote poetry, which she was willing to read to visitors for a tip.)

Commercial portrayals of local inhabitants could be crudely exploitative in their eagerness to display whatever would "sell" the island. Artistic portrayals were sometimes kinder, at times even respectful of the inhabitants they depicted, but they shared a similar preoccupation with the quaintness of Nantucket natives. The paintings of Eastman Johnson, who summered on the island between 1870 and 1887, reflected this preoccupation.[39] His best-known paintings are of islanders engaging in quaint, obsolete farm tasks—like his 1880 "The Cranberry Harvest"—or of old mariners, like his "Nantucket Sea Captain." Typically, the models for paintings like Johnson's "Nantucket School of Philosophy," a collective portrait of old Nantucket whaling-men, were bathed in a nostalgic light that emphasized their frailty and age, and the sense that they belonged to another world.

In some sense these portrayals reflected a reality of Nantucket life. And many islanders acknowledged that Nantucket's people did have a unique history that had made them different from other people. Edward Godfrey reported in his 1882 guidebook that there were still many people left in

This much-reproduced photograph of Billy Clark, the town crier, has been featured in Nantucket guidebooks since the 1870s. It was apparently the most popular of the four photographic images of Clark for sale, "one representing him with horn and papers, one with auction bell, and two in 'dress up' costumes." Clark sold copies of these photographs to visitors, along with newspapers and sundries. From Henry S. Wyer, *Nantucket Picturesque and Historic* (Nantucket, 1901). Courtesy, American Antiquarian Society.

town "whose lives possess a romantic interest . . . who could entertain one for hours with moving tales of shipwreck, disaster, suffering, and adventures of all kinds."[40] He reported that Mrs. Eliza McCleave, who had a seashell collection that the public was welcome to visit, was herself "the most quaint and curious of all" in the collection.[41] But while Godfrey admitted that Nantucketers were indeed "hospitable, honest, intelligent, brave," he concluded on a decidedly unromantic note: They were "after all just like the rest of the world, neither better nor worse." He acknowledged the existence of special "characteristics and peculiarities" on the island, but he neither romanticized nor condemned them. He attributed them to the island's isolation; such traits were "always noticeable in isolated localities."[42]

By contrast, outsiders often imagined the character of Nantucket people nostalgically, as something no longer quite of this world. Samuel Adams Drake wrote that Nantucket's "isolation from the world surrounds it with a mysterious haze."[43] The island possessed "many of the conditions of an undiscovered country"—not unlike the "primitive" regions encountered on vacations in the American West or in the islands of the Pacific. (Perhaps the figure of Nantucket's "Last Indian" was consistent with this vision of Nantucket's other "natives.") Their character—simple dignity, manly frankness, openhearted hospitality—appeared at once admirable and faintly ludicrous, as if it were the product of a childlike ignorance.

Both Nantucketers and their visitors agreed, for example, that islanders were especially hospitable. But it was outsiders who typically portrayed the "honest . . . open countenance" and traditional hospitality of the Nantucketers as traits that qualified them by nature to be porters or hotel keepers. Islanders, as Frank Sheldon described them for *Atlantic Monthly*, were free from the profit motive: They "do not look upon a stranger as they do upon a stranded blackfish—to be stripped of his oil and bone for their benefit." They were good guides, and they were glad to recount stories of their whaling days. Moreover, their native hospitality prompted them to offer all these services, as Sheldon put it, "good-humoredly and *gratis*."[44]

Nantucketers knew that their prices must be kept low if they were to compete with other, more convenient resort locations. But for Sheldon, Nantucket's low prices were a sign, not of the island's depressed economy, but of their naiveté and utopian simplicity: Nantucket was the home of "[t]he blessed old prices of my youth . . . long since driven from the continent."[45] Sheldon linked Nantucket natives to the "natives" to be "discovered" on faraway islands like Bali and Hawaii, where the local population were thought to be similarly naive about profit and loss. When Sheldon's traveling companion was informed of the price of renting a cottage on Nantucket, he could not believe his good fortune. His reaction of surprise and glee was "similar to those of Captain Cook or Herman Melville when they first landed to skim the cream of the fairy islands of the Pacific."[46]

Of course, Nantucketers were not utopian islanders who knew nothing of business or profit. They were quite open about their motives for bringing tourists to the island. Nothing could have been more direct than the *Inquirer's* editorial reminder in 1866 that "we want the money that strangers will leave."[47] William Macy recalled in later years the fascination that the new "strangers" had held for him in his childhood. They were better dressed and noisier than townspeople, and they spoke differently, too. "They called the commons 'moors' and everything was 'quaint.'" But all that would have been of no interest had they not also had outlandish tastes for the small services young boys could render: "They would buy pond-lilies at two-for-a-cent . . . so the town boys . . . waxed prosperous."[48]

Edward Bellamy's account of Nantucket hinted at a different comparison with the exotic experiences travelers encountered in the South Seas. His novel was titled *Six to One: a Nantucket Idyl.* It was idyllic mostly because the hero is the one man in a social circle of six young Nantucket women, casualties of the unbalanced sex ratio resulting from the exodus of Nantucket men in search of work. Bellamy let his readers in on the perspective of both the male visitor and his local hostesses: The hero assumes that the young Nantucket women have arranged their social lives around him purely out of an innate desire to please him—out of natural "hospitality." The reader is quite plainly informed, though, that their generous hospitality is the result of a deal the women struck before the young man reached the island: They have agreed to share the visitor evenly among themselves, in order to get the greatest benefit (in this case social rather than financial) out of his stay.

While both islanders and visitors considered Nantucketers to be welcoming and gracious, there are signs that Nantucketers were not eager to embrace the new professional hospitality. The young women of Bellamy's novel frankly acknowledge to the hero of the story that they are not at all pleased to find themselves in the position of professional hostesses. When he asks whether they like summer visitors, one replies, "No, we don't any of us, except the hotel keepers and owners of fishing-boats." (Actually, they take a vote: Four dislike the visitors, while one thinks they break up the monotony, and one dislikes them only because she wishes she could leave with them at the end of the season.) But like them or not, the locals were quite practical in their determination to get what good they could out of what floated ashore.[49]

According to one observer, Nantucketers had been quite slow to come up with a polite term for the strangers in their midst. In pretourist days, non-Nantucketers had been referred to as "coofs." Only the need for their money had created a demand for a more neutral term: "off-islanders." As this observer put it, "'Coofs' are now 'off-islanders' just as Jews in New York are called Israelites when they move into Fifth Avenue," an analogy that implied a grudging acceptance at best.[50]

Another tourist reported that islanders had too much self-respect to serve tourists on demand. It was important not to give them orders but to humor them with *requests* for their services. "These people need and want to make an honest living, and you are the most convenient material at hand out of which to make it. But they are descended from blood that ruled the wave and humbled the Leviathan[,]" and they did not like taking orders.[51] This was in part simply another romanticization: "Natural" hospitality was not incompatible with "natural" dignity. Samuel Adams Drake constantly juxtaposed the ancient rectitude of the natives of the New England coast with the sad decline brought about by tourism: "We may, perhaps, live to see a full-fledged lackey in Nantucket streets."[52] But outsiders' talk about the dignity and self-respect of islanders was as ambiguous as their admiration of island hospitality. Old-fashioned dignity was laudable, but in this case it was merely quaint, since it was based on economic status and power that no longer existed except as a nostalgic fantasy.

The reality, as this tourist acknowledged, was that tourism was the nearest—indeed, virtually the only—means of making a living on the island. Outsiders sometimes admitted that Nantucket hospitality was born of desperation more than of native character. Sometimes a glimpse of the true situation on Nantucket filtered through the journalistic enthusiasm: A *Harper's* article published in 1860 described in unusually graphic detail the "battered and dismantled hulks of whale ships . . . the quiet, listless seeming people . . . with an aimless air very uncommon in New England."[53]

A promotional pamphlet put out by the Old Colony Railroad, called *Pilgrim Land*, managed to reveal those desperate circumstances in a dazzling display of double-think that expressed some of the unique appeal of Nantucket for many travelers. The writer pointed out that Nantucket's dependence on tourism as its only livelihood made life more pleasant there for tourists. It provided the "dreamy, quiet, conservative conditions" that tourists wanted, and it allowed what he called "the free devotion of every natural feature and facility and advantage of the island to the interests of the summer sojourner and pleasure-seeker."[54] In short, islanders had no choice but to serve the needs of tourists, and that was good news for the tourist.

In this context, the focus on Nantucket's native character—its hospitality, its simplicity, its timelessness, even its former heroism—took on a special meaning. Nantucket appeared to be untouched by the vices of the age. No trace of Gilded Age industrial struggle intruded on this island retreat, neither the cutthroat competition of late nineteenth-century business nor the violent conflict of late nineteenth-century labor relations. Far from participating in a scramble for money, Nantucketers appeared to live—and to be hospitable—almost without any visible means of support. Because they had no business to pursue, they were happy to perform small services for tourists without payment. One need not pay them much, but their "character" made it unnecessary to see them as victims. (Even the old whalers' ardent pursuit of profits was reinterpreted; they had not been capitalists, either, but heroic and manly seafaring adventurers.)

The experience Nantucket offered to Gilded Age tourists was clearly in part an idealized experience of "old-fashioned" class relations, a return to the imaginary time when the interests of employer and employee were one—and that one was the employer. (Not coincidentally, that image masked a situation in which the island's employees had few alternatives.) The author of *Pilgrim Land* painted just such a rosy picture of class harmony: "Now both the permanent population and the transient residents are at one . . . and the main business of Nantucket, on the part of all concerned . . . is to make of her situation a garden of delights."[55]

This was a far cry from the resignation expressed by the editors of the *Nantucket Inquirer*, who acknowledged that they had little choice but to serve the tourist trade, but who drew a sad comparison with "the busy days of our commercial activity" and saw the island's dependence on tourism as a sign of failure. "It must be confessed," they wrote, that their hopes of using tourism as a stepping stone to some better trade had "proved a failure, and the prospect of such a consummation has grown fainter and fainter." There was no choice: "We must submit gracefully to our fate."[56] The editorial concluded with a forced enthusiasm whose ironic tinge made it anything but convincing:

But we forget that we must not talk or write in this strain, at the risk of being called croakers. . . . So we retract any heresy of which we may have been guilty, and straightway lay plans for another campaign to entertain the guests of 1878.[57]

The editors of the *Inquirer* had initially encouraged the growth of tourism, but they now saw it as a trap. Other islanders who had invested in tourism also expressed reservations. Isaac Folger, editor of another Nantucket paper, the *Island Review*, wrote a guidebook he published in 1874. The *Handbook of Nantucket* was designed specifically for summer tourists and featured advertisements for tourist services on every other page. But even within its pages, Folger could not resist a regretful backward glance, admitting in his prologue that he longed for the "good old days when we were all engaged in the busy pursuits of life . . . when our streets resembled the crowded thoroughfare of a city."[58]

That some islanders had qualms about the tourist industry is clear, but there is little evidence of open conflict between those who supported the tourist industry and those who were not so enthusiastic, or between tourists and islanders. There are only a few signs of discontent with the new industry—and one intriguing hint of sabotage. In 1881, the *Inquirer* ran a news brief entitled "Villainous," which reported that "there appears to be a desperate character in our midst, who is endeavoring to wreak vengeance on the Nantucket Railroad Company for some real or fancied injury." It seems that this "villain" had obstructed the railroad path on two separate occasions. Both times, the train had been carrying tourists to Surfside.[59]

There were occasional signs of a less villainous, but equally real, reluctance to make tourists comfortable on the island. In 1876, the *Nantucket Inquirer* pleaded several times in one issue that people preserve an atmosphere of "good feeling" at the beginning of the summer season, in order not to frighten off tourists. In one such article, the paper announced the steamboat company's policy of keeping islanders behind a line on the pier when tourists came in, because their "crowding about the gangways" had "become so annoying to passengers." The steamboat company was attempting to prevent Nantucketers from showing up to look over the "cargo" of an arriving boat, a custom that apparently died hard on the island, although it was quite clear that tourists did not like being greeted this way. The newspaper requested that people honor the company's demand out of a "sense of propriety," and "thus prevent any resort to compulsory or police force."[60]

Whatever their discontent, Nantucketers quickly became aware of what their visitors expected from them. Perhaps the most difficult part of the new enterprise was the discomfort of being made quaint. As one of the girls of Bellamy's *Idyl* put it:

We don't like to be regarded as curiosities, or have strangers come just to play for fun at a sort of life we live in sober earnest the year round. People don't like to have what is practical to them patronized as amusement by others. It cheapens it in their own eyes.[61]

But, as the editors of the *Inquirer* argued, there was no help for it. If island "peculiarities and whimsicalities" were caricatured before the whole world, they wrote, there was no choice but to "join in the smile at our own expense." After all, in the business they were now embarked on, any publicity was good publicity, and if mainland newspaper correspondents reported stories that were patronizing, or simply untrue, that was all part of the job: "If we put up for notoriety, we both desire and expect to be talked about."[62] The editors concluded wistfully, expressing their fears that there might not be enough quaintness left to make the island alluring. Not much of Nantucket's distinctive architecture, and not many of Nantucket's unique characters, remained to give the tourist a taste of the flavor of "Old Nantucket." Nantucket, they concluded, had become just like everywhere else.

"Manufactured for the Trade"

That was one problem that need not have concerned the editors of the *Inquirer.* Nantucket's unique atmosphere was already being re-created all around them. If a quaint atmosphere were in demand, it could be produced. Edward Godfrey reflected on that demand in his 1882 guidebook. Nantucket, he reported to tourists, had once been filled with antiques, rich in "old crockery, clocks, furniture . . . and curiosities of all kinds." And in fact, a lot of antiques were still for sale, but "when one wants a *history* to what one buys,—well, the dealers here are just as honest as elsewhere, and stories, like goods, can be manufactured for the trade."[63] What was

true of antiques was true of quaintness in general. Nantucket's unique atmosphere, in the words of Godfrey's guidebook, could be "manufactured
for the trade."

The process by which Nantucket was made quaint, and even the process
by which individual islanders turned to this particular "trade," is difficult
to trace. It has shaped the Nantucket of today far more than the local investors' speculation in cottage lots, but compared with the deeds and
blueprints of the resort trade, there are not many remnants of its construction. That is not entirely accidental, since this trade, unlike the resort trade, thrived on its invisibility. "Manufacturing" old-fashioned
hospitality, quaint mannerisms, and nostalgic atmosphere worked best,
then as now, if the manufacturing was not too apparent. And those on
the front lines of the transformation, the people who were most often
mentioned by guidebooks as quaint, have left no traces of their own
thoughts. It is not clear whether Mrs. Eliza McCleave thought she was
selling her own peculiarities as well as a look at her shell collection. And
although one can speculate, it is not clear whether Billy Clark, the town
crier, was aware of how many books featured photographs and descriptions of him. The old sea captains who sat for portraits, took tourists fishing, and told whaling stories have not recorded how they came to these
occupations. But by the early 1880s, some islanders had clearly begun
to respond to tourists' notions of Nantucket, and even in some respects
to shape them.

One of the landmarks of that transformation was a reunion of the Coffin
family, held in August 1881. On the face of it, the Coffin reunion was little
more than a promotional scheme, scheduled to take advantage of the
opening of the Nantucket Railroad, which brought visitors out to its railroad depot on the open plains of what was envisioned as Surfside. The investors of the Surfside Land Company hoped to sell cottage lots. The
master of ceremonies, a local lawyer named Allen Coffin, was running for
governor of Massachusetts on the Prohibition ticket. The reunion followed
two other similar big events that summer: on July 4, the railroad was
opened amid great fanfare; and on August 1, a roller-skating rink was
opened at the depot of the Nantucket Railroad. A clambake and a dance
were held to celebrate.

The reunion was very much like those other summer entertainments,
although it required more organization. Members of the "clan" had been
summoned from all over the country. Out of 233 signatures on the guest
register, ninety were from outside New England and New York. Most in

evidence, though, were the seventy Coffins from New York, Brooklyn, and Boston, while only twenty-one Nantucketers signed the register, along with one Martha's Vineyard Coffin.[64] Many of the visitors were in-laws or only tangentially related to the Coffin family; perhaps they found the idea of belonging to a "first family," even such a minor one, appealing.

The reunion program took place at the terminus of the Nantucket Railroad, where the Surfside Land Company had divided up cottage lots for sale. From August 15 through 18, visitors combined the standard seaside entertainments—picnics, clambakes, excursions to other parts of the island—with speeches and ceremonies that appealed to a more sentimental interest.[65] One speaker traced the English roots of the Coffin family; another discoursed on the nature of American citizenship. The opening speech, delivered by Judge Tristram Coffin of Poughkeepsie, New York, combined the usual appeals to the healthful atmosphere of the island with a more nostalgic reflection on the past: "The dear little island still stands!" In the past, "commercial prosperity smiled upon it; the names of its merchants were known throughout the world," but, he continued, "that fair day has passed by, perhaps not to return. Its storehouses were closed, its docks fell to decay, its once thriving center became 'An ancient town, a very ancient town,/With rotten wharves, and quiet grassy streets,/And quaint old houses wrinkled in the sun.'" Nowadays, however, all that was changing: "Hosts of congenial visitors attracted by its exhilarating health-giving climate" were "thronging" to the island. Judge Coffin held out the hope that future generations of Coffins would produce thousands of summer visitors.[66] After his speech, the band played "In the Sweet Bye-and-Bye." (That was an apt choice. The song promises that "we will meet on the beautiful shore," which is exactly where they were meeting. It reinforced both the roles Nantucket had come to play, as seaside resort and as "old home.")

The Coffin reunion met with some skepticism from Nantucketers. Some of them saw it as a ridiculous pretension on the part of the family, and most seemed to recognize its promotional nature. One correspondent of the Nantucket Inquirer suggested sarcastically that the islanders continue to hold reunions year after year, one family at a time, for the sake of the tourist revenue it would generate. Henry S. Wyer published an extensive parody of the reunion, making fun of both its promotional aspects and its family sentimentality. He wrote a mock program for "Ye Second Coffyn Reunion," at which various figures were caricatured, including the agent of the Old Colony railroad line and two hotel keepers, who were portrayed on the lookout for tourists. Orations were entitled: "Where there's a (Coffyn) will there's a way" and "Was Shakespeare a Coffyn?"[67]

The reunion apparently failed to generate much interest in Surfside. But it had other, more important effects on the tourist business. For one thing, the reunion engaged many islanders in the tourist trade through a gradual process that required neither large initial investments nor a major shift in self-perception. The Coffin reunion committee went door-to-door asking families to take in a boarder or two for the event—as a personal favor for returning relatives rather than a decision to open a boardinghouse. One effect of such a move was illustrated by the story of the Chapmans, a retired farm couple who had recently moved to town from Long Island Sound. Chapman and his family were persuaded to allow reunion guests to stay in their house on Step Lane, and when some of their guests returned the next summer, the Chapmans decided to go into business. Soon they bought more property, enlarged the house, and expanded one of its chief attractions, its open platforms overlooking the harbor. The Chapmans' house became the Veranda House in the 1890s, a hotel that could accommodate as many as 150 guests at a time but maintained the kind of personal, "family" connections between host and guest that allowed them to appear as equals.[68]

More important, though, the Coffin reunion was clearly an attempt to take control of the romanticization of the island's history, not simply to profit from it, but to redefine it. Some Coffin reunion leaders hoped to shift the emphasis away from the quaint characters who filled the guidebooks to a more dignified emphasis on family lineage and heritage. Nantucket's first families were attempting to stake their claim as families "as refined and conservative as those of Old Virginia, or Eastern Massachusetts generally."[69] (Indeed, the tourist who made that assertion for Nantucket's families went further: She imagined Nantucketers as the social *superiors* of their guests, who revealed by their eagerness for local antiques that they "presumably possess no family antiquities" of their own.)

While the Coffin reunion did not radically alter the image of the island, it did finally help to shift the focus of nostalgia on the island away from its problematic focus on people's characters. It did that by beginning the process of transforming and reinterpreting the architectural heritage of the island. Nantucket's reputation in the next several decades would come to rest on its physical appearance, which would take on the associations once attributed to Nantucket's quaint, seafaring people.

Nantucket's physical appearance was already in the process of being transformed by the time of the Coffin reunion. William Macy recalled from his childhood during the 1870s that "[t]he old town began to spruce up, houses, barns and fences were repaired and painted, and something like prosperity dawned once more." This change was due entirely to tourism: "New hotels were built or projected, old mansion houses were turned into boarding houses, and at the height of the season all were filled to capacity."[70] From an outsider's perspective, Samuel Adams Drake described the same process with less enthusiasm: "Old brasses were being furbished up, and cobwebs swept away by new and ruthless brooms." Those brooms were wielded by the tourist industry, and "though the inhabitants welcome the change, the crust and flavor of originality can not survive it."[71]

In some ways, then, Nantucket looked newer after tourists began to flock to it, more like it did in its commercial heyday, less like it did in its days of "quaint" decay. But the Coffin reunion helped to shape a new approach to the structures now designated as "historic" by transforming the "Oldest House," a farmhouse on the edge of town that had been built by Jethro Coffin in 1686. During the Coffin reunion, the house was recognized as a family heirloom, and a year later Judge Tristram Coffin of Poughkeepsie purchased it in order to preserve it. At that point, the house had been unoccupied since 1867, when the farm family that owned it had abandoned it and moved to a less expensive house in town.

In the 1860s, the house had looked very much like the rest of Nantucket—a little battered, but no more so than other buildings still in use. By the time it was bought in 1881, the building needed substantial repairs, both because of its age and because it had become well known in the 1870s as the Oldest House, and the traffic had done some damage. It was the practice of tourists, for instance, to write their names on the inside of the house and to take a shingle with them as a memento. By 1881, when the repairs began, the house had already been transformed from a battered farmhouse to the relic of a bygone era—a tourist attraction, although a very dilapidated one. In 1881, the shingles were replaced (with old shingles from another very old house in town, which was not entitled to the protection granted to the Oldest House), and a new roof was added. In 1886 the interior was repaired and the graffiti removed. In that year, it was opened to the public as part of a celebration of its two-hundredth anniversary—a much newer-looking, refurbished Oldest House.[72]

But in another sense, the Oldest House looked still "older" in 1885 than in 1865.[73] Now clearly set off from other structures, it was no longer an

The Oldest House appears simply as a battered old farmhouse in
this photograph, taken around 1865. It was known to be the
"oldest house" but had not been set aside or marked in any way.
The farm family who lived there abandoned it about the time this
photograph was taken.

abandoned farmhouse but a relic whose significance was interpreted
by local guides and by a sign on the door. The town as a whole went
through a similar process. By the 1880s, both islanders and visitors were
very much aware of the historic and nostalgic significance of Nantucket's buildings. More and more historic architecture was being identified as such: The Oldest House, the old Friends' meeting house, the
Old Mill, were recognized as attractions, and the "colonial" features of
many Nantucket structures were more clearly defined. When the
Nantucket Historical Association was founded in 1894 to protect these
features, it had already become clear which buildings were most historic, and why.

During the 1870s, the Oldest House began to acquire status as a historic building, but it was not yet treated as a museum. It was customary for visitors to take away a shingle as a souvenir, as the bare patch on the right side of the house reveals. When Judge Tristram Coffin of Poughkeepsie decided to refurbish the house, workers took shingles from another old house in town—one without the status of a relic.

By then, the island's appearance was a well-understood symbol of its history. Of course, much of the appearance that seemed so antique and timeless in 1885 had been brand-new only fifty years earlier, when the town had been built with whaling money in its days of prosperity. But to visitors, Nantucket's appearance in 1885 carried a weight of historical and nostalgic associations not only with the Nantucket of the 1840s, but also with the Nantuckets of 1680 and 1775. One author described his subject as that "quaint Nantucket which existed for two hundred years before the island was discovered by 'the summer boarder.'" The look of Nantucket seemed to embody timelessness rather than a particular historical moment—not the conspicuously extravagant days when whaling money built downtown Nantucket but the "old days," when life was serene and unhurried, when people did not scramble for money, when all was harmonious. It was manifestly "old," but it was no longer decaying. It carried associations with the romantic past, but no more associations with failure and defeat. It seemed to corroborate the claim of the author of *Quaint Nantucket*, who wrote in 1896 that the island's "history [had] stopped nearly half a century ago."[74] And in that regard, Nantucket had adapted remarkably well to its dual functions as a seaside resort and a nostalgic escape. The image it had "manufactured for the trade" was one that was to serve it well for the next century.

"95% Perfect"

The transformation of Nantucket was repeated in scores of New England's villages and towns in the last quarter of the nineteenth century. In Litchfield, Connecticut, emigres from New York created a "New England village" appearance for their summer colony that was more "colonial" in 1870 than it was in 1770.[75] In Deerfield, Massachusetts, residents responded to the loss of their competitive edge in agriculture and manufacturing by transforming the village into a living memorial to the past.[76] Plymouth had begun its ascent to national prominence as the home of the "Pilgrims" as early as the 1850s. And in Marblehead, Ipswich, Salem, and many other "quaint" towns, old houses were sought out and catalogued as the sites of romantic tales or the homes of eighteenth-century heroes (or villains and victims, in the case of Salem's witchcraft relics).

All these historical attractions shared an appeal that rested at least as much on a sense of nostalgic timelessness as on a sense of history, but the new nostalgic trade they shared took different forms. Some places, like Plymouth, and later Deerfield, came to market their historical attractions as part of a national heritage and to stake claims for their significance within a national political context. In some places, wealthy and influential summer people came to identify with the area's history so deeply that they transformed the place into a powerful statement of their vision of the past. (Chapter 6 describes such a case in York, Maine.) In other places, nostalgic associations, romantic history, and old buildings were used primarily as a way of enhancing the tourist's resort experience. Nantucket's history remained "quaint"—an expression of local uniqueness, useful primarily as entertainment. Like Deerfield, Litchfield, and other "antimodernist" havens, it served as a refuge from an increasingly complex, modern urban world. But Nantucket was as much an exotic island retreat as the homestead of the ancient paternal virtues.

Nantucket's need to provide both resort entertainments and a sense of the past never worked entirely smoothly. The need for tourist money has both required and interfered with the preservation of its unique flavor. (A modern visitor sometimes senses a jarring contradiction between these two roles. Looking at Nantucket, one sees its pristine white clapboards, grey shingles, and red brick; listening to Nantucket, one hears the sounds of rented cars on cobblestones, buzz saws and hammers, and bars and restaurants full of vacationers eager to eat, drink, and tan.) The definitive statement on the relationship between these two functions was made in a 1935 preservationist plea called *95% Perfect:* Nantucket's tourist trade hinged on the island's ability to look quaint—and its economic survival depended on the tourist trade.[77] Sheer economic necessity dictated the preservation of old houses no matter what the cost.

In this relationship may lie one of the differences between Nantucket and many other places re-created by such nostalgic forces. Nantucket was too dependent on the money of outsiders to shape a new history of its choosing, even if the images outsiders held were sometimes contested by Nantucketers. Nantucket's fate, like that of many New England towns and villages at the end of the century, was in the hands of outsiders only casually interested in its history, which they found more charming than inspiring.[78]

For that reason, the history of Nantucket's nostalgic tourist trade reveals some truths that are obscured in many other histories. In "nostalgic" tourist places like these, local history and culture were a crucial part of the tourist industry, but they were also ultimately at the service of that industry. Nostalgic writing about Nantucket might serve many purposes, but whatever else it did, it served the tourist trade which had become essential to the economic survival of the region. Quaint features were an asset to these towns, but up-to-date services were a necessity; architecture might be historically correct, but it *must* be pretty. Its people should be proud of their illustrious past, but they must be willing to wait on tables. And the special nostalgic ambience of "quaint bygone days" must be "manufactured for the trade."

5

THAT DREAM OF HOME

Northern New England and the Farm Vacation Industry, 1890–1900

I n 1899, the governor of New Hampshire, Frank Rollins, made national
news with two startling moves. In April he revived an old New England
custom—a day of fasting in the spring—to call attention to the decay
of rural church life in New Hampshire. Two months later he called a
special statewide meeting to create an entirely *new* New England custom.
It was to be called Old Home Week, and it was designed to deal with a complex mix of economic and social problems in the northern New England
states. The governor's two innovations confronted with unusual candor
the troubles that had overtaken northern New England in the past two
decades. They also helped to bring those troubles into a national spot-
light.

What was going wrong with rural northern New England? Unlike Nantucket's business leaders, New Hampshire's governor could point to no
single catastrophic moment of decline in the region. What he confronted
instead was a nebulous sense of looming crisis, compounded of long-
standing economic difficulties, a shifting population, and gloomy social
analysis. Writers in the agricultural press bemoaned the flight of young
people to the cities and the West. In the past few years, articles had begun

REPORT ÷ ÷ ÷ ÷ ÷

"But far more bright, more dear than all,
That dream of home, that dream of home"

OLD HOME WEEK
IN
NEW HAMPSHIRE

. . Come back again . . .

THE OLD RED SCHOOL HOUSE

"HOW DEAR TO MY HEART ARE THE SCENES OF MY CHILDHOOD."

AUGUST 26 TO SEPTEMBER 1

1899

Old Home Week promoters were not noted for their subtlety. This cover of the first official report of Old Home Week in New Hampshire features the motifs most often employed in state promotional campaigns. It quotes from popular songs about the old farm home: "But far more bright, more dear than all,/That dream of home, that dream of home"; and "How Dear to My Heart Are the Scenes of My Childhood" (see page 141). The photographs elaborate on the theme: In the middle is the "Old Oaken Bucket," associated with rural childhood in yet another song; to the left is the "Old Red School House"; and to the right is the old homestead itself. From New Hampshire Old Home Week Association, *Annual Report of Old Home Week in New Hampshire* (Manchester, N.H.: Arthur E. Clarke, 1900). Courtesy, American Antiquarian Society.

to appear outside the region in the national press, uncovering even more serious underlying problems. Writers warned of "decadence" and "decline" in rural northern New England and hinted at social and moral "degeneration" caused by isolation and poverty in the countryside.

This sense of crisis was not entirely misplaced. Serious economic problems *were* confronting rural northern New England. Over the previous generation, the villages and towns of the region had become the victims of a kind of late nineteenth-century deindustrialization, casualties of the ever increasing centralization of population and work. Local factories, mills, and workshops had been gradually driven out of business by larger producers in the growing industrial cities of southern New England.[1] Northern New England was being drained of its small-scale industry; with each passing decade, it depended more heavily on farming. There were exceptions, of course: Southern New Hampshire's Merrimack River textile cities resembled the highly industrial Massachusetts cities to their south; up-country New Hampshire and inland Maine were given over to large-scale lumbering operations; and the tourist trade played an increasingly important economic role along the coast and in the White Mountains. But these regional variations only highlighted the increasing dependence on agriculture in the farming regions.

And farming was in trouble, too. Northern New England had suffered through a generation of decline in the price of wool, its primary cash crop, along with damaging competition for grain crops from the Midwest. Agricultural experts urged northern New Englanders to convert from wool and grain to dairy farming, but that was a difficult process.[2] Perhaps more disturbing, parts of rural northern New England were losing people at what seemed to be an alarming rate. During the last quarter of the century, the specter of the "abandoned farm" arose to haunt, first the politicians and planners of the northern states themselves, and later the reform writers of the national magazine circuit.

In retrospect, it appears that the depopulation problem (and the abandoned-farm crisis) was somewhat misunderstood.[3] The population of the three northern states remained stable or grew slowly throughout the period from 1860 to 1900. But there was massive out-migration. Between 1850 and 1900, about forty percent of all those born in Vermont left it in every decade. The frontiers of Maine continued to gain in population, as did the growing factory towns of southern New Hampshire and the larger towns of Vermont. But within these states, the more remote hill towns and villages—those without easy access to the railroads that made competition possible—were losing people to the larger towns and cities. Some towns were quite literally "going downhill" toward the valleys that provided railroad access.[4]

This pattern of migration out of the state, to the West and to the cities, was actually a typical one for settled agricultural areas. It was happening in New York, Ohio, Indiana, and even farther west by the early twentieth century.[5] And local experts even at the time pointed out that many of those "abandoned farms" had been on marginal, unproductive land. Often they were not abandoned at all; they were simply owned by farmers who had allowed some of their holdings to revert to forest in order to maximize output from their better land. But because these empty farmhouses and overgrown fields were located in rural New England, they struck many people outside the farm regions as alarming signs of moral and social decay. Rural New England had come to hold a special meaning for many Americans. Its "decline" raised disturbing questions that went beyond economic strategies to threaten cherished values. And for the farmers of northern New England, increasing hard work for declining (or nonexistent) profits, helplessness in the face of international market forces, and the loss of sons and daughters to cities created a parallel sense of crisis all their own.[6]

Old Home Week

Frank Rollins came into office determined to attack both the clear economic problems of his state and the murky psychological and cultural issues that seemed linked to those problems. Old Home Week was the linchpin of his plan. It was not a completely new idea. As early as 1853, the city of Portsmouth, New Hampshire, had sponsored a "hometown reunion" for its scattered natives, and an increasing number of family reunions (like the Coffins had held on Nantucket) had served similar purposes. But Governor Rollins was the first to institutionalize such reunions and to link them with a consistent, organized profit motive.

Old Home Week had several objectives. It was intended to raise spirits among the natives of rural areas, by giving them a chance to interact socially with representatives from the wide world, and by encouraging a sense of pride in their surroundings. That contact was supposed to ward off the mental and ethical "degeneracy" that was thought to grow out of the isolation of rural life. But a more important goal of Old Home Week was to inspire *former* residents to spend money in their hometowns, by endowing a library or school, by underwriting the cleanup of a graveyard or a piece of common land, or by buying a summer home there, perhaps the "old home" itself.

Frank Rollins was in a good position to create such a program. He was the leader of a state that seemed to be in deep economic trouble. He saw Old Home Week and related programs as one way of improving its economy. But he was not only the governor of New Hampshire, he was also a published author, a graduate of Harvard Law School, the son of a United States senator, and a Boston banker—an elite urbanite who understood the vacationer's perspective. Rollins was well suited to the task of harnessing and profiting from the nostalgia of fellow city dwellers. (As one laudatory biographer put it, "We, who are part of the soil of our native state, welcome [Old Home Week], but scarcely one among us all *feels* what it means."[7]) Rollins was able to *feel* his state's appeal to potential vacationers.

That appeal was a deeply nostalgic one. Southern New England had become a region of large industrial cities, populated increasingly by immigrants and their children. The great industrial cities of the Merrimack River had spread through northeastern Massachusetts and well into southern New Hampshire. By 1890, Rhode Island had become the most urbanized state in the union, and Massachusetts was in second place. The northern New England states, although they were not as sparsely populated as many western states, were still overwhelmingly rural. Vermont, the most rural state in the region, had an urban population of only 7.9 percent.[8]

Southern New England was alarmingly ethnically diverse. Sixty-eight percent of the population of Boston in 1890 was made up of first- or second-generation immigrants. In a mill town like Fall River, the percentage reached an amazing eighty-three percent. But up north (or out in the country), the population was still reassuringly "Yankee." True, even the northern parts of New England were ethnically diverse. Almost a third of the citizens of Vermont and New Hampshire in 1890 were first- and second-generation French-Canadian immigrants. But in comparison with southern New England's cities, rural Vermont and New Hampshire still seemed "Anglo-Saxon" and Protestant.

Of course, the geographical distinction between "northern" and "southern" New England was never clear. The northern New England states included ethnically diverse factory cities, frontier lumber towns, and elite vacation resorts, as well as classic white-painted New England towns surrounded by picturesque small farms. (And there were plenty of such "New England–looking" towns and farms in Connecticut, Rhode Island, and

Massachusetts, too.) But at a time when an imagined "old New England" of small towns, rural virtues, and ethnic purity formed an increasingly attractive antidote to the new industrial city, the location of that imaginary New England seemed to be moving north.

Once northern New England had been looked on as the backwater of the region, where residents were little removed from barbarism. Timothy Dwight, in his famous early nineteenth-century travels through New England, saw little sign in the northern back country of the literacy, godliness, sobriety, and thrift he found in southern New England.[9] But in the late nineteenth century, the "real" New England was apparently being pushed out of the crowded cities of Massachusetts and Connecticut, into the villages of Vermont and New Hampshire. Northern New England was increasingly considered the true home of New England's heritage, both moral and racial. Because of that perceived shift, the fate of the northern New England states was becoming increasingly significant for the many people, both outside and inside the region, who looked to the region for the preservation of values threatened by the explosion of the great industrial immigrant cities. It was these sentiments Governor Rollins was bent on exploiting.

The Old Home Week plan was simple. Each state set formal dates for a week to be designated its official Old Home Week. If a town wished to participate, it could send away for a packet of information from the state, with instructions on how to get appropriations from its town meeting and how to plan a program. Town committees canvassed the residents and gathered the names and addresses of natives who had left. Invitations from each town were sent out to all the native sons and daughters of the state who could be located, asking them to "come back again" to the towns they had left, "to return and visit the scenes of their youth."[10] A reception committee greeted homecoming visitors at the train and escorted them to their accommodations at the houses of relatives or friends, or of volunteers if they no longer knew anyone in town.

In northern New England, a town might appropriate anywhere from fifty dollars to as much as a thousand dollars for its Old Home Week celebration. It might choose to celebrate the entire week mandated by the state (in New Hampshire, it was the last week in August; in Vermont, it was the week including August 16, the anniversary of the Battle of Bennington) or simply one or two of the days. Sunday church services were always included, along with a whole array of entertainments. Picnics, band music, and speeches were affordable even for the most impoverished towns.

Wealthier towns (or more enthusiastic ones) could lavish time and money on historical pageants, new memorial statues, and floral parades.

The first Old Home Week celebration of Dunbarton, New Hampshire, was typical. It began with a hilltop bonfire. On Sunday, there was a special "union service" (incorporating all the town's Protestant denominations). Tuesday was designated Old Home Day: A local band played, and there was a bicycle race, a shooting match, a dinner, and a "museum of local antiquities." Governor Rollins gave a speech. (Dunbarton is only ten miles outside Concord, the state capital.) A typical town would have had a somewhat less distinguished guest speaker, perhaps a local boy who had become a wealthy businessman or successful lawyer.[11]

The appeal to potential visitors was twofold. The invitations appeared, as one enthusiast put it, "just when the absentees are beginning to think longingly of their summer vacation," exploiting the desire for a summer escape from the city.[12] But the pitch was also unabashedly sentimental, particularly in the hands of Rollins, who played on the guilt of potential visitors by insisting that "when we ask you to come home, it is your mother's voice."[13] References to home, mother, and childhood were the staples of Old Home Week marketing. An often-repeated joke at the time was that at least one local industry had been given a tremendous boost by Old Home Week: poetry-writing.

Old Home Week advertisers borrowed lavishly from a variety of popular sources. One illustration, typically unrestrained, embroidered on the theme of childhood's home with engravings both of the "little red school house" and the "old oaken bucket," well-known sentimental motifs associated with rural childhood. Those engravings were surrounded with excerpts from popular songs: "How dear to my heart are the scenes of my childhood" and "But far more bright, more dear than all,/That dream of home, that dream of home." Governor Rollins echoed these sentiments in his speeches at the first Old Home Week celebrations: "When you think of the old home, you bring back the tenderest memories possessed by man,—true love, perfect faith, holy reverence, high ambitions—the 'long, long thoughts of youth.'"[14]

Old Home Week was greeted with a great deal of enthusiasm in its first years, both from local promoters and from national magazine writers and reformers. Within five years, all the New England states (and some other older rural states like Ohio and Pennsylvania) had copied it. During those first years, as many as seventy of New Hampshire's towns and forty of Vermont's participated in Old Home Week in some form.[15] The program did not fulfill its planners' dreams by becoming an annual event, at least not in most northern New England towns and villages (the strains—both financial and psychological—began to tell after a few summers), but Old Home Week continued to be celebrated regularly throughout the early twentieth century. A number of towns still celebrate it today, usually as "Old Home Weekends."

The effects of Old Home Week ranged far beyond its original goal of attracting former residents. The pitch was aimed at the pocketbook of the returning native, but it was also aimed more broadly, at all potential visitors. Rollins anticipated that the widespread publicity Old Home Week generated might prove to be more lucrative in the long run than individual gifts from former residents. Old Home Week, as he argued, would make "the name of home . . . synonymous with that of New Hampshire in the minds of newspaper and magazine readers far and wide"—and that was a connection that could be put to practical use.[16] The real task facing its organizers was to make rural northern New England seem like "home" to everyone, and to inspire in all potential visitors a sense that going "home" to such a town or village would provide something like a return to their own childhoods.

In this regard, Old Home Week was only part of a larger effort launched by all three northern New England states. During the 1890s, each state had taken steps to shore up the regional economy by capturing a share of a new and growing tourist market. Old Home Week was simply the crowning publicity achievement of these programs. Its creators were already deeply involved in the promotion of regional tourism. In Vermont, for instance, two regional magazines—the *Vermonter* and the *Inter-State Journal*—played an important role in getting the state involved, arguing that "the establishment of Old Home Week is in line with what has already been done toward bringing many summer visitors into the State."[17] In the years before Old Home Week's debut, these northern states had taken the innovative step of building governmental infrastructures to attract tourists and to shape tourist demand to fit their own specifications.

Fertile Farms and Summer Homes

Northern New England already boasted several thriving tourist industries by the 1890s. New Hampshire's scenic White Mountain trade had been booming for forty years. Along the coast of Maine, resorts like the elite Mount Desert (now Acadia National Park) and the more plebeian Old

Orchard Beach had become prime summer territory. But the state-sponsored programs of the 1890s encouraged the rise of a new kind of tourism. Their clients looked to the northern farm in itself—not to scenery or to fresh air alone, but to a pastoral, nostalgic vision of rural life—for their fulfillment. All three states set up programs to encourage this new tourism. But it was in Vermont, New England's most rural state, that the pastoral vacation outdistanced all other kinds of tourism. Vermont was the most visibly rural of vacation destinations, and state officials there centered their efforts on the farm vacation. Because of that, the Old Home Week cluster of images—the little red school house, the old homestead, and other rosy memories of rural childhood—came to be associated even more specifically with the state of Vermont than with neighboring New Hampshire or Maine.

Appropriately enough, the promotion of tourism in Vermont was largely the work of the state's Board of Agriculture, which launched an ambitious and innovative campaign during the 1890s to interest both potential tourists and Vermont farmers in the new business.[18] The Board of Agriculture's role in encouraging tourism grew out of its mandate to preserve farming in the state, the purpose for which the board had been created by the state legislature in 1871. The board's mission was to preserve the viability of Vermont farming by disseminating advice and information to farmers. It sponsored meetings, ran seminars, and published yearbooks, all designed to increase the profitability of farming by introducing new crops and techniques.

In particular the board concerned itself with the problem of abandoned farms. Its attempt to repopulate marginal areas was what first led it into the summer vacation business. The board issued a series of pamphlets beginning in 1891, first called *Resources and Attractions of Vermont* but later renamed *Vermont . . . a Glimpse of Its Scenery and Industries*. These were written by Victor I. Spear, statistical secretary of the Vermont Board of Agriculture and the guiding hand behind its tourist development policy. During the early 1890s, Spear was responsible for a number of efforts to encourage tourism in Vermont: a groundbreaking statewide survey of tourist services, with findings published as the *Report on Summer Travel for 1894*; the series that began as the *Resources and Attractions of Vermont*; and another series of pamphlets designed specifically to market abandoned farms.

The first pamphlet of the abandoned-farm series, *A List of Desirable Vermont Farms at Low Prices*, was mailed out in 1893 to prospective farmers in a plain brown wrapper. By the 1895 edition, a crucial change had taken place: The pamphlet had become *Vermont, Its Fertile Farms and Summer Homes*, and instead of its plain binding sported a wildflower sketch and fanciful lettering on its cover. The promotional campaign that had begun as a search for farmers to settle on abandoned farms quickly transformed itself into a search for vacationers to buy them as summer houses. The new, tourist's version of the pamphlet listed summer resorts, hotels, and boardinghouses as well as abandoned farms for sale.

During the 1890s, the board advertised farms to tourists, but it also advertised tourism to farmers. Its mission was to encourage experimentation with new and more profitable crops, and tourism was one of the more promising of these. Indeed, Victor Spear argued in an article on "Farm Management" that "there is no crop more profitable than this crop from the city."[19] Tourism in his vision was well suited to a newer, highly diversified intensive farming system that maximized profit on a number of high-quality products for a discerning market: maple sugar, fresh dairy products, eggs, fresh vegetables, and ultimately even the fresh air and scenery of the farm itself.

Objections to the state's promotion of farm tourism came not from conservative advocates of old-fashioned subsistence farming, but from advocates of a more streamlined, factorylike agriculture. These critics argued for a massive move to a more scientific agriculture based on higher capitalization and more technical training. In northern New England, that meant dairying. Summer boarders were an impediment to such a transformation because they competed for scarce labor on the farm, a key constraint in the switch to labor-intensive dairy farming.[20] But most progressive agricultural writers in the region preferred to champion an equally scientific, equally profit-oriented, but more mixed agriculture—one that would, in their view, be more practical for the typically undercapitalized, understaffed farm family. Rural tourism could become an important part of such a system.

The new crops explored by advocates of that system tied farmers to new consumers. Producing for the market was not new to Vermont farmers. They had been involved for two generations in the national and international wool markets. But these new products sold to urban markets essentially "rural" experiences. They relied on the farmer's ability to guarantee consistent high quality, and they relied as well on an image of rural purity. Vermont farmers came to depend on their reputation for producing the sweetest butter, the freshest milk, the purest maple syrup. And the state learned to guard that reputation as an important financial asset. At a time when nationally known brand names were beginning to compete with local products, the state itself, in cooperation with producers' associations like the Vermont Maple Sugar Makers' Market and the Vermont Dairymen's Association, was doing its best to become a kind of brand name, a guarantee for the quality and "authenticity" of the product.[21]

In the same way, the state of Vermont came to present itself as the provider of the most "authentically" rural farm experiences. In this context, tourism was just one in a long line of new specialty "cash crops" promoted by the Board of Agriculture. Tourists bought abandoned farms on marginal land and then bought vegetables and labor from farmers. Or better yet, they boarded at the farmhouse and made use of farm products that would otherwise go to waste. As an advocate of the tourist trade explained, summer tourism would provide the farmer with retail prices for the products he ordinarily shipped to the cities, and also exploit "products" of the farm that he could not otherwise sell at all—"his pure spring water, clear fresh air, and beautiful scenery . . . at retail price."[22]

The Board of Agriculture was not alone in its attempt to bring tourists to Vermont. Local promoters and other state officials played supporting roles, often combining enthusiasm for tourism with their own projects. The secretary of the Vermont Fish and Game League, for example, pointed out that stocking fish for out-of-state fishermen had trickle-down effects for everyone, since fishermen patronized railroads, hotels, guides, and country stores.[23] And the state's railroads launched major advertising campaigns at the same time, publishing yearly pamphlets like the Rutland Railroad's *Heart of the Green Mountains*, and the Central Vermont Railroad's *Summer Homes among the Green Hills*.

For the most part, though, the tone of the campaign was set by the programs of the Board of Agriculture, which was in charge of Vermont's tourist industry until the creation of a separate Board of Publicity in 1911. And the unusual circumstances that had drawn the state into its involvement with tourism—rural depopulation, declining farm profits, and widespread nostalgia for rural life—also called forth the special themes used by the board and echoed by other promoters, by farmers, and by tourists themselves at the end of the century. For the two decades during which the state of Vermont's tourism promotion was under the aegis of its Board of Agriculture, it reflected the interests and values of Vermont's farm-policy makers. It was these values that shaped the experiences of vacationers and of their rural hosts.

Come Home to Your Mother

People who wanted to encourage tourism in Vermont had available to them a variety of marketing themes. Promoters emphasized the clean, healthful "mountain" air of the "Green Hills" (a popular strategy as maladies like hay fever and consumption came to play important roles in vacationing toward the end of the century). And they echoed the familiar references to New England's founding fathers, the language of ancestry used to such advantage in Deerfield and Nantucket. Vermonters were presented as sturdy members of the "Anglo-Saxon race" and as the vigorous guardians of democratic traditions and religious freedom. (Hills and mountains had long evoked fantasies of freedom and vigor, as they did in the White Mountains next door in New Hampshire, where the granite Great Stone Face was imagined as representing the independence and integrity of its citizens.)

But Vermont's promoters used another theme more often than any of these. Like Nantucket, Vermont staked its future on nostalgia. In Vermont, though, it was nostalgia for a different past. Nantucket's adventurous and hardy whalers, Deerfield's courageous pioneers, embodied a vision of the nation's virile youth, when the founding fathers had acted with rugged virtue and self-reliance. Vermont's image relied on a more immediate past—the childhood days of those who were now tourists and of farmers who were now hosts. It was not the founding fathers but home and mother who called Vermont's visitors back to the past. The marketing pitch of the Vermont Board of Agriculture anticipated the Old Home Week strategy, imagining the state of Vermont as a mother longing for her children, now scattered far and wide.

There was no inherent reason why this should have been so—no reason why Vermont's Green Mountain boys could not have matched Nantucket's whalers in the manly virtues, or why Vermont's granite hills could not have inspired the same homilies to rugged character as did New Hampshire's.[24] (After all, the pioneering innkeeper who founded the White Mountain tourist trade had been named Ethan Allen Crawford, after one of those Green Mountain boys.) Some of the state's promotional literature, in fact, did use more masculine themes. Promoters pointed out that Vermont's Civil War regiments had never lost a battle flag and that Vermont had lost a higher percentage of its population in that war than any other state. They praised the pioneer spirit, the hardiness and self-reliance of the first settlers, who came to "A rough land of rock and stone and tree,/Where breathes no castled lord nor cabined slave."[25] But most often, they employed a softer vision of the past and of their state, extending even to their depiction of the mountains of Vermont as the "Hills of Home"— protective, gentle, and nurturing.

This understanding of Vermont, and of northern New England generally, was deeply rooted in its actual demographic and economic conditions. Northern New England farms *were* the childhood homes of thousands of people living in cities to the south. (Well over half of the native-born Americans who had migrated to Massachusetts in 1890, for example, were from New Hampshire, Vermont, or Maine.) But it was also rooted in the sensibility and values of the state officials who contributed most to the tourist campaign. Their promotional vision of Vermont reflected their own regional and occupational pride, and their understanding of the meaning of farm life. Not coincidentally, it also proved to be a close, if not perfect, match for the nostalgic fantasies of potential tourists.

These agricultural writers espoused a perspective that had been shared by New England's farm writers since the middle of the nineteenth century and even before. There was a long history to their association of the Vermont farm with "home." Northern New England had been competing with the West for generations, not only for markets, but also for the sons and daughters of New England farmers. For years Vermont's agricultural reformers had been campaigning for innovations that would keep farm children from straying by making the farm more "homelike" for the family itself. The first report of the Board of Agriculture, in 1872, advised farmers to keep their sons and daughters down on the farm by making their farms "not merely a place in which to stay, but a home, around which will cluster all the hallowed associations of life," and a center from which progress and improvement would "emanate."[26] It seemed to be relatively easy for the board writers to switch over to tourist promotion from there. They would still promote the virtues of the farm as "home," but their audience would now include potential tourists along with the footloose sons and daughters of Vermont farm families.

In addition, as Hal Barron has suggested in his study of Chelsea, Vermont, *Those Who Stayed behind: Rural Society in Nineteenth Century New England*, the farm periodicals and Board of Agriculture bulletins of late nineteenth-century Vermont outlined a general philosophy as well as a farm program. They called for more modern intensive farming techniques to compete with the West, but they did so in the name of a traditional "producer's ethic": a set of values that they clung to in direct opposition, as they saw it, to the spirit of the age. Against the allure of western speculation and urban riches which drew young Vermonters from the farm, they championed the values of contentment, stability, and home.[27]

But home and the old ways could be maintained only by experimentation—by new farming techniques, new crops, and new social arrangements.[28] These Vermont farm writers were not exactly engaged in a rear-guard defense of "traditional" rural values against capitalism, although it often sounded like that. They had long ago embraced the structure of economic competition and profit-making that surrounded them. They were expressing a criticism of the dominant values, but it was a criticism already deeply embedded in mainstream nineteenth-century culture. Their critique mirrored another much-discussed ambiguity in Victorian culture: the mismatch between the values of the home (in theory the world of women and children) and those of the capitalist working world (the world of men).

Vermont farm writers embodied these conceptions of home and world, woman and man, in a regional form as well. They gave to their own region and to New England farmers a task that recalled the work of middle-class women: the task of protecting the values associated with home—peace and contentment, community cohesiveness, republican simplicity—against mobility, greed, and individualistic competition. In that regard, they were caught in an internal conflict very common to the late nineteenth century. The board's tourism promoters wanted Vermont farmers to be the guardians of a stable rural home and of the noncommercial values they associated with that home. They also wanted them to work at the cutting edge of an increasingly competitive, highly profit-oriented agricultural enterprise. Their critique of the values of the marketplace was thus a deeply ambivalent one, but one that would have struck a sympathetic chord in many people, both farmers and potential tourists.

Victor Spear, the prime mover of the board's tourist program, was one of "those who stayed behind." Educated at Dartmouth, he had hoped to pursue a career as a civil engineer but was prevailed upon by his parents to take over the family farm. As a farmer, he achieved prominence by his consistent championing of new high-profit farm enterprises, first in raising breeding merino sheep for the West, then in lumbering and in maple sugar. He served in a number of offices during the last quarter of the century: in town offices in his hometown of Braintree; in both houses of the state legislature; on the Board of Agriculture; and as the treasurer of the Vermont Maple Sugar Makers' Market. As the Statistical Secretary of the Board of Agriculture, he was active in encouraging Vermont farmers to take on new crops: maple sugar, dairying, and of course the "crop from the city"—tourists.[29]

For Spear, this vigorous advocacy of new marketing devices, crops, and technologies in no way interfered with his belief that the Vermont farm stood—perhaps alone—against the speculative bent, the wanderlust, and the greed of the age. In his advice to farmers, Spear presented a clear choice between the Vermont farm and the world of money. As he put it, "there are not millions in farming. Men who have ambition to simply run up a big bank account . . . to pile up money for the sake of the money, farming is not the place for it." With that self-confident dismissal of the forces of greed and ambition, Spear drew the moral lines very clearly. Those who stayed behind knew how to value what they had: "For a man who has an appreciation of home . . . Vermont farming is a good occupation."[30] Spear had put aside his dreams of becoming an engineer, perhaps of "piling up money," in favor of his own "appreciation of home," and he based his defense of farm life on that choice. What is more interesting is that he also used that argument to encourage farmers to take in summer tourists, and even to encourage tourists to come to Vermont.

Writing for farmers, Spear described tourist work as an extension of homemaking, almost as a charitable enterprise:

[Our city cousins] want a little good food, they want a little milk to drink that has not been skimmed; they want to get out of the city . . . Let us see if next season we can not . . . benefit ourselves and do good to others.[31]

In Spear's vision, Vermont farms were the proper homes, and farmers the proper homemakers, not only for the farm family itself, but for vacationers as well. Of course, this was not really homemaking, and it was not charity. To preserve the values they cherished, Vermont farmers had, in effect, to sell them. Spear's enterprise was filled with irony. In order to preserve the Vermont farm as a haven against speculation and greed, Spear pressed farmers to rationalize production, delve more deeply into speculative involvements in the market, and finally to plunge into what was probably the most modernizing and disruptive business available to them: the tourist industry. To safeguard the home and its values, Spear encouraged farmers to bring the forces of urbanism into those very homes.

When Spear wrote for an outside audience, he used a similar language, with a similarly ambivalent defense of the rural home against the city. The board's advertising pamphlets, from one angle, seemed to express sentiments that had prevailed for decades in the farm advice journals of northern New England. Spear's very first publication, *Resources and Attractions of Vermont*, put forward that claim in its starkest form:

> Vermont from her beautiful hills cries to her absent sons and
>   daughters,
> Come back to your mother, ye children, for shame!
> Who have wandered like truants, for riches or fame.[32]

This plea might have been written in the 1870s with the intention of bringing home farmers who had gone out west to settle. In that context, it might have been taken quite literally, as an attack on profit-seeking and mobility (echoing Spear's earlier pointed remarks about those who seek to "pile up money for the sake of the money"). Even in the 1890s, it might still have retained a critical edge. But by then, the invitation to "come back" had become much more ambiguous. This was not so much a plea to the exiles to return to the farm as it was an invitation to tourists to come "home" for the summer. An audience of prospective tourists must be able to read this verse as a mildly humorous mock criticism—anything but a serious critique of their choice to "wander like truants." (After all, they would certainly not have had the money to vacation at "home" in the summer had they not wandered off in search of "riches or fame.") Spear's words, both for farmers and for tourists, recalled an older critique of marketplace values and urban life, but in such a way as to reassure, rather than alarm, potential city visitors.

New England Decadence

Of course, the Vermont Board of Agriculture was not the only source of information on the New England farm experience. The future of northern New England's farms and of rural life and values was the subject of heated debate among outsiders at the end of the century. Popular magazines filled their pages with articles on the decline of New England (by which they now meant rural, and especially northern, New England). Between 1890 and 1910, titles like "Broken Shadows on the New England Farm" and "Is New England Decadent?" were an almost constant presence in the popular magazines.[33]

Urban reformers often described the "decline of rural New England" primarily as a problem of character. The best and the brightest had moved west or to the cities, and those remaining were unadventurous and small-minded at best, mentally or morally defective at worst. Unlike the farm writers, who saw their region's problems as primarily economic—low profits, too much competition, inefficiency—these reformers discovered widespread social, religious, and moral problems in the region.[34] In one particularly harsh account, a reform-minded minister described a New England town as a "misfortune," harboring tribes of incestuous half-wits, "pests and delinquents and dependents and defectives and degenerates."[35] The New England farmers such writers discovered at the turn of the century seemed to them too much like the urban poor—morally indiscriminate, religiously inclined toward skepticism or too-fervent revivalism, badly educated and badly fed—and not enough like the independent Yankee yeomanry on whom they thought the nation depended.[36]

New England farm writers usually dismissed these gloomy assessments as the product of ignorance, referring sarcastically to a writer-reformer like Alvan Sanborn as "a bright young man, who . . . writes for the Atlantic Monthly all sorts of things that aren't so, about New England rural life."[37] But urban reformers did share with Vermont's own farm writers some of their beliefs about rural New England. Both reformers and natives accepted the idea that the region should be, if it was not, a special repository for "traditional values" that were, they thought, besieged in the cities.

That belief informed much of the voluminous fictional writing on New England rural life, too. From Sarah Orne Jewett's loving evocation of a dying countryside to Edith Wharton's grim depictions of the emptiness and savagery of village life, a wide variety of writers reflected on the lives of contemporary rural New Englanders in these years. "Local color" writers like Jewett, Elizabeth Stuart Phelps, and Rose Terry Cooke differed widely in their assessment of the relative simplicity and beauty, or narrowness and poverty, of New England rural life. In any case, their meticulously crafted observations were only a trickle in a flood of sentimental memoirs and tales of childhood memorializing the nostalgic features of the New England farm. What most of these works had in common, though, was a sense that New England rural life was significant beyond its meaning for those who lived it.

The notion of the decline of New England rural life was based in fact on a shared belief in a sort of golden age, when New England's institutions and values had created a democratic rural utopia, whose beneficent influence

Clifton Johnson traveled the "highways and by-ways" of New England capturing images of vanishing ways of life. This photograph was taken in the Berkshires of Massachusetts, but it was only one version of an image of bucolic boyhood that became ubiquitous during these years. From Clifton Johnson, *Highways and By-Ways of New England* (New York: Macmillan Co., 1915).

had radiated out over the entire country. (That vision of New England was perhaps best expressed in the regional novels of Harriet Beecher Stowe, whose work had a profound influence on the next generation of women writing in the "local color" genre.[38]) Many types of writings—history, sociology, personal reminiscences, "local color" stories—reflected this shared belief. The argument was about *when* "the old order of life, with its romantic charm, its simplicity, its godliness, its reposeful calm," had been replaced, as one harsh critic put it, with "the beautiless affectations of a crude and very modern civilization."[39] The reformers believed it was going or gone; the nostalgic writers argued that somewhere in northern New England one could still find a "veritable rural utopia."[40]

For these writers, whether sentimental or scientific, the countryside of New England was primarily a resource for the nation's political health and for the city person's moral and psychological health. New England's countryside was imagined as a kind of underground cultural aquifer that fed the nation's springs of political courage, personal independence, and old-fashioned virtue. Reformers feared that this source was becoming tainted, but they shared with more sentimental writers the hope that the region could yet be made to yield the proper medicines to treat the illnesses of modern urban life. It is easy to see in these writers the same impulse that would draw increasing numbers of urban vacationers to the New England countryside in search of rural peace and contentment.

That outsider's vision of the role of the New England farm bore some resemblance to the vision of farm reformers like Victor Spear, who did portray the role of farm hosts as a kind of social service to city dwellers. Enthusiastic tourists often seemed to be employing the rhetoric of the Board of Agriculture. Herbert Wendell Gleason, for instance, wrote glowingly about Old Home Week in a 1900 article in *New England Magazine*. Gleason argued that "the spirit of commercial greed has wrought sad havoc with the ideals of our fathers," especially of "the old New England idea of home, with its cheerful simplicity, quiet atmosphere, strong ties of affection and ruggedness of virtue."[41] Here Gleason's urban nostalgia met the Board of Agriculture on its own ground, using some of the same language.

But Gleason was not advocating a return to rural life—far from it. City dwellers like Gleason were actually turning the Board of Agriculture's rhetoric upside down. Farm writers like Spear viewed tourism as a means to an end: the preservation of the farm. Outsiders like Gleason viewed farm life and farm families as resources for the health and well-being of urbanites like themselves. In one way or another, they hoped to extract these values and experiences from rural life rather than to return to the farm for good. It was a pattern characteristic of Victorian social compromises: Just as women in the middle-class home were supposed to impart moral training to men on their way out of the home into the world, Vermont farms were to confer peace and contentment on visitors who would then return to the corruption and competition of their urban lives.

There was a real gap between rural and urban perspectives on rural life. That gap was obscured by the success of the state programs, but its presence was often felt. Although local inhabitants made the preparations for Old Home Week festivities, for example, those ceremonies could hardly be described as celebrations of rural life. The flattery and the attention were focused on the returning conquering heroes—Boston bankers and Chicago railroad magnates—not at all on "those who stayed behind." Edith Wharton's 1917 novel, *Summer,* described an Old Home Week celebration that laid bare a stark contrast between the sentimentalism of city visitors returning home to "North Dormer" and the constricted and hopeless lives of those who still lived there. As Wharton told the story, "the incentive to the celebration had come rather from those who had left North Dormer than from those who had been obliged to stay there, and there was some difficulty in rousing the village to the proper state of enthusiasm." It was outsiders who spoke, in one visiting character's cynical phrase, of "the old ideals, the family and the homestead, and so on."[42]

Anyone considering a vacation in rural Vermont in the 1890s was likely to have been influenced by at least some of these debates over the meaning and uses of the New England countryside. Such urban tourists had been exposed to impossibly contradictory descriptions of New England farm life. What were they expecting when they set out on vacation? Perhaps they harbored an essentially sentimental attitude toward the farm and their own childhoods, not unlike the images disseminated by Old Home Week committees. At the same time, their distance from the farm and its values was apparently not so great that they were immune to the Board of Agriculture's implicit critique of modern urban life (and of their own choices). After all, such a tourist might have chosen to go to the coast or to a scenic resort rather than "home" to the farm for a vacation. Perhaps it is most useful to see the farm vacationer as someone standing on contested terrain in the most literal sense, taking a position that could be understood either as a kind of muted resistance to some aspects of urban industrial life or as a pleasant retreat from some of its symptoms.

The Summer Boarder

During the 1890s, the summer tourist industry in northern New England became a major business. Although the states' methods of counting were rudimentary, they were sufficient to show the importance of the summer tourist industry to the region. New Hampshire's Bureau of Labor estimated in 1900 that the total income from tourism for 1899 was $6,600,000 and the total number of summer guests was 174,000 (at a time when New Hampshire's permanent population was 411,588).[43] Vermont's industry was smaller and grew more slowly at first. Its statistics were probably less reliable, but it seems clear that during the 1890s, between fifty thousand and sixty thousand visitors were in Vermont each summer, and that there were as many as 650 hotels, resorts, boardinghouses, and farm boarding places in the state during the 1890s—enough to justify Victor Spear's opinion that summer tourists were second only to dairying in bringing money into the state.[44] These lodgings ranged from large hotels accommodating 150 or 200 people to farmhouses with room for a single family, or even a single boarder.

While the Board of Agriculture's program encouraged tourism in all its forms—camping out, patronizing resort hotels, buying summer homes—the most characteristic form of this new vacation was summer boarding on farms. This was both a less formal and a far less expensive type of vacation than a hotel visit. Farm families who wanted summer boarders simply advertised in newspapers of nearby cities, and then screened the letters they received for the type of visitors they wanted. Arrangements varied a great deal. Some households had room for only two or three people. Some were actually small hotels, with room for as many as twelve or fifteen. Prices also varied, from as low as $3 per week for a family to over $12, still substantially less expensive than even a moderately priced hotel (at around $3 per day). For those prices, the boarders received fairly simple accommodations, including a shared room and access to a common parlor. They also received fairly elaborate meals, often served to them separately while the farm family ate in the kitchen. Advisers repeated frequently that good food was far more important than lavish accommodations and that city boarders would be content with clean, rather spartan living conditions if only they were given good "country-style" meals.

The Board of Agriculture's promotional program, like Old Home Week, seemed particularly to invite former residents of Vermont to board on farms, but there is little evidence as to whether they really attracted returning natives. Farm boarders seem to have varied somewhat in social class. Sometimes they were people who could have afforded a more lavish vacation—wealthy ladies who wanted to milk cows and make their own preserves—but most often they seem to have been from middle- to fairly low-income groups. The families of businessmen often came from nearby Vermont cities like Burlington or Brattleboro. Wife and children could then stay for an extended period while the husband came out for weekends. From more distant cities, as far away as Boston, Springfield, or Hartford, came single women or men. These boarders tended to have distinctly white-collar occupations with rather marginal incomes—"schoolteachers, bookkeepers, and clerks," as one farm wife reported, "all intelligent and refined."[45] Some summer boarders were actually related to the farm family. These were clearly "coming home" in a very different sense.

In fact, the farm vacation exhibited a remarkable flexibility in its ability to cater both to those people for whom it was actually some form of going home and to those for whom it was a safely distanced fantasy of home and the old days. The actual relationship of urban tourists to the farm vacation may have depended in large part on the degree of distance between them and their own farm pasts, but visitors of all kinds were in a position, perhaps for the first time, of being able to envision the countryside as a playground rather than as a mass of conflicting obligations, restraints, and memories.

For that reason, if for no other, there were necessarily some important differences between the expectations of farm families and those of their guests. Both groups had recourse to the same notions of the special qualities of farm life: its healthfulness, its peacefulness, its preservation of important values. But that rhetoric did not always mean the same things to farmers as it did to visitors.

Northern New England's tourist promoters, having helped to create a new demand for a nostalgic farm experience, were then obliged to respond to it. Tourists who wanted to experience life on the old farm, or wanted their children to experience it, traveled in increasing numbers to the hill towns at the end of the century. They brought with them a whole host of expectations and assumptions about farm life and the New England countryside, many of them engendered by the promoters themselves. But the fulfillment of these expectations was not always easy. Promoters were acutely aware of the need to give summer boarders a nostalgic experience. *New England Homestead* advised its readers: "Make the house a home for your 'paying guests,' but above all, make of it a purely country home; do not make the mistake of trying to make a city home of it. They left the city to get into the country."[46] But what constituted a "purely country home"? What did these "city cousins" want from their visit?

Rural hosts were often uncomfortably aware of the wide difference between their perspective on rural life and the perspective of their "city cousins." For one thing, there was the simple difference between daily life and vacation life, between work on a farm and play on a farm. One farm woman's heavily underlined sarcasm made it clear that her visitors were not getting what she considered the "real" rural experience:

They find the morning *so* fresh after you have served their late breakfast, and the glass of milk *so* refreshing after their afternoon nap, and the cream is *so* delicious, and the piazza *so* cool, you think some day you would really like to enjoy it yourself for a few minutes.[47]

As far as Mrs. Gibbs was concerned, her own hard work was the *real* farm experience, not her visitors' leisurely days.

And of course, that was true. In theory, farm visitors wanted to experience a way of life they associated with the old days, with the virtues of rural simplicity and closeness to nature. But they did not really want to "go home" to the drudgery and isolation of farm life—they wanted to go on vacation. Their decision to board on a farm simply indicated that they had certain vacation preferences. Farm vacations were inexpensive, and they also seemed healthy and natural, especially for children. And farm vacations offered some very special attractions, none more important than the food everyone called plain country fare.

Plain Country Fare

Frank Rollins spelled out the preferences of vacationers in a *New England Magazine* article encouraging farm families to get involved in the tourist industry. City visitors, he wrote, wanted "plain country fare"—good butter, good bread, fresh vegetables and eggs—and they wanted it cooked "simply," which was to say, *not fried.* "Throw away your frying-pan; go bury it in the pasture twenty feet deep." And furthermore, they wanted fresh flowers and service "by as pretty a girl, a farmer's daughter, as you can find, neatly and prettily dressed."[48] (Rollins was only one among several

The caption reads, "'I'm going a-milking, Sir,' she said." This farmer's daughter appeared—without explanation or comment—in an article advising farm families to take in summer boarders and explaining their preferences and expectations. Apparently the point was self-explanatory. From C. T. Wiltshire, "The Summer Boarder As An Asset," *New England Homestead* 64 (18 May 1912).

promoters to add the "farmer's daughter" to the list of farm products more effectively exploited at the point of production. *New England Homestead* illustrated its article on boarding tourists with a photograph of a jaunty farmer's daughter standing at the doorway of the barn. The caption read, "I'm going a-milking, sir, she said."[49])

"Plain country fare," according to those who advised farmers on how to produce it, consisted of fresh milk, fresh eggs, fresh vegetables and fruits of all kinds. Its preparation was to be as "simple" as possible, in city terms. Clearly it was not the kind of food prospective tourists were accustomed to eating in the city, since it was denoted country fare. Just as clearly, it was not the kind of food farmers were accustomed to eating in the country, since they needed so much help in figuring it out. In reality, visitors hoping for fresh, seasonal simplicity had to contend with the monotonous, high-fat diet of most farmers. Urban reformers recorded with repugnance the endless round of pork, biscuits, doughnuts, and pies the average farmer ate.[50] One writer described her former boarding experience as "a bad dream," recalling the "tough beef," "blue milk," and "the ubiquitous prune and pie" (that is, dried fruit and dried fruit pie) she had endured.[51]

Food could easily become the stumbling block on which the entire vacation foundered. William Dean Howells rented a house in Shirley, Massachusetts, for his family during the summer of 1876. As with a growing number of his contemporaries, Howells's position as editor of the *Atlantic Monthly* gave him both the flexibility and the money to go away for the summer but kept him within a day's travel of his offices in Cambridge. In June, he wrote to his father that his family had the "promise of a very pleasant summer" before them. The local woman who cooked for them would have to be taught their "ideas of cooking," but she was willing to learn, and "so far, all goes well." Six weeks later, Howells suddenly informed his father that the family had fled their summer home because of their "extreme discontent" with their landlord and his family. The landlady was not, after all, willing to learn their ideas of cooking. As Howells described it, "everything on the table was sour, dirty, or rancid."[52] The problem so intrigued Howells that thirty years later he framed a novel, *The Vacation of the Kelwyns*, around his family's attempts to compel their summer landlady to give them "plain country fare, with plenty of milk and eggs and berries" in the place of the "cowy milk," bitter tea, greasy eggs, and rancid butter she provided.[53]

Food was not the only subject on which urban and rural understandings of the farm collided. Alvan Sanborn, who reported on the deplorable eating habits of rural New Englanders in *Atlantic Monthly*, was equally displeased with the "up-to-date gewgaws" and "smart sets of parlor furniture" he found in farm homes.[54] *New England Homestead* argued with its readers that tourists did not expect city accommodations in the country—"in point of fact they do not want them"—and suggested that they get rid of their "stuffy draperies, dusty carpets and superfluous furniture" and brighten up the place with painted woodwork and tasteful wallpaper.[55] The stuffy draperies and dusty carpets were in all likelihood the most up-to-date and urban of the farm's furnishings, and they seem also to have been the very kinds of objects most associated with domesticity in the urban parlor.[56] But city tourists were not interested in modern farms. Farm furniture, clothing, and customs must be old-fashioned and quaint, in order to give the visitor a nostalgic experience of the past. Howells's Kelwyns were disappointed to find that the house they had rented from the Shakers in New Hampshire came complete with new furniture straight from the warehouse, in place of the "Shaker quaintness" of "rag carpets and hooked rugs" they had expected.[57]

Tourist promoters were eager to smooth over these difficulties. The Central Vermont Railroad reported in its pamphlet *Summer Homes among the Green Hills of Vermont* in 1894 that it had, "at no inconsiderable expense," recruited a number of Vermont families to "open their comfortable, and often luxurious homes" to the summer boarder.[58] And increasingly, the state involved itself in attempts to train Vermont farm women to cook plain country fare properly, and in general to train farm families to entertain tourists. More informal networks also dispersed information. In the last years of the century, *New England Homestead* readers wrote to the magazine in large numbers every summer, reporting their experiences with summer boarders, their advice on how to set up such a business, and their evaluations of its worth.

By the end of the century, no would-be rural vacation provider could have been ignorant of the kinds of food and accommodations city people liked. Every summer issue of the farm magazines carried advice about fresh cream, eggs, chicken, vegetables, and fruit, and more: how to rotate the food to create variety, how to capitalize on the boarder's imagination. One farm woman observed that "the vegetables that passed directly from the garden to the stove, under the direct observation of the boarders, were considered to be far superior to any others." It had sometimes been inconvenient to cater to the boarders in this way, she acknowledged, "but it paid, you know."[59] The same sort of advice was available for decorating:

"The old furniture proved very interesting and the painted floors were just the proper thing."[60]

The advice was so well understood that one farm woman reported her experiences to the contrary with some astonishment: "My boarders ate pie!" In her article, entitled "Pie a Standard Dessert," Mrs. A. M. Lewis of New Hampshire reported that her boarders had eaten her pie with relish, although they had been a bit defensive about it, one of them explaining "somewhat humbly" after eating three pieces, "I did not know before that pie was so good to eat." After that day, she reported, she "felt no fears"; she served them pie, and even baked beans and doughnuts. "To tell the whole truth," she concluded, "they liked everything that was good"—but she hastened to concede that perhaps she had been unusually fortunate in her boarders.[61]

The battle over plain country fare was not essentially a matter of ignorance. It was at least in part a battle for control of the vacation, and ultimately over the meaning of rural life. For if vacationers did not expect "city" food or urban parlor furniture, their notions of "simple" cooking and "plain" furnishings demanded a great deal of extra work for both the men and women of the host family. Producing a constant supply of fresh food for the boarder's table required planting and tending a different sort of garden. As one Vermont farmer reported it, "city people . . . eat three times as many vegetables as do the farmers . . . (and) eat three or four times as many sorts." He advised farmers who wished to cater to the summer trade that they must "plant every sort of fruit and vegetable . . . that may ordinarily be found in the city markets," that they had to plant early and repeatedly, and that the whole business involved a great deal of planning, constant attention to the garden, and familiarity with a variety of vegetables their own families had rarely seen.[62] (The vacation trade, along with similar ventures into market gardening near cities, may account for the numerous articles printed in the Vermont Board of Agriculture's *Reports* on how to grow southern exotics like eggplant in a climate where even corn barely had time to ripen.)

For farm women, boarders were not simply extra people for whom they cooked and cleaned. They added entirely new demands: for fresh towels every day, for variety at mealtime, and for patience with those who wanted to "help out" in the kitchen. Susan Warner's 1882 novel, *Nobody*, touched on the difficulties of accommodating a city boarder on a New England farm. The strains both of anticipating urban tastes and expectations and of providing for urban amenities on a rural cash budget were illuminated in a conversation between the daughters of the family. It was reasonable for the skeptical daughter in this novel to wonder: "'She is a city body, of course. Do you suppose she will be contented with our ways of going on?'" New curtains for the parlor windows, new tablecloths and napkins, silver-plated forks instead of steel, and soft-coal fires instead of wood were only part of the list of changes necessary to accommodate the new boarder.[63]

One rather smug magazine correspondent set herself up as a model landlady, claiming that she "constantly studied to cater to [her boarders'] delicate appetites." For breakfast she provided for those delicate appetites an astounding array of foods: "broiled chicken, broiled ham or steak or fresh trout [not fried, of course] . . . delicious cream toast, eggs in a variety of ways, baked potatoes or apples, graham gems or muffins with white clover honey"—and her pièce de résistance, "fresh fruit picked with long stems, arranged in my best cut-glass dish and garnished with leaves." In addition to such aesthetic feats, she went so far as to change the furniture in her sitting room to suit the weather, from wicker on sunny days to plush when it rained.[64] Most people with summer boarders probably did not go this far, but the farm magazines were filled with tips for extremely time-consuming work: where to set up lawn furniture, how to vary your desserts, how to convince your husband to take your guests for a drive.

Most of the helpful hints on such subjects were recorded in the women's sections of farm magazines. Everyone in the farm household could expect to come into extra work if they decided to take in boarders, but it was additional washing, cooking, and decorating that made up the largest work load, and that, of course, was done by women. There is some evidence to suggest that the decision to take in summer boarders was made by farm women, in recognition of the greater impact on their work inside the house. It appears that the women of the family may have pocketed the cash from the boarders, just as they would have claimed the butter or egg money earned through their efforts.

In any case, summer boarding brought cash into the farm household during a time when the family's needs were becoming ever more tied to the cash economy. One farm woman took in summer boarders long enough to earn $35 for a bicycle (although the writer who reported her story asked, "Was that compensation for rising before 5 o'clock every morning, baking, brewing and serving separate meals to farm help?").[65] Susan Warner's fictional heroines found that the twelve dollars a week they would make from their boarder would compensate them entirely for a disastrous year in which their only cow had died and both their apple and hay crops had failed. Instead of the apple crop that year, it was the boarder's fee that paid for the family's winter clothes.[66]

At the same time, though, boarders contested the farm family's control over their own house and the relationship between host and guest. There was no simple definition of this relationship. Were the farm woman and her husband servants, or hostess and host? From the standpoint of the boarder, the farm family resembled servants; they were responsible for feeding and cleaning up after the boarders. From the standpoint of the farm family, they were hosts with guests (although these guests sometimes made unreasonable demands). The work they did, while it entailed many adjustments, was essentially consistent with their ordinary farm work, no more a matter of personal service than was any other farm work. And although they debated in the magazines whether the extra work was worth the extra income—weighed the "worries and small trials," the "petty annoyances," with the profit to be gained—no one suggested that the work of boarding tourists was essentially different from ordinary farm work.

Farm women who described their experiences in *New England Homestead* painted extremely varied pictures of the relationship of boarder to host. In some cases they reported a clearly equal relationship between their own family and the tourist family. One woman wrote that she had made "several warm friends" among her boarders and that she often visited them when she was in town.[67] More often, the general advice was to keep a distance, not out of any sense of inferiority, but out of a sense of appropriate privacy, and out of a desire to protect one's own family. It was appropriate to "cultivate lasting friendships with those who are so inclined," as long as one could make sure that they were "the right sort and sincere."[68]

It is clear not only from the promotional literature but from the words of these farm women themselves that they viewed their position as at least equal to that of their visitors from the city. They were quite capable of assessing the class status of their visitors and of evaluating their desirability on that basis. One woman wrote in a column called "First Class Boarders" that "there are several classes of people who spend, the less favored a week or more, the more favored from one or two months to all summer, in the country." She recommended the "more favored" group as being on the whole easier to please; and she cautioned against mixing classes, since it would be "pleasanter if all the members of your household are congenial."[69] (Apparently she included her own family among those who would be congenial to the "more favored" classes.)

If urban tourists expected old-fashioned hospitality from a naturally humble farming class, they often met with something rather different. And this conflict was heightened by the structure of summer boarding itself, which included so many uncertainties as to the status of the boarder. It was simply unclear who was in charge. "The visitors with one accord, however humble their social status in the city, [regard] themselves as vastly superior to the farmer," but "the farmer regards [the city person] as essentially ill-bred, and . . . laughs to scorn his pretensions to superiority."[70]

This perspective could be very frustrating to the boarders, who sometimes expected a level of personal service quite out of keeping with the farm family's understanding of the situation. Small details could become momentous: Once having decided that the boarders would eat alone, and the farm family in the kitchen, who would serve them—and how continuously? Howells's vacationing family complained that they had to go into the kitchen for second helpings or hot water for their tea.[71] Farm women complained that boarders invaded their "sanctum"—the kitchen— "at any or all hours."[72] In these small details, the wide disparities between rural and urban visions of the farm worked themselves out.

Ultimately, these struggles reflected a contest over the farm family's identity and over the meaning of the farm. Farm women knew that some of their boarders wished to see them as quaint representatives of a simpler world, but they had their own reasons for appearing otherwise. If their boarders preferred old-fashioned furniture, clothing, and customs, they themselves may not have wished to appear out of step and "countrified." From their perspective, modern conveniences and fashions did nothing to threaten the essential value of farm life. Their own magazines were full of advertisements and advice on how to keep up with the modern improvements of the cities: "A Country Girl Can Dress Just as Smart as a City Girl" went one *New England Homestead* advertisement for *Ladies' Home Journal*. Farm families were well aware that these tourists, whatever they said, were quick to condemn any truly old-fashioned foods and habits they encountered.

These areas of contention revealed themselves in trivial issues, but they were nonetheless powerful and real. A glance at the contents of the summer issues of *New England Homestead* for 1905 shows a new familiarity with summer boarders and a more critical perspective. Instead of an array of advice letters and accounts of experiences designed to encourage and reassure the farm family, there is a series of cartoons on summer boarders and their foibles. In the cartoons, the boarder, not the farm family, is on trial. One cartoon, in addition to mocking the city boarder's ineptitude, manages to belittle his much-discussed dietary preferences at the same time. The city boarder is in search of plain country fare, in this case roast chicken, but he gets stuck with the much-despised pork through his own inadequacy. The other cartoons in the series also emphasize the summer boarder's ignorance of farm life (and they hint that there may have been some conflict over the summer boarder's desire to "help out" with farm chores). Farm families may have accepted summer boarders and tourists, but not necessarily the values and perspectives of their guests, and certainly not their guests' definitions of farm life and rural people.

The hidden incongruity between the meaning of the farm "home" for northern farmers and for visiting tourists became an all-too-concrete struggle over pies, towels, and carpets. But in spite of these conflicts, the fit between the Vermont farmers' experiences and their visitors' experiences held fast. The summer tourist business prospered in northern New England, and for the most part, both visitors and farmers seemed to get what they expected. If their understanding of the meaning of their experiences was not the same, that did not destroy the alliance they had made.

In the end, northern New England, and especially Vermont, took on a role touched by elements of both rural and urban perspectives. The nostalgia

"The helpful city boarder plans for roast chicken but gets pork instead." On one level, this comic strip simply mocks the city boarder's inability to handle simple farm tasks; but it also lampoons the urban visitor's taste for "plain country fare"— fresh poultry, fresh fruits and vegetables—and the urban aversion to pork. From *New England Homestead*, 17 July 1905.

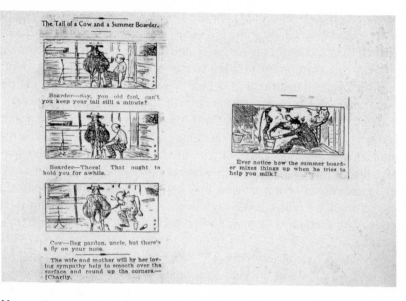

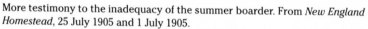

More testimony to the inadequacy of the summer boarder. From *New England Homestead*, 25 July 1905 and 1 July 1905.

that surrounded the region was deepened by the ways in which the tourist industry needed real, "old-fashioned" farming, and by the growing dependence of farming on tourism. Even after the direct connection between Vermont agriculture and Vermont tourism was severed with the creation of a separate Board of Publicity in 1911, the two industries remained intertwined. In 1930, for instance, the Vermont Agricultural Extension Service arranged two statewide conferences on the subject of entertaining tourists, including such topics as "How to Attract and Hold the Tourist," "Presenting an Attractive Exterior," and "Meals for the Tourist." (The farm families of Vermont, like the modern woman, were being encouraged to become more active. Rather than waiting quietly for their customers to come calling, they were to "attract and hold" them with an "attractive exterior.")[73] By that time, small-scale tourist businesses played a major role in the economy of the state.

Northern New England farmers were able to use the tourist industry not only to bolster their faltering farm economy, but also to confirm their understanding of farm life as a uniquely useful and rewarding occupation. In that sense, their situation was much more fortunate than that of Nantucket's local providers of tourist services, who were more or less at the mercy of the fantasies and projections of affluent visitors. Because of a fortuitous "fit" between the needs of the northern farm economy and the desires of urban tourists, the two were able to take advantage of one another—at least for the time being.

But the deeper incongruity remained. The nostalgic rhetoric used by farm promoters and by returning tourists sounded the same, but it led in radically different directions: one toward a viable and renewable agricultural economy, the other toward a nostalgic imitation of rural life—a place where urban people could play out their fantasies of rural values and experiences. If the story had ended in the early twentieth century, the incongruity might not have emerged at all. Nostalgic tourism thrived in northern New England, and it also bolstered the region's farm economy, giving farm advocates what they most wanted from the new industry. It is only in recent years that this alliance has come apart. Or rather, it has only recently become clear that there was no real alliance to begin with—that hay fields and scenery cannot always be preserved by the same policies. In northern New England today, the nostalgia industry and agriculture are more often in open and bitter conflict than in apparent harmony, but for a short time, the double-edged rhetoric of farm nostalgia seemed to make everybody happy.

6
THE PROBLEM
OF THE SUMMER

Race, Class, and the Colonial Vacation in Southern Maine, 1890–1910

hen William Dean Howells became editor of the *Atlantic Monthly* in 1871, his salary became high enough for him to take his family on their first real vacation. It was a momentous change, but one that he had anticipated for years. In 1869 Howells had written to Henry James about a short excursion to the beach, "It was with a kind of dismay that I learnt the pleasure was quite within my means."[1] If he had known what lay in store for him and for his family in the coming years, he would have been dismayed indeed. Over the next forty years, Howells and his family would sample the fare of almost every tourist region in the Northeast, from the White Mountains to the Berkshires, from Long Island to the coast of Maine. They would endure every kind of vacationing misfortune, from the "wave-whipped desert" of Long Island to Jaffrey, New Hampshire, with its "mosquitoes so large that you can see them tuning their harps . . . on the top of Mount Monadnock, four miles away."[2] Following the Howellses' vacation saga is a tour in itself, through all the vacation industries of the late nineteenth century, and through all the most pressing concerns that haunted affluent vacationers.

Old houses were even more appealing when they could be associated with an aristocratic colonial figure like Sir William Pepperell, a Loyalist who had been made a baronet by the English crown for his wartime assistance in retaining Canada in English hands. These houses scattered over Kittery Point bear testimony to Pepperell's great wealth. "Old Historic Mansions, Kittery Point, Me." from *Attractive Bits Along Shore* (1900). Courtesy, American Antiquarian Society.

In the early years, the young couple had made do with inexpensive makeshift vacations while Howells established himself as assistant editor of the *Atlantic*. In 1867, they had summered in Brattleboro, Vermont, an eminent resort town well-known for both its pastoral beauties and its celebrated water-cure establishment. But they had not chosen Brattleboro for those attractions. That first vacation was a gift from Elinor Mead Howells's parents, who had moved out of their house and boarded somewhere else so that the couple could spend some time relaxing in the country.

Once Howells was secure in his position as assistant editor and the young family was settled in Cambridge, they were able to take short trips to the beach and countryside. The summer of 1869 found them sampling what Howells referred to in a letter to Henry James as "the simple joys of a trip down the harbor to Nantasket beach."[3] The hint of mockery in that description came from Howells's awareness that the "simple joys" of plebeian Nantasket Beach were strictly off-limits for people of his rising social status. Years later, he made use of his Nantasket memories for one of his best-known novels, *The Rise of Silas Lapham*, which traced the tribulations of a parvenu millionaire so ignorant of Boston social standards that he took a summer cottage in barely middle-class Nantasket rather than in elite Nahant or Bar Harbor.

Soon, Howells was promoted to editor of the *Atlantic*, and the real vacations—and the troubles—began. For twenty years, the family searched for the right summer place. Their first attempts landed them in the farming region of southern New Hampshire and north central Massachusetts, where they hoped to find rural quiet, space for the children, and the "plain country fare" they associated with farm life. The summer of 1874 found them in Jaffrey, New Hampshire, home of those giant mosquitoes. The next year they tried another rural retreat not far away, in Shirley, Massachusetts. It appeared at first to be the perfect location, and it might have been had Howells not become hopelessly embroiled in the violent domestic disputes of the host family. Weighing the experience, Howells reported that it was "a tragedy, dreary and squalid beyond conception. Still, the vegetables and cream are of the first quality."[4]

Perhaps it was the memory of the vegetables and cream that convinced the family to return to the same village one more time. This time the Howellses boarded with another couple who appeared more amiable. But they, too, turned out to have serious problems. These were the hosts who gave Howells the material for his novel *The Vacation of the Kelwyns*, a tale of a disastrous summer vacation discussed in Chapter 5. When Howells wrote to his father in June, shortly after their arrival, he described the couple as "good-natured" and, although ignorant, "very willing to learn." By late July, however, Howells reported to his father that the landlord had "turned out a surly ruffian, and his wife a slut. Everything on the table was sour, dirty, or rancid, and the discomfort of our whole life intolerable."[5] In place of the "plain country fare, with plenty of milk and eggs and berries" Howells had hoped for, they suffered through meal after meal of "cowy milk," bitter tea, greasy eggs, and rancid butter. Finally, the family fled. They managed to spend the rest of the summer at another farmhouse in a nearby town, but their enthusiasm for rural life was considerably dampened.

For the next decade, each summer found the family somewhere new. In 1877, they turned toward the seaside, boarding in a farmhouse on Conanicut Island, "near Newport." They went to Duxbury, on the south shore of Massachusetts, "where Miles Standish lived"; to the White Mountains of New Hampshire; to Great Barrington in the Berkshires; to Mount Desert and Old Orchard Beach (Howells called it "Old Orchard

Beast") along the coast of Maine. In the first years, this continual movement reflected simple dissatisfaction and restlessness. Later, it reflected
a more serious problem. After 1885, their mobility was caused by their
anxiety over the oldest daughter, Winifred, now in her teens and increasingly ill with a mysterious disease.

For three years, the family spent summer vacations conveying Winifred
from one hospital or spa to another: health resorts in Lake George, Danville
in the Adirondacks, and Nahant, north of Boston. Many affluent and
leisured people had extensive experience with that sort of "vacation,"
spent in the pursuit of health. Although Victorian resorts are often portrayed as the haunts of rich hypochondriacs, they actually treated a wide
variety of urgent medical problems—physical, mental, or both. "Change
of scene," or sea or mountain air, might be prescribed for diseases ranging in seriousness from hay fever to ulcers to tuberculosis. The six months
Edward Bellamy spent on Nantucket (described by Bellamy in *Six to One:
A Nantucket Idyl*, the novel discussed in Chapter 4) had been prescribed
by his doctor to treat his nervous breakdown and exhaustion from overwork. Howells's close friend Mark Twain spent years traveling throughout the United States and Europe in search of health for his daughters.

Resorts that specialized in medical treatment often offered innovative
regimens or techniques—water cures, electric therapy—designed to
combat chronic illness. Winifred Howells underwent several such treat-
ments as her health declined, culminating in the celebrated "rest cure" of
S. Weir Mitchell. (Mitchell's prescription of complete bed rest, force-feed-
ing, and sensory deprivation was highly acclaimed at the time of Winifred's
illness, but is remembered today mostly because of a harrowing tale of
a woman driven insane by it: Charlotte Perkins Gilman's *The Yellow
Wallpaper*.) In spite of all the Howellses' care, Winifred died in 1889, of
causes that are still unclear.

In the years that followed, the grieving family continued to seek out appropriate summer vacation places. Their vacations in these years centered on their attempts to find congenial company for their two remaining
children, now reaching adulthood, and on the aging and depressed couple's attempts to find a place to retire: "We are drifting about from one
place to another, this summer, trying to discover some spot within a few
hours of New York where we might pitch our ragged tent for the few summers that yet remain to us."[6]

By that time, Howells had left Boston and was working in New York City,
first for *Harper's* and then for *Cosmopolitan*. The family tried several re-

sorts near New York. Long Island seemed like a "wave-whipped desert" to Howells, who remembered the New England coast as "so much lovelier." Far Rockaway gave Mrs. Howells neuralgia. (She ended up having to take a vacation in the White Mountains to escape her summer place by the beach.)[7] At one point, Howells thought he had found the perfect summer place on Cape Ann, along the North Shore of Massachusetts: "a most beautiful place," quiet and isolated, where Mr. and Mrs. Howells thought of making a permanent home. But as Howells wrote to his son, Cape Ann had a fatal defect: "If it would develop socially, and give poor Pil [his second daughter Mildred] a chance for her life, I should try for it. But it is the most manless place I ever saw."[8]

It was not until 1898, after Howells's income as a free-lance writer had freed him from the need to commute to New York, that the family at last found the spot they were to prefer for the rest of Howells's life, and to which his son, John, would return even after the deaths of his parents. (Mildred Howells remained single and maintained an extremely mobile existence, traveling extensively on her own and with her parents in Europe, the United States, and the Caribbean.) In 1898, Howells wrote to his sister that "'Yorke Harbor' is a beautiful little seaside village. In fact, everything on this coast is beautiful."[9] Howells confided to Henry James that summer that he had a "notion to write pretty closely" about the town.[10] The next summer the family rented a house in nearby Kittery Point, "beside a reefy and shippy shore, with sails by day and lamps by night. . . . The air is such as you breathe nowhere else in the world, and the fisherfolk life quaint and old as the 17th century."[11] Within a few years, Howells and his wife had bought a house in Kittery Point, and Howells had conceived a deep love "for Kittery and golden joys!" The ordinarily reserved Howells wrote to his sister in 1906, "John and I are going down to Kittery Point at the end of the month, hurrah!"[12]

Kittery and Golden Joys

What made the quiet, reticent Howells use so many exclamation points when he wrote about his newfound summer place? It is easy to imagine what his own answer might have been. The southern coast of Maine harbored fewer mosquitoes than inland New Hampshire (although even in Kittery, as Howells later wrote, there were occasional mosquito population explosions); the protected inlets and coves of the area offered protection from the windy, "desert-like" conditions Howells had found on Long Island.

Howells was fond of the "neatness and self-respect" of New England villages. And Kittery Point had that incomparable air.

Of course, any seaside resort in the north provided air very much like it. The towns of York and Kittery Point were not very different from much of the rest of the coast of New England. They could not rival Mount Desert's spectacular combination of mountain and seacoast scenery, which the Howellses had seen; nor were they much different from the well-to-do cottage colonies of Massachusetts' North Shore, where the family had also stayed. Scenic beauty and fresh air were *prerequisites* for a vacation community that hoped to attract the sort of affluent and leisured people the Howellses had become by the end of the century, but they were not enough to distinguish one vacation resort from another.

For Howells, York and Kittery did have at least one important advantage over other attractive seaside spots. A great many of his friends and professional associates were there. The Howellses rented their Kittery Point cottage that first year from *Atlantic* contributor George Wasson. In 1902, one of Howells's closest friends, Mark Twain, was in nearby York Harbor, only "forty minutes from Kittery Point" by trolley, as Howells reckoned it.[13] The same trolley would deliver Howells to another old friend and business associate, Sarah Orne Jewett, at her inland ancestral home in South Berwick. Everywhere he looked, Howells saw someone he knew, or whose work he knew. In 1900, he wrote to *Atlantic* contributor Edmund C. Stedman, "I can see your house [across the harbor in New Castle] from my porch. I wish I could see you in it!"[14]

It is not surprising to find people of the same social circles and professions at the same resorts. That had been one of their chief attractions since the days when pioneering resorts like Wesleyan Grove had carved out their highly specialized social niches, designed to surround the vacationer with congenial company—and to keep out influences and people such vacationers might find disturbing or "uncongenial."

At their crudest level, such social niches might be based solely on class and income. Resort promoters, for their part, made no secret of their attempt to segregate vacationers by class. Addressing a wealthy clientele, they used the term "exclusive" to signal that they would be protected from any contact with middle-class or working-class vacationers; most of all, they promised to exclude "excursionists," a code word for working-class vacationers, who took day trips to the beaches on inexpensive round-trip "excursion" passes. Not far up the coast from Kittery, for example, a flagrantly wealthy new summer resort was bankrolled by the Kennebunkport

Seashore Company, a group of Boston investors connected with the Boston and Maine Railroad. In the Kennebunkport summer newspaper, *The Wave*, the company reported bluntly in 1886 that it was the "intention of those interested in Cape Arundel to make it exclusive. Every precaution has been taken to guard against an invasion of excursionists."[15] (Their precautions apparently paid off. Part of Cape Arundel is better known today as Walker Point, where former President George Bush has his ancestral summer home—not an area likely to be invaded by excursionists anytime soon.)

York and Kittery were certainly exclusive, too. But their social distinctions were at once less explicit and more nuanced than the crude distinctions used by the Kennebunkport Seashore Company. At York Harbor, where Howells and his friends stayed, a cluster of opulent architect-built cottages surrounded a small private beach and a luxury hotel, the Marshall House. Those who vacationed next door at York Beach, or Long Sands, as it was called, were in a different world—the world, as Howells described it, "of people several grades of gentility lower than ours." York Beach was "lined with rows of the humbler sort of summer cottages . . . supposed to be taken by inland people of little social importance." Down even farther on Long Sands were the excursionists, who came to the beach by trolley to spend "long afternoons splashing among the waves, or in lolling groups of men, women and children on the sand."[16] Kittery Point offered even more exclusivity, in a less ostentatious form, simply by having no beach at all to attract local vacationers.

Howells, by nature and political conviction disinclined to assert class privilege, poked fun at these elaborate social distinctions. He was offended by the sort of announcement used by the Kennebunkport Seashore Company and by the arrogance of vacationers who trumpeted their class privileges: "I confess that I cannot hear people rejoice in their summer sojourn as beyond the reach of excursionists without a certain rebellion." And yet, he confessed, he was "rather glad that my own summer sojourn was not within reach of them." His experience at Far Rockaway had convinced Howells that the sheer numbers of vacationers found at working-class resorts would destroy his enjoyment: "It is not because I would deny them a share of any pleasure I enjoy, but because they are so many and I am so few that I think they would get all the pleasure and I none." (Not entirely satisfied with this bit of sophistry, Howells ended with a little self-mockery: "I hope the reader will see how this attitude distinguishes me from the selfish people who inhumanly exult in their remoteness from excursionists."[17])

The atmosphere at popular Old Orchard Beach was livelier than that of more exclusive beaches, not unlike the crowd scene one would have found at Far Rockaway. William Dean Howells's "lolling groups of men, women, and children in the sand" are certainly in evidence here, but there are also some middle-class vacationers on the left who have found more respectable seating. Old Orchard Beach was not far up the coast from exclusive Kennebunkport, but socially it was worlds away. From Ernest Ingersoll, *Down East Latch Strings: or Seashore, Lakes and Mountains* (Boston: Boston and Maine Railroad, 1887), 39. Courtesy, American Antiquarian Society.

Howells enjoyed the privacy and quiet that exclusive vacation communities promised. But resorts could be exclusive in more ways than one. If the Howellses had simply wanted to hobnob with the wealthy, they might have been equally comfortable at Newport, among New York City's rich industrialists, or at stodgy old Nahant, which still claimed the loyalty of Boston's Beacon Hill society. What Howells found at Kittery Point was far more precisely fitted to his needs: not simply a wealthy summer community, but one that catered to the literary and professional men and women with whom he socialized at home in Boston or New York. But late nineteenth-century resorts were so finely attuned to the needs of an increasingly varied clientele that even literary types like Howells's friends and associates had a variety of choices available to them. Howells could have encountered similar collections of professional and literary families at other resorts: He might have joined James T. Fields, who had first hired him at the *Atlantic*, in the cottage community Fields called "Manchester-by-the-Sea," on Cape Ann; the Howellses would probably also have been comfortable in Conway in the White Mountains, where Howells had often visited William James.

Kittery Point and York and their neighboring towns had yet another advantage over such rivals: They were not simply *inhabited* by Howells's literary friends and acquaintances, they were also *defined* by them. Years before he came to Kittery Point, Howells had been reading stories and sketches about the surrounding area. In fact, he had been publishing them. Thomas Bailey Aldrich's popular reminiscences of his childhood in nearby Portsmouth, New Hampshire, had been published first in serial form in the *Atlantic*, under Howells's direction. By the time of the publication of *The Story of a Bad Boy*, he and Aldrich were already close friends. (Howells had first met Aldrich when the two of them were young editors working for Osgood, Fields, and Company—Aldrich as editor of *Every Saturday*, Howells working for James Russell Lowell as assistant editor of the *Atlantic*.) Sarah Orne Jewett also sent her first local color pieces to Howells at the *Atlantic*, a series of sketches based on the area surrounding her hometown of South Berwick, a few miles up the river from Kittery. Howells had published those sketches in the *Atlantic*, before they were collected as *Deephaven*, Jewett's first book. He remained in close touch with both Jewett and Aldrich, on personal and professional terms, throughout their lives.

So Howells had not exactly discovered the towns of York and Kittery on his trip in 1898. He had already "seen" the area through the eyes of his literary friends.[18] As Howells wrote to Aldrich from Kittery Point in 1902, "You have no idea how your personality peoples Portsmouth for me with the young Aldrich. We are boys together there."[19]

The Ghost of the Old West India Trade

Kittery and York belonged to a region with a common history and a clearly delineated geography, defined by tidal rivers and dominated by the Piscataqua River, which divides New Hampshire from coastal Maine. The largest town in the area, Portsmouth (on the New Hampshire side), is at the mouth of the Piscataqua. Most of the old towns in the area were built along smaller tidal rivers, like York with its own York River; on tributaries, like South Berwick on the Salmon Falls River; or on the protected coves and inlets of the Piscataqua River itself, like Kittery on the Maine side and New Castle on the New Hampshire side. Because these tidal rivers offered the best possible access to the sea and its trade opportunities, most of the towns of the area were founded very early in the seventeenth century by settlers with an eye for a commercial investment.

The prosperity of the Piscataqua River towns peaked in the eighteenth century, when even the smallest towns took part in the lucrative West India trade—one leg of the infamous "triangle trade," supplying the sugar plantations of the West Indies with raw materials in return for slave-produced molasses and rum. The merchants of Dover, Berwick, York, Kittery, Portsmouth, and New Castle shipped local produce—lumber from upriver and salt fish from local fishing fleets—to West Indian planters. Even the most remote places in the region were brought into this international market: The Isles of Shoals, a cluster of small islands outside Portsmouth Harbor, were barely capable of sustaining life, but they were settled as processing plants for vast quantities of fish bound for the West Indies.

During the boom years of the West Indian trade, even the small towns took on an imposing and prosperous appearance. Ship's captains and wealthy merchants built large and elegant houses overlooking their wharves and warehouses. But almost as soon as the houses were built, the sources of the fortunes that had financed them began to dry up. Like most boom economies, this one was fragile. Economic disaster hit the region with the Embargo Act of 1807, and the War of 1812 sealed its fate with the destruction of many ships and the complete disruption of trade patterns.

That sudden shock, which the Piscataqua River towns shared with all of New England's seaports, was not the only blow. At least one of the area's major commodities, lumber, was already fast disappearing. By the time of Timothy Dwight's first tour through the region in 1796, he reported that the "commerce of Dover consists chiefly in lumber [which] is daily diminishing, and in a short time will probably fail." And by the time of his second visit in 1810, Dwight described some towns as in serious decline. The town of York in particular was almost completely deforested, "naked and bleak," with an air of "stillness and solitude," even of "antiquity."[20] The generation following the War of 1812 saw the Piscataqua River towns at a low point, losing population and unable to find viable substitutes for their former trade.

By the later nineteenth century, though, the literary sons and daughters of the Piscataqua River towns were finding that they could turn the early and profound economic depression of their region to advantage. Local color literature thrived in places that seemed "old" and out of touch. In *The Story of a Bad Boy*, for example, Aldrich wove together tales of his boyhood with memorable images of the commercial decline of Portsmouth, lingering lovingly on the details of decay: "barnacles and eel-grass cling to the piles of the crumbling wharves, where the sunshine lies lovingly, bringing out the faint spicy odor that haunts the place—the ghost of the old dead West India trade!"[21] Jewett's description of South Berwick thirteen years later wrapped her town in a similar nostalgic mist: "From this inland town of mine there is no sea-faring any more, and the shipwrights' hammers are never heard now. It is only a station on the railway, and it has . . . grown so little that it is hardly worth while for all the trains to stop."[22]

The nostalgia of these local writers grew out of their own childhood experiences, but it was also part of a literary sensibility they shared with the editors and writers of the *Atlantic*, where both these sketches first appeared (Aldrich actually became editor of the *Atlantic* after Howells resigned). Their unique blend of realism and nostalgia taught Howells how to interpret the Piscataqua River towns once he arrived there. In the imposing old mansions and rotting wharves, he saw Aldrich's "ghost of the West India trade." When he encountered the quaint "fisher-folk" of Kittery Point, he was delighted but not surprised: He had read about such archaic figures in Jewett's *Deephaven* sketches.

The Spirit of a New Trade

But what Howells must also have seen as he journeyed through Portsmouth and up the coast to Kittery and York was something Aldrich and Jewett did *not* examine in detail, though it was apparent to the two of them as well. By the time their descriptions were published, and certainly by the time the Howellses bought their cottage in Kittery Point, the Piscataqua River towns were no longer the perfect subject of a local color sketch, isolated and out of touch with the modern world. Within a mile or two of the location where Jewett described the peaceful solitude of the Salmon Falls River, that same river had, as she herself acknowledged, "made itself of great consequence by serving to carry perhaps a dozen or twenty mills, of one kind and another."[23] Little South Berwick was actually a mill town. It also served as a major junction for the Boston and Maine Railroad, on the heavily traveled route from Boston to the White Mountains. Its population was not declining but increasing.

A traveler uninfluenced by local color sketches would have seen less genteel decay and more signs of a thriving Victorian economy than were depicted by Aldrich and Jewett. Decaying wharves did line the riverfronts, but they often stood in the shadows of textile mills. The naval shipyards at Kittery went into a slump after the Civil War but were gearing up for full production in the years of imperialist enthusiasm at the end of the century. In other places, another sort of "water power" was fueling economic recovery: Old fishing towns along the coast were finding new ways to exploit their old resource, the sea. The vacation trade, perhaps the most modern of all late nineteenth-century industries, had moved into the oceanfront towns.

In fact, the summer trade had been booming in York for two decades when the Howellses arrived in 1898. It began with the erection of an elegant modern hotel by one of York's leading citizens, Edward Marshall, in 1870. That same year, Charles Grant, another York native, bought a run-down farm fronting the ocean and built a three-story hotel he called the Sea Cottage. At nearby York Beach, investors pursued a similar course: Hiram Perkins, an inland shoe manufacturer, retired to York Beach, purchased a half-mile oceanfront tract of land, divided it into cottage lots, and made his house into a hotel at the popular beach known as Long Sands.

The boom swept over the area in a single generation. Men who had grown up in the traditional vocations of a farming and fishing region found themselves launched into entirely new trades. Captain Theodore Weare had retired from the sea to farm his ancestral acres when he noticed that the old farm was worth more for its ocean views than for its produce. Jesse Frisbee, proprietor of the Hotel Park Field at Kittery Point, had gone to sea at the age of eleven as a cook; William Varrell, owner of the Yorkshire Inn, began his working life as a sailor on a merchant vessel; Elias Baker, proprietor of the Albracca—the hotel where the Howellses stayed during their first summer in York—had gone to sea with his father at the age of twelve; Horace Mitchell, a Maine Congressman and owner of the Hotel Champernowne at Kittery Point, spent two years "coasting" (aboard a ship that plied an intercoastal trade) before he came ashore and worked his way up through clerkships at a variety of local hotels.[24]

The town of York was at the center of resort development, with its clusters of vacation industries at Long Sands and York Harbor. Almost no one in York was left out of the reorientation of the local economy. Farmers came to specialize in products for summer visitors; town shops stocked luxury goods for urban clients; and owners of large old farmhouses found they could make a little cash by boarding a few visitors during the summer. By the end of the century, the editor of the *Old York Transcript* summed up the tourist industry's widening circle of influence: "The railroad, the newspaper, the porter, the hackman, the trader, the merchant, the boot-black, the trolley, the livery stable, the barber . . . everyone gets some of [the summer guest's] money."[25]

York Harbor's summer aspect by the time the Howellses arrived in 1898 was a jumbled mix of high fashion, urban crowds, and the studied infor-mality of affluent cottage life. But Howells's vision of quiet and antiquity was not just a fantasy engendered by local color writing. One guidebook captured the juxtaposition: "Only a mile from the Long Sands [York Beach] . . . slumbers the historic hamlet of York, with its half-dozen shops and a somnolent post-office."[26] What the guidebook did not say was that the "historic hamlet" of York was fast becoming an attraction in its own right, equal to the sun and surf up the road. By the last quarter of the nineteenth century, the Piscataqua River towns were not slumbering, however quiet they might have been. They were deeply engaged in both the summer resort trade and the burgeoning industry of vacation nos-talgia.

Historical attractions were almost as important as beaches to these towns. Local writers had worked to publicize the historical and architec-tural features of Portsmouth. Charles Brewster's *Rambles about Ports-mouth*, published in 1859 and 1869, and Sarah Foster's *Portsmouth Guide Book*, first published in 1876, offered walking tours for the tourist intrigued by the elegant old houses of Portsmouth, built in the prosperous days of the West India trade. Outside the old city, visitors could take day trips to the revolutionary-era forts and the mansions of colonial dignitaries scat-tered around the harbor.

Vacation promoters by the 1880s had already become adept at distin-guishing the towns of the Piscataqua from their competitors at Mount Desert or the White Mountains by their rich history and by their abun-dant evidence of that history. Local entrepreneurs simply added the re-gion's "relics of the earliest colonial history" to its "coast scenery of the rarest beauty" in their advertisements.[27] A hotel keeper might name his modern hotel the Garrison House, to evoke memories of the romantic "Indian-fighting" relics nearby, or the Old Fort Inn, because it was built where an old fort had once been. No local publications failed to mention that York was the "oldest city in America" (even if they would not go so far as to claim, as one promoter did, that York was "the Most Famous Summer Resort on the Atlantic Coast").[28]

The town of York (or "old York" as it began to be known in these years) benefited most directly from the historic trade, in part simply because it hosted one of the largest and most affluent tourist communities. York could not compete with stately old Portsmouth's collection of handsome Federal buildings, nor with the picturesque village streetscape of New Castle, but York had a specialty of its own. In York were the McIntyre and Junkins garrison houses, relics (it was thought at the time) of the hardy Indian-fighting pioneers. And York had an even more ancient landmark: an old jail (by its restoration in 1900 it had become the "Old Gaol"), which was thought to have been constructed as early as 1653. The Old Gaol was York's real claim to fame, allowing visitors to experience "the early days of our colonial life and customs . . . when witches were imprisoned and a public whipping post and stocks were familiar objects in every colonial settlement."[29]

The Old Gaol, like the "witch houses" of Salem, promised an experience of the darker and more macabre aspects of the past. Old York's garrison houses called forth emotions similar to those evoked by the Indian massacre relics on display in "Old Deerfield" in Massachusetts. The historical attractions of York and Kittery, Portsmouth and New Castle, were much like those to be found elsewhere in New England. Like the quaintness brought on by Nantucket's economic decay, the antiquity of the Piscataqua River towns was reported to foster a quaint, otherworldly atmosphere that made visitors feel as if they were actually living in the past.

But there was one difference, not so much in the attractions themselves as in the sorts of people who dominated these summer communities. The summer people of York and its surrounding towns were not the wealthiest vacationers in the United States, nor the most flamboyant. But they wielded as much cultural power as any group of vacationers in the country. The Howellses and the Aldriches, the Clemenses and the Stedmans, Miss Jewett and Mrs. Fields, made up one part of a circle that extended far beyond their immediate acquaintance. Celia Thaxter's home on Appledore was the center of a circle of its own, around which family and friends settled on the other Isles of Shoals and on the mainland at the "point" of Kittery Point. Barrett Wendell colonized the village of Little Harbor, bringing with him his circle of Harvard professors and Cambridge architects and painters. Charles Woodbury opened one of two competing summer art schools at Ogunquit in 1898.

Like many affluent Americans in the late nineteenth century, these writers, editors, painters, photographers, historians, and architects were interested in experiencing the past. But unlike many other vacationers, they were not in the market for mass-produced history. What they wanted was not simply to visit the past but to shape it into a usable common vision. The historical artifacts of the Piscataqua River towns attracted them in part because of their potential uses: Old houses could be bought and restored as summer homes; they could be used in photographs and paintings or as settings for stories and sketches, or as models for new architectural plans. In short, they could be used to create the movement now referred to as the "colonial revival," a movement designed to resurrect the architecture, the aesthetic sensibility, and what were thought to be the social values of the "colonial" period at the end of the nineteenth century.[30] In the hands of such summer people, the towns of the Piscataqua River became not just old or quaint but recognizably "colonial."

Capturing the Colonial

The pursuit of the colonial was distinctly different from other kinds of relationships with the past. For one thing, the colonial label was at once hazier and more precise than other historical categories used by vacationers. The haziness was chronological: Colonial might refer to almost anything within the entire stretch of time between the first landing of Europeans in America and the Industrial Revolution. To contemporary historians, turn-of-the-century colonial enthusiasts often seem deplorably inaccurate—willing and sometimes even eager to sacrifice the realities of seventeenth- and eighteenth-century society to their passionate pursuit of an idealized colonial past. But in the context of the late nineteenth century, colonial revivalists were usually far more concerned with historical accuracy than most of their nostalgic contemporaries.[31]

Rather than conjuring up memories of childhood in a timeless, unchanging world (like Old Home Week), or exotic fantasies of an island paradise protected from the corruption of modernity (like Nantucket), the colonial movement focused on specific historical events and personalities. Colonial enthusiasts liked to know the exact dates when John Paul Jones stayed in the John Paul Jones House in Portsmouth. They were attracted to architecture and relics associated with real, although often near-legendary, people like the Tory Sir William Pepperrell, whose house in Kittery Point was a popular landmark. Accuracy was important to them, whether they were interested in genealogy, in architectural details, or in the lives of historical personages.

In pursuit of accurate information, colonial enthusiasts were drawn into an activist approach to the past: They founded local historical societies, collected antiques, restored houses, and created museums. Rather than simply "consuming" the history of the region, such summer people helped to produce it. Amateurs played a key role in such efforts: Maine Senator James Phinney Baxter took time from his political life to write an article on "Piscataqua and the Pepperrells" for the *Maine Historical Society Collections*. Scores of vacationing artists—amateur and professional painters, writers, and photographers—used their summer vacations to attempt to capture the spirit of the colonial.

Photographer Emma Coleman, who summered at Kittery Point, found the old houses of the area the perfect backdrop for her photographic images of the past. She provided the illustrations for a special 1893 edition of Sarah Orne Jewett's *Deephaven*, working in close collaboration with Jewett. Coleman's images were deeply nostalgic, yet they were carefully constructed to reflect the most accurate information available to her. Set with colonial houses as backdrops, her photographs featured her friends dressed in colonial garb, sometimes staged so that they appeared to be engaged in traditional handcrafts. Coleman also worked as an amateur historian, collaborating closely with her lifelong companion, C. Alice Baker, on a series of research projects stemming from Baker's involvement with the historical rediscovery of her hometown of "Old Deerfield," in Massachusetts.[32]

More than anything else, of course, colonial meant architecture. The restoration of old houses was the most visible of all summer people's efforts to acquire a piece of the past. Scores of old houses were reshaped into summer homes for wealthy vacationers. (Such a "restoration" usually involved substantial modernization: servants' wings, modern plumbing and lighting, and features like sleeping porches were common.[33]) The most elaborate and large-scale restoration effort undertaken in the Piscataqua River region was the work of Emily and Elizabeth Tyson, a mother-daughter team whose colonial mansion, the Hamilton House in South Berwick, was bought at the suggestion of their friend Sarah Orne Jewett. Beginning restoration in 1899, the two turned the Hamilton House into a showcase. Lavish spending, years of study and consultation, and a lifetime of art collecting created a Hamilton House larger, grander, and far more aristocratic than anything the builders of the original house could have imagined.

Mary and Elizabeth Perkins, another mother-daughter team who came to "Old York" from New York in 1898, bought a comparatively modest eighteenth-century house along the York River for their summer home. After its restoration they turned their attention to a more public enterprise: the "preservation" of the Old Gaol. The Old Gaol, like the Oldest House on Nantucket, had already been a tourist attraction for many years before a coalition of summer people and a few influential natives decided to transform it into a museum. That transformation involved many members of the community in the work of the colonial revival. As the *Transcript* reported, "all York has been infused with the spirit of research, and has for two weeks been burrowing into the depths of old chests and trunks," seeking out "the costumes, books, utensils of our grandfathers."[34]

By official report, William Dean Howells was the originator of the idea to restore the Old Gaol and open it to the public as a museum. (He was said to have come up with the suggestion in a conversation with Elizabeth Davidson, whose husband owned the bank next door to the Old Gaol. Mrs. Davidson was the leading local supporter of the Old Gaol's restoration.)[35] Aside from that contribution and the obligatory speeches on ceremonial occasions, Howells did not play an active role in the shaping of Kittery and York as a colonial region. He did make an indirect contribution, though, in the form of his son, John Mead Howells, who became a prominent architect. John Mead Howells participated in several important local restoration efforts, most notably the restoration of the Lady Pepperrell House, just down the street from his Kittery Point summer home. He specialized in modern office buildings, but he also developed expertise as a colonial revivalist, restoring historic buildings in his summer community, and occasionally designing new colonial revival buildings (like Paine Hall at Harvard University) as well.[36]

Colonial enthusiasts were prolific producers of culture, but behind all this creative productivity was a shared belief. The artifacts of seventeenth-century "pioneer" days—the Old Gaol, the houses that were thought to have been Indian-fighting forts—bore little physical resemblance to the elegant Federal and Georgian houses of the eighteenth and early nineteenth centuries, built from the profits of the West India trade. But in the eyes of those who cherished them, all these varied styles represented a common set of values.

From one angle, those values may be characterized as "antimodernist," using T. J. Jackson Lears' term for the nostalgia that was widespread among educated and well-born Americans at the turn of the century. Something was missing in the urban, sophisticated life of the wealthy antimodernist. Colonial enthusiasts hoped to find that lost sense of commitment, or

York's Old Gaol was fitted out as a museum in 1900. In 1907, the women who organized the museum enacted a colonial tea party—a sort of early "living history" demonstration. The exhibits on the walls in the "parlor" display domestic objects collected in York. A clear concern for historical accuracy pervades the Museum of Colonial Relics, but these colonial enthusiasts were also taken with the idea of acting out "colonial" fantasies of grace and leisure. Courtesy, Old York Historical Society.

authenticity, or intensity of experience, in their pursuit of the past.[37] Thomas Nelson Page, a York Harbor summer resident of many years, wrote a short story in which his character voiced the classic antimodernist complaint about her comfortable life among the affluent: "'I feel so tired all the time—so dissatisfied. . . . It is all so hollow and unreal.'"[38] Those feelings motivated Page's character to purchase and restore an old house, a solution embraced by many vacationers.

But the pursuit of the colonial was not based simply on vague dissatisfaction with modern life. Colonial artifacts pointed to a clear set of colonial values, embedded in the very architecture and craft styles that attracted so much attention. The aesthetic language of symmetry, order, and harmony translated for many colonial enthusiasts into a social language. In the colonial they saw, not a treatment for an ill-defined psychic

ailment, but a clear political agenda: To recapture the colonial was to recapture the class stability and harmony of a world without industrial conflict, the graciousness and dignity of aristocrats whose claims to authority
had never been challenged.

Sarah Orne Jewett's regret for the lost West India trade was clearly tinged
with regret for the apparent peace and dignity of a world in which the
claims of the "best families" had gone unchallenged. In "River Driftwood,"
an *Atlantic* sketch of 1881, Jewett described her favorite cardinal flowers
growing along the banks of the Salmon Falls River as "fine court ladies in
their best gowns, standing on the shore. . . . They are no radicals; they are
tories and aristocrats; they belong to the old nobility among flowers." For
the flowers, Jewett took a position she never explicitly championed in the
world of politics: "It would be a pity if the rank marsh grass overran them,
or if the pickerel weed should wade ashore to invade them and humble
their pride."[39]

William Dean Howells was no elitist; by the time he discovered Kittery
Point, Howells had become a Tolstoyan socialist and a powerful voice
against the injustices of industrial capitalism. Yet even Howells's affection for Kittery Point was clearly tinged with his admiration for the unchallenged elite status of its colonial inhabitants. Writing of the vast
holdings of the legendary Tory figure Sir William Pepperrell of Kittery
Point, he acknowledged the attraction with characteristic honesty: "In
my personal quality I am of course averse to all great fortunes; and in my
civic capacity I am a patriot. But still I feel a sort of grace in wealth a century old."[40]

Sentiments like these drove the summer penchant for the colonial. Old
houses stood for the "old nobility," for "wealth a century old." In fact, the
need to see the colonial inhabitants of the region as aristocratic out-
weighed even traditional regional affiliations. More than one author who
summered in York or Kittery described the area as more like the elite
Tidewater regions of the "Old South" than like rugged, egalitarian New
England. That notion was supported in part by the area's landscape. The
Piscataqua River region *is* a sort of small-scale "tidewater": Its large (for
New England) tidal rivers create wide-open marshlands uncharacteristic
of the New England shore. But the assertion that the region was a uniquely
"Southern" part of New England was based more on politics than on land-
scape.

Colonial enthusiasts left the mark of their politics on the past in a rather
startling rejection of the religious heritage of New England. Summer

people often imagined the Piscataqua River towns as New England without the Puritans. Although they sometimes liked to look at relics from the barbarous past, they preferred to think of the former inhabitants of the area as secular, enlightened members of an elite colonial social network that had transcended region. As the author of *Down East Latch Strings* explained it, Portsmouth was a better place for tourists than, say, Salem. Portsmouth was as "venerable and quiet" as the Massachusetts towns but not so gloomy because, he argued, it was not a "Puritan" town: "It was not a religious but a money-making community, and hence the picture of the earliest civilization here has a brightness that does not belong to that of its Pilgrim neighbors."[41] Sarah Orne Jewett took pains to distinguish the builder of her favorite Hamilton House from the inhabitants of those other New England shores: "I have heard that he came from Plymouth in Massachusetts, and was a minister's son, but if ever a man's heart gloried in the good things of this life it was his, and there was not a trace of Puritan asceticism in his character."[42]

Rejection of Puritan influences by colonial enthusiasts had several sources. Puritanism was in some disrepute at the end of the nineteenth century, in part because glorification of a Puritan past exacerbated sectional tensions that many conservative Gilded Age Americans (including some who vacationed in York, as we shall see) would have liked to have forgotten. Puritan heritage was also out of style because it reminded wealthy New Englanders of the distinctly non-elite backgrounds of their ancestors. Puritan ancestry implied a heritage of narrow and rigid morality, a social code distinctly out of step with the lives of many affluent colonial enthusiasts. Colonial ancestry implied something far different—an elegant and aristocratic social world that might be shared with the "best families" of the Old South as well as the old New England families. And it was precisely the notion of a proper colonial ancestry that most attracted summer people to the colonial experience in the Piscataqua River towns.

Many affluent summer people saw in the past colonial glories of York or Portsmouth an appealing vision of a harmonious and stable world completely different from their own chaotic, ethnically diverse urban environments. Like Nantucket's visitors, the summer people of York and Kittery were deeply disturbed by the apparently insurmountable chasm that separated urban rich and urban poor at the turn of the century, and perhaps even more by the violent class conflict that characterized industrial society. They responded to the violence and brutality of contemporary class relations with elaborately constructed (quite literally *constructed*, in the case of restored colonial mansions) fantasies of an aristocratic colonial world where harmony and stability had prevailed.

For some, that vision was all the more compelling because they had deep family roots in the Piscataqua River towns. Many of the "summer people" had inherited a complex relationship with the region. Some, following Governor Frank Rollins' directive to return "home" bringing cash, used their vacations to reestablish links with their family's past by buying back or restoring family properties. The family of Barrett Wendell, a Harvard literature professor, had summered at their spacious and modern New Castle cottage since his childhood in the 1880s. But their connection to the Piscataqua River towns went back further than that: The Wendells also owned an old house in Portsmouth, passed down from their ancestor Jacob Wendell and lovingly preserved and transformed in the last quarter of the nineteenth century by two generations of Wendells living in New York and Cambridge.

The Wendells visited their modern oceanfront cottage during the summer months and their ancestral home in the autumn; they were in a sense both summer people and returning natives. In fact, the Piscataqua River summer communities were characterized by the presence of people who were both natives and vacationers. Sarah Orne Jewett, for example, maintained a lifelong allegiance to the town of her birth, spending parts of every year in the old house in South Berwick, while for over thirty years she spent most of each winter with Annie Fields in Boston and visited numerous friends and acquaintances at their summer cottages up and down the coast.[43]

Such complex ties of allegiance helped to create in some summer people a peculiarly strong commitment to the Piscataqua River towns and their history. Even for people like the Howellses, who had no family ties there, the attractions of local history were still personally accessible through the experiences of friends and acquaintances with roots in the area (as Howells acknowledged when he wrote to Aldrich that the personality of the young Tom Aldrich "peopled" Portsmouth for him). And for some summer people, the ancestral connection with the colonial past became the most compelling part of the summer experience. It was natural for them to see a connection between their ancestors and the old houses that dotted the region and perhaps equally natural for them to imagine that their own ancestors had held the reins of unassailable authority in the stable world of the past.

Ancestors and Immigrants

The search for ancestors reflected common, and increasingly urgent, pre-occupations with class and "race" in the last quarter of the nineteenth century, particularly among the old-stock wealthy and educated vaca-tioners who peopled the towns around York. Barrett and Edith Wendell's restoration of their Portsmouth house, for example, reveals a deep con-nection between their enthusiasm for the colonial and their passionate search for aristocratic ancestry. When they took possession of the house, the Wendells were delighted to discover that they had also inherited a houseful of antiques—"furniture of anywhere from 1750 to 1825"—and a treasure trove of family papers. Their work in restoring the house, cata-loguing the manuscripts, and organizing the antiques was motivated by their devotion to the idea of ancestry. As Barrett Wendell put it, his fam-ily "combined honestly professed belief in democratic principles with un-broken persistence in aristocratic feeling."[44] That "aristocratic feeling" led many wealthy vacationers into pursuits like those of Edith Wendell, who later became deeply involved in efforts to preserve national and local colo-nial landmarks and was for many years president of the Massachusetts Society of Colonial Dames.

At its worst, a preoccupation with ancestry could become a way of de-fending reactionary and racist political interests against the challenges presented by immigrants and radicals. Thomas Bailey Aldrich had made Portsmouth famous with his *Story of a Bad Boy*. But his most important political statement was a poem, also deeply rooted in his childhood mem-ories of Portsmouth. "Unguarded Gates" argued, in elegant sonnet form, for legislation to cut off the flow of immigrants from southern and eastern Europe. "Wide open and unguarded stand our gates," the poem began, "and through them presses a wild motley throng."

Aldrich subscribed to the popular racial theories that divided hu-manity into a ladder of "races"—"Malayan, Scythian, Teuton, Kelt, and Slav"—with the "Anglo-Saxon" race at the pinnacle, carrying in its blood-lines centuries of development of mental agility and aptitude for polit-ical democracy.[45] His poem warned of the gathering power of darker races incapable of cherishing freedom, bringing with them "unknown gods and rites," "strange tongues," and "tiger passions." It ended with a warning against "the thronging Goth and Vandal" who had once "tram-pled Rome": "Liberty, white goddess, is it wise/to leave the gates un-guarded?"[46]

"Unguarded Gates" was not Aldrich's only word on the subject of immigration. His 1880 novel, *A Stillwater Tragedy*, described a New England stonecutting yard in which native-born workers were led astray by a dangerous Italian worker who had convinced them to form a union. Aldrich identified strongly with his New England parentage and background, although he had spent most of his childhood in New Orleans. He shared with many of his peers a profound sense of personal loss in the transformation of the United States, and particularly of New England, from a rural, ethnically homogeneous population to a "wild motley throng" of immigrants working in vast mills. He especially resented the intrusion of foreign "types" among the reassuringly familiar Yankee "characters" he remembered from his childhood in Portsmouth.

And Aldrich was certainly not alone in these opinions. Thomas Nelson Page, a York Harbor summer visitor of many years, shared Aldrich's racial politics, although his background was quite different. Page was deeply attached to his own southern heritage. He was perhaps the best known among a school of southern local-color writers who memorialized the spirit of the South in the years following Reconstruction. Unlike Aldrich, who made only occasional forays into political writing, Page's short stories almost always delivered a heavy-handed political message. At the height of his career, in 1892, he took time from his fiction writing to publish an essay on "The Race Question." There he outlined what became the standard white supremacist argument against equal rights and opportunities for southern African-Americans, an argument based on racial inferiority and an imagined golden age—the days of slavery—when race relations had been kindly and mutually beneficial.

As Page saw it, his goal was to "defend the south" from its northern accusers and to garner sympathy for elite southern whites in the north. Political "redemption" had ended Reconstruction with the return of southern governments to the hands of former slaveholders. Page hoped (in conjunction with other southern local color writers) to effect a cultural "redemption" of the south—to bring the hearts and minds of white northern readers into sympathy with the white rulers of the south. Albion W. Tourgée, a rival southern writer whose sympathies were with the Reconstructionist Republicans, acknowledged his own defeat in 1888, writing that Page and his comrades had succeeded in converting northerners to a perspective that was "distinctly Confederate [i.e., white supremacist] in sympathy."[47]

Page did the same work while on vacation. In York, where he and his wife spent many summers, Page continued his campaign to forge alliances along the color line and across regional divides. As a guest speaker at the celebration of the 250th anniversary of the settlement of York, he made the politics of his vacations very clear: "I never expected the day to come when I'd feel the deep affection that warms my heart for these Yankees up here." But in York, Page claimed, he had come to recognize a greater loyalty that superseded his old sectional faith: White native-born northerners and southerners "are all of the same race; all have the same history; all have the same traditions."

Now, Page argued, it was time to unite against a common enemy—not black Americans this time (they were a "southern problem"), but the inferior races who were pouring into the cities of the Northeast. "Elsewhere in our country are large numbers of people of other races and with other traditions; people who have not the past that we have." Page pictured New Englanders—natives and summer people alike—as united with him by common bloodlines, "with the blood and brawn and principles that made . . . this York . . . the oldest continuous chartered settlement of the Anglo-Saxon race on this continent." He made much of the similarity between this York River and "another York River in another colony planted by the same people," the York River in the Tidewater of Virginia, Page's family home.[48]

It is difficult to tell whether the compliment was returned by the native "Yankees" who lived on *this* York River. Page's kind of ancestral rhetoric did not always go unchallenged. The natives of the region may have shared with the summer people some assumptions about race and history, but they might also disagree about who "owned" that history. In 1899, for example, the editor of the *Old York Transcript* set down in no uncertain terms the contest over who owned Old York's heritage. "Of the men one meets in York nine out of every ten can tell you of their father, their grandfather, and—yes their ancestors way back to the founding of this republic," he wrote, "yet not one of them will thrust a coat of arms before your gaze or send you a note of invitation adorned by a family crest."[49]

Here, the editor of the *Transcript* was at least ostensibly attacking the pretensions of summer people like Page on behalf of natives. But the attack was calculated not to cause too much offense to visitors with aristocratic pretensions. First of all, the categories used by Page and his supporters were not challenged: Part of the editor's purpose was surely to make it clear that the natives of York *were* racially "pure." If he also envisioned the natives as rather prickly and proud, that characterization dovetailed nicely with the racial notions of many visitors.

Nearly every description of the natives of York and Kittery portrayed them in the same terms: Local Yankees were fiercely independent, resenting the slightest hint of condescension, refusing all work that infringed on their notions of self-respect or autonomy. In contrast with the Yankees of Nantucket, who were imagined as naturally hospitable, ingratiating, and helpful, York natives were pictured as supremely indifferent to the presence of the summer people, stoically unimpressed by their wealth, their education, and their fashions.[50] In spite of—or in fact because of—their taciturnity and abrasiveness, such Yankees delighted summer visitors. But those characteristics meant different things to different people.

For adherents of scientific racism, the prickly independence of Yankee workers signified the racial superiority that made it impossible for "Anglo-Saxon" workers to be subservient. The pride such Yankees kept up in the face of their evident dependence on tourists proved that even the poorest and humblest farmers of "Anglo-Saxon" blood were born to rule—or at least not born to serve. On the other hand, William Dean Howells managed to draw a progressive political moral from some of the "Yankee character" anecdotes current in York, using the tourist/native relationship as a model for more equitable class relations in the industrial world. Howells recorded with approval an anecdote "of the lady who said to a summer visitor, critical of the week's wash she had brought home, 'I'll wash you and I'll iron you, but I won't take none of your jaw.'" His point was genial, but quite serious: "As in all right conditions, it is here the employer who asks for work, not the employé; and the work must be respectfully asked for."[51] For less ideological summer people, such anecdotes simply provided an amusing relief from urban class antagonisms. From any standpoint, though, the stock description of York Yankees reflected the awareness of summer visitors highly sensitized both to a "racial" language and to class-based political conflicts.

The summer people of York, with or without family crests, were clearly not all fervent backers of Page's vision of racial solidarity. Howells was near the opposite end of the political spectrum from Page, along with his dear friend Mark Twain. During the same year that Page was writing jingoistic poems defending the "Anglo-Saxon" domination of the seas, Howells and Twain were outspoken in their opposition to war with Spain and colonial war in the Philippines.[52] Neither was Jewett a purveyor of racist or anti-immigrant doctrines. She wrote sympathetically and forthrightly of the value that Irish and French-Canadian immigrants brought to her beloved Maine countryside.[53] Insofar as she recorded opinions on the subject, she leaned toward the notion that environment shaped character as much as or more than heredity or "race."

But the similarities between many of Jewett's stories and Page's far less skillful ones are more than accidental. Page's defense of the antiquated manners of a high-born southern lady, for example, found echoes in a number of Jewett's sketches. (Page wrote, "Even you, Miss or Madam, for all your silks and satins . . . are at best an imitation; Miss Thomasia is the reality. Do not laugh at her, or call her provincial. She belongs to the realm . . . of old-time courtesy and high breeding."[54] Jewett wrote in *Deephaven*: "It is a great privilege to have an elderly person in one's neighborhood . . . who is proud, and conservative, and who lives in stately fashion; who is intolerant of sham and of useless novelties, and clings to the old ways of living and behaving."[55]) Jewett even wrote several short stories set in the "Old South," a place she imagined as a region not unlike her own, with a faded gentry lost in its memories of the past.[56]

Guarded Gates

Given those similarities, it is perhaps not so surprising that it was the southerner Page who wrote the story that best captured the complex appeal of the colonial vacation in the Piscataqua River towns. In a short story titled "Miss Godwin's Inheritance," first published in *Scribner's Magazine* in 1904, Page wove together all the experiences and associations that most enchanted the wealthy vacationers of York and Kittery. In this story, the main character embarks on the restoration of a colonial mansion; she rediscovers a connection with her elite ancestry; and she uses her influence to reassert harmonious and hierarchical class relations, in this case between herself as the new "lady of the manor" and the "natives" who become her grateful dependents.

Page's main character, Mrs. Davidson, was clearly modeled on Emily Tyson, who with her daughter restored the Hamilton House in South Berwick. (Sarah Orne Jewett also appears in the story as Miss Hewitt, a benevolent invisible presence.) The story revolves around Mrs. Davidson's decision to buy the Hamilton House and her plans for its restoration. It opens with a vivid description of her motive: "'I feel so tired all the time—so dissatisfied.'" Mrs. Davidson complains of the vacuity of life among the affluent: "'[This strenuous life] is all so hollow and unreal.'" Her doctor has recommended that she travel in Europe, to "go to some

European watering place ending in 'heim,'" but she has rejected his advice. "It is 'heim' that I want, but it is an American 'heim.'"[57] In search of something "calm and natural," something authentically American, she sets out to restore a colonial mansion.

Mrs. Davidson has "discovered" the old house on her own, but she has a kind of ancestral claim to it; her grandfather visited the place in his

The Hamilton House had a special attraction for many influential summer people. It was elaborately "restored" by Emily Tyson and her daughter, on the advice of Sarah Orne Jewett, and it also inspired a variety of literary and artistic efforts. This illustration was by the painter Charles Woodbury, who summered in nearby Ogunquit; it was used to illustrate Jewett's historical novel, *The Tory Lover*. From Sarah Orne Jewett, *The Tory Lover* (1901). Courtesy, Old York Historical Society.

youth, and remembered it fondly. By introducing a gentlemanly colonial ancestor for Mrs. Davidson, Page was able to establish his character's elite genealogy *and* to make one of his favorite connections: The grandfather's letters, it seems, confirmed the "southernness" of this corner of Maine— and the social meaning of that southernness. "Imagine my surprise," the grandfather wrote, "when I discovered that the place and the people are more like those among whom I was brought up in my youth [the elite families whose mansions lined the York River in Virginia] than in any other part of New England." The house "though not large, would have done justice to any place in Maryland or Virginia." These northern aristocrats were neither Puritan nor democratic, as he discovered; they had all the trappings that distinguished southern elites, even "coats of arms and other relics of the gentry-class."[58]

Her grandfather's early visit, Mrs. Davidson discovers, had led to a romance with the daughter of the house, whose love for flowers had prompted the grandfather to call her Hortensia—Mrs. Davidson's given name. (That name was an inside joke intended for the real-life owner of Hamilton House, Mrs. Tyson, who had a passion for gardening; the Hamilton House "restoration" gardens were a showpiece of the region.) Real-life colonial house restorers might have hoped for a more direct historical connection with their house, but hardly a more romantic one.

There are two Yankee characters in the story: an almost allegorical figure named Silas Freeman, who conveys the judgments of the Yankee natives, and the title character, Miss Godwin, who is reminiscent of many Jewett characters. Miss Godwin has been oppressed all her life by relatives whom everyone refers to as "them"—the former owners of Mrs. Davidson's mansion. Her poverty is so abject that she cannot afford a stamp with which to mail a request to Mrs. Davidson. "They" would not allow Miss Godwin to continue to live in the mansion but instead have sold it off to the highest bidder, Mrs. Davidson.

One might expect, then, that "Miss Godwin's Inheritance" will feature a conflict between native and newcomer over the rightful ownership of the house. But Miss Godwin makes no such claims (and Page recognizes none). She has only a humble request for a rosebush on the grounds of the old house. Mrs. Davidson is deeply touched by Miss Godwin's plight, at one point exclaiming in tears, "I wish I could give her the house." But in Page's framework, that is not only unthinkable, it is not even what Miss Godwin really wants.

Miss Godwin's plight, instead, is a test for Mrs. Davidson: Can she live up to the social position she has bought? True aristocrats, in Page's southern stories, combined natural authority with concern for the needs of their dependents. Mrs. Davidson must prove her right to the role of lady bountiful by finding a way to help Miss Godwin without either upsetting the social hierarchy or offending the dignity of the Yankee poor. Mrs. Davidson is able to give Miss Godwin what she really wants by restoring to her both the rosebush and a proper relationship with the "great house"—a position as a valued but dependent member of the household. In the process, she also proves her worth to the natives of the town, expressed in the final judgment delivered by Silas Freeman, "'I guess you was about right . . . you wa'n't altogether city folks.'"[59]

"Miss Godwin's Inheritance" is deeply marked by Page's racial and class politics. It closely resembles the stories he turned out celebrating the selfless nobility of southern gentry in their relations with their dependent poor. Its Yankees differ from the freed African American slaves of the other stories only because they have a different role to play in the drama of racial politics. But one did not have to share Page's reactionary politics to find this story—and the vacation pursuits it describes—appealing.

Much of that appeal rested on experiences that could be enjoyed even without the colonial ideology that gave them resonance. Page's Mrs. Davidson (like her real-life model) was able to exercise her creative talents by "restoring" the past to life; the extensive work she conducted and supervised in the house and gardens offered her greater opportunities for creativity than anything she would have encountered at home in the urban drawing room.[60] The urge to "get in touch with her roots," to explore her family's past in a lifelike and romantic setting, was one that Mrs. Davidson shared with many real vacationers, with or without the political strings attached.

At the same time, these colonial pursuits, as Page imagined them, offered a powerful fantasy of class reconciliation—disguised as a reconciliation between city people and country people, and set in terms most attractive to elite vacationers. Mrs. Davidson's takeover of the resources of the countryside reestablished the old-fashioned class relations that seemed to most people of Page's background to have been inherently harmonious, friendly, and stable. Mrs. Davidson was unmistakably the owner of the "big house"; her dependents, unlike real-life servants and workers anywhere in the world, could be counted on neither to make too many claims on her charity (they were self-respecting Anglo-Saxon Yankees, after all) nor to challenge her right to her position.

That fantasy might appeal to a wide variety of affluent urban vacationers, from the reactionary to the progressive to the simply escapist. Page, at one end of the spectrum, believed that the racial and class hierarchies of the past could heal—or at least suppress—contemporary social conflicts. He was far from alone in that conviction; the Piscataqua River towns were filled with summer people whose colonial vacations were rooted in such beliefs. Somewhere in the middle, perhaps, were the countless affluent vacationers who simply wished to escape modern conflicts, to replace the painful realities they saw too much of with a colonial fantasy. At the other end of the spectrum, one might place a vacationer like Howells.

The Problem of the Summer

In 1902, looking back on a lifetime of vacationing, Howells wrote an essay called "The Problem of the Summer." In it, he sympathized at elaborate and mocking length with the plight of the privileged few who were burdened with the necessity of choosing where to go on summer vacations. For those who must choose, life was much more difficult than for those "who have no choice, but must stay the summer through where their work is, and be humbly glad that they have any work to keep them there." The sufferings of those "sweltering in upper rooms over sewing-machines," or "stewing in the breathless tenement streets" were not to be compared with those of wealthy people faced with the "curse of choice."[61]

Howells was no escapist, as this essay alone amply demonstrates. He was almost unflinching in his attention to the painful realities others of his class often avoided. Even in an essay titled "Confessions of a Summer Colonist," he pondered the perspectives of lowly excursionists and the fate of the Spanish prisoners of war who were being held at the naval yards near his Kittery home. But Howells, who identified more and more with those left behind in the sweltering cities, was nevertheless faced with the "curse of choice." And faced with that curse, he chose a place that offered him at least a respite from industrial conflict and urban poverty.

Ultimately, Howells chose Kittery Point and York for the same reasons Page did; its appeal for him was the same as its appeal for Jewett, for Aldrich, for Emma Coleman, Barrett Wendell, and Emily Tyson. Vacations could be used by the affluent to find marriage partners or congenial companionship. They offered rest for the exhausted and medical treatment for the sick. They might offer diversion, or even a reprieve from haunting memories, as they did for Mr. and Mrs. Howells after the death of their oldest child. But a vacation in the Piscataqua River towns offered more. There one would find a respite from intractable political and social realities, a vision of a world untouched by the seemingly unresolvable conflicts that racked the cities of industrial America. And Howells felt the power of that appeal as much as any of his more conservative social peers.

Howells was not altogether comfortable with the peace he found in Kittery Point. In "The Problem of the Summer," he dropped his characteristic gentle wit, writing with a bitter sarcasm more characteristic of Mark Twain's later writings than of most of Howells's work, a sarcasm that took its own author as its first target. Those who must go through the "terrible stress" of choosing a vacation resort are truly to be pitied, Howells wrote: "They it is whom I am truly sorry for, and whom I write of with tears in my ink." "Their case is hard," he continued, not only for the difficulties they face in this life, but because of their moral dilemma: Think of "how foolish they will look . . . at the judgment-day, when they are asked about their summer outings."[62]

That image of vacationers at the judgment seat, being called to account for their vacationing choices, brought Howells back to his sense of the ridiculous. "I do not really suppose we shall be held to a very strict account for our pleasures because everybody else has not enjoyed them, too." But Howells could not be sure of that. He found no way to absolve himself of the responsibility of enjoying what others could not have. In the end, he recommended the course he took in real life. Vacationers like himself must embrace the uncomfortable responsibility that comes from privilege, even on vacation: "It might be . . . amusing, for one stretched upon the beach or swaying in the hammock to inquire into the reasons for his or her being so favored." In that way, perhaps they might make a truly good use of their vacations, and discover a solution to the "question that has vexed the world ever since mankind was divided into those who work too much and those who rest too much."[63] As Howells knew, that would be a novel use of the vacation indeed.

EPILOGUE
Tourism in the Twentieth Century

By 1900, the tourist industry had penetrated almost every corner of New England, from the coast of Maine to the hill towns of Connecticut. Railroad guidebooks marketed every stop along their tracks as the perfect vacation destination. With titles like *By-Ways of Central Vermont, Here and There in New England,* and *Down-East Latch Strings,* promoters hoped to make it clear that *anywhere* along these "by-ways," the tourist would encounter the special experience now imagined simply as "New England," whether mountain village or colonial seaport.

There were exceptions, of course. Much of inland Maine remained (and remains) untraveled frontier, only a few of its countless lakes and rivers exploited fully by hunting and fishing tourists. The industrial towns and cities, from Nashua to Lowell to Pawtucket, were also assiduously ignored. By tacit consent, such immigrant-filled communities were written out of the definition of New England. Tourists traveling through these cities averted their eyes and kept their thoughts on their destinations in rural, ethnically homogeneous New England.

There was a third exception, too, one that may seem especially striking to travelers in the late twentieth century. Not much of Cape Cod had become familiar tourist ground by the turn of the century. True, Henry David Thoreau wrote with great admiration of the landscape of the Cape after his walking tours there in the 1850s. But Thoreau's Cape Cod essays describe a place very different from the Cape of today. The popular beaches of what is now the Cape Cod National Seashore appear in Thoreau's descriptions, not as lovely scenery, but as an empty and savage land—the "most uninviting landscape on earth."

Thoreau himself preferred the desolation he encountered on Cape Cod to the more civilized charms of heavily traveled regions like the White Mountains or Newport. In fact, he made that contrast a central theme of his Cape Cod essays, playing up the difference between fashionable resorts and the beaches of Cape Cod: "They commonly celebrate those beaches only which have a hotel on them," he wrote. "But I wished to see that seashore where all man's works are wrecks." Although his essays took the form of the sort of travel writing that was intended to entice tourists to a region, Thoreau emphasized that he had peculiar tastes few travelers would share: "Every landscape which is dreary enough has a certain beauty to my eyes." He really hoped no one would be converted to his taste for Cape Cod: "I trust that for a long time [fashionable visitors] will be disappointed here."[1] And for a long time they were.

The Road Not Taken

Most of Thoreau's contemporaries were looking for scenery with a special sort of meaning, for landscapes endowed with the "interesting associations" of poetry or romantic history or legends. Cape Cod certainly possessed the raw material for such a trade: sublime seascapes, native legends, the tales of weather-beaten "old salts." But, with the notable exception of Thoreau, no one exploited that raw material in the 1840s and 1850s. Mid-century travelers imagined Cape Cod, when they thought of it at all, almost as "antiscenery"—the direct opposite of the kind of nature they craved. One 1863 children's book, for example, used the Cape's landscape as a symbol of emotional deprivation: The heroine suffered through a loveless, stunted childhood, growing up where there was "no sweet singing of birds in the air; but the harsh cry of curlews. . . . No soft murmur of little brooks; but only the measured roar of the wild ocean waves. No rustle of leafy woods . . . only the dreary beach-grass and blue moss."[2]

Not all coastal landscapes appeared so unattractive to nineteenth-century travelers. In fact oceanfront resorts were springing up almost everywhere except Cape Cod in the second half of the century. To the south, on Martha's Vineyard, the Methodists colonized Oak Bluffs. Their hotels and cottages competed with a variety of nearby Rhode Island resorts, all the way from ritzy Newport to popular Narragansett Pier. Not far to the north, Nantasket Beach and Cohasset on the Massachusetts coast plied their vacation trade with great success. Cape Cod certainly had beaches fine enough to rival any of its competitors. But few promoters saw their possibilities.

Twenty years after Thoreau made his famous tramp, the situation had not changed much. National guidebooks gave Cape Cod very little attention. In *Appleton's Illustrated Hand-Book of American Summer Resorts,* published in 1876, the whole area of the Cape rated only one page. (The White Mountains, in contrast, were allotted fourteen pages; Mount Desert rated three.) The single page devoted to Cape Cod was composed of a series of passages the editor lifted from Samuel Adams Drake's *Nooks and Corners of the New England Coast,* a book dedicated to exploring out-of-the-way and quaint sections of the shore. Yet even Drake found it tough going to promote the Cape. "To one accustomed to the fertile shores of Narragansett Bay or the valley of the Connecticut," he admitted, "the region between Sandwich and Orleans . . . is bad enough." But, as he put it, "beyond this is simply a wilderness of sand."[3]

In spite of Appleton's bad reviews, the last quarter of the century did see signs of change. A cluster of hotel and cottage colonies patronized by wealthy summer people appeared on the highlands looking west over the waters of Buzzard's Bay and southward over Nantucket Sound. These resorts were basically spin-offs of the Martha's Vineyard and Nantucket trade, built along the railroad route from Boston to the islands. At the tip of the Cape, Provincetown began its long relationship with painters and painters' friends, arriving by steamboat from Boston. Between that end and the other, though, most of Cape Cod remained more or less untouched. The Old Colony Railroad guidebooks did the best they could to play up whatever attractions existed along their line, but the towns between Hyannis and Provincetown—including Yarmouth, Dennis, Harwich, Chatham, Brewster, Orleans, Eastham, Wellfleet, and Truro—were clearly not expecting many guests.[4]

One might have expected to find one sort of tourist industry in the more isolated towns of Cape Cod toward the end of the century: the business of quaintness. Nearby Nantucket had made it a specialty. Cape Cod, like Nantucket, had quaint "old salts" and rotting wharves. It even had the economic desperation to make such an enterprise seem worthwhile. Between 1860 and 1920 the Cape's population dropped by twenty-six percent; its major industries, including coastal shipping, commercial fishing, whaling, salt-making, and a variety of manufactures, all declined drastically in the second half of the nineteenth century.[5]

A few communities did turn their energies toward developing an "old-fashioned" Cape Cod. In 1890 a guide to Provincetown described it as a "quaint old town by the sea" with the usual claim to an Anglo-Saxon population that could "trace their lineage back to the early settlers," and old sailors who could entertain one with tales of seafaring adventures.[6] The town of Harwich attempted to generate summer business with an Old Home Week celebration, noting hopefully that although "some fifty years and more ago a host of New England men and women . . . went west," now the tide was turning, "and these same people with their children are turning their thoughts and steps to the scenes of their childhood and the places of their nativity."[7] But these were scattered, isolated efforts. Instead, most Cape Codders continued to eke out livings with small-scale fishing, farming, and foraging. And some left, seeking better opportunities in the cities or in the West.

If anyone had cared to investigate, there were plenty of opportunities for tourist development on Cape Cod. The transportation system that took so many natives away from the Cape might also have brought tourists in. The Old Colony Railroad had reached the tip of the Cape in Provincetown as early as 1873, making all points easily accessible by rail. Steamboats moved efficiently between Boston and Provincetown, and between Falmouth and the cities of southern New England. In fact, the whole area was arguably more accessible to travelers in the late nineteenth century than it is today. But in spite of the potential, Cape Cod lagged far behind neighboring areas in the development of tourist industries.

The reasons for that backwardness are complex, involving the choices made by fifteen different towns and thousands of individuals. A complete exploration of those reasons would require a full-scale study of the process by which a place did *not* become a tourist attraction: the role of off-Cape promoters in not developing the region, the availability of capital that remained unused, the other means of livelihood available to Cape residents. But for the purposes of this book, there is one simpler lesson to be learned from Cape Cod's initial sluggishness in the pursuit of what was later to become its defining industry. To a modern eye, there may appear to be something inevitable about the growth of tourist industries. Wherever they have flourished, they seem to have emerged naturally out of the attractions of a particular place—its mountains, sea air, or quaintness. But nothing could be further from the truth. Just as rivers do not mandate textile mills, beaches alone do not make a resort. Nature alone does not make "scenery," and picturesque history alone does not make a quaint tourist destination.

Tourism is not destiny, imposed on a community or a region by its geography or its history. Tourist industries were built by people. Sometimes they were created by individual entrepreneurs: innkeepers in the White Mountains or farmers in Old York. Sometimes corporations like the Oak Bluffs Land and Wharf Company or the Kennebunkport Seashore Company played a major role. State governments dabbled in tourist development. Even families—the Coffins on Nantucket, for example—built tourist industries. But in every case, the industries were the product of human choices, made not only by visitors, but by natives as well. Those choices were often made under extreme economic duress; they were often made by outside investors "for" the inhabitants of a place, or by a small minority of more powerful inhabitants against the will of others. Certainly they were influenced and shaped by economic and even geographical forces larger than the communities themselves. But they were not predetermined. And although it may seem in retrospect that Cape Cod must always have been the "natural" home of tourism, for most communities on the Cape in the nineteenth century, tourist industries were a road not taken.

Taking to the Road

In the twentieth century, of course, Cape Cod's communities have ardently pursued the path of tourist development. The Cape has become famous for its great natural beauty, its wide range of resorts for all social classes and "lifestyles," even for its quaint "Old New England" atmosphere (and eventually for its crowds and traffic jams as well). But that did not begin to happen until the 1920s, when a technological breakthrough—the automobile—transformed the experience of tourism.

Within a decade of its introduction, the automobile had become the most popular means of transportation for tourists. And automobile tours were different from railroad or trolley tours. Railroads had brought the traveler to fixed points at fixed times. Most tourists in 1900 had expected to journey to a single destination for a weekend, a week, or a month, and to use that destination as a home base for their explorations of mountains or beaches or historical buildings. Early automobile travelers, in contrast, imagined themselves as more adventurous than staid Victorian vacationers, idealizing the speed and mobility of modern travel. They liked to "explore" back roads and towns off the beaten track, staying for only a night or two at each stopping-place. Modern guidebooks encouraged that sense of freedom, nudging travelers to be more adventurous. "Why follow a tour, anyway?" asked the WPA guide to Massachusetts. "Be your own gypsy," "abandon all rules and directions and . . . make up your own tours."[8]

The new approach had far-reaching consequences for the tourist industry. Its first casualties were the great hotels that had come to epitomize the tourist experience at the turn of the century. The fate of the great hotels was inextricably bound up with the fate of the railroads; these hotels were crucial components of railroad networks and were commonly built and operated by railroad companies. But their future had been in jeopardy even before the advent of the automobile. On Martha's Vineyard, for example, Cottage City as a whole was in good shape at the end of the nineteenth century: Private summer cottages continued to be built; small hotels and boardinghouses prospered. But the Oak Bluffs Corporation projects had not fared so well: The island railroad had gone bankrupt, the Sea View Hotel had burned down, and the projected development of other parts of the island had collapsed, leaving nothing but scattered hulks of abandoned hotels on the beaches.

The Sea View's fate was typical of many Victorian hotels at the end of the century. Few leave any trace in the landscape today. Nantucket's Surfside Hotel collapsed in 1899. Most of the great White Mountain hotels burned down. Such large frame structures had always been susceptible to winter fires (often suspiciously well-timed to wipe out financial obligations without much danger to guests or workers), but by the end of the nineteenth century, they were no longer being rebuilt the next season. (Only a few of them remain in the White Mountains today: Perhaps the most impressive is the massive and elegant Mount Washington Hotel, built in 1905, the last of a long line of hotels at the west entrance to the Crawford Notch, near the place where Ethan Allen Crawford's inn first stood.)

The automobile complicated the problems of the great hotels in two ways. In the short run, it added to their cash-flow problems. Instead of large numbers of stationary guests who stayed for a month or more, the automobile brought unpredictable, vagrant overnight guests, a less reliable and less lucrative business that hastened the hotels' decline. More significant in the long run, automobile travel accelerated an already long-standing consumer movement away from the grand hotels. Alternatives to hotel life—summer cottages, boardinghouses, farms—were already competing successfully with hotels in the late nineteenth century. Auto touring simply encouraged the further development of such alternatives, by adapting them to the auto tourist's informal, nomadic preferences.

Farmers or town dwellers who were already accustomed to accommodating summer boarders arriving by train could easily take in motoring tourists overnight. Small-town homeowners in heavily traveled regions put up signs on their Main Street houses: "Tourists Accommodated." Frontage on a well-traveled road could become the basis for a wide variety of new businesses. Roadside restaurants, souvenir shops, and tourist cabins, or "auto camps," could all be operated next door to the old farmhouse. In 1931, the New Hampshire Extension Service—always abreast of the latest trends in rural tourism—conducted a conference designed to train such entrepreneurs, with talks on "How Roadside Shops Can Be Turned into Money Making Magnets," and the "Successful Management of a Tea Room."[9]

Cape Cod's vacation industry emerged within the structure of this new automobile trade. At both ends of the Cape—in Falmouth and Provincetown—promoters had already established old-style resorts fed by railroads and steamboats. But from the beginning of its popular era, the automobile took Cape Cod by storm. In retrospect, it *does* almost seem inevitable: Cape Cod's very geography seems to call out for automobile tourists. The simple, linear route of the old stagecoach roads created an ideal "natural" loop of the kind most favored by automobile guidebooks, allowing tourists to pass through almost every town and village on Cape Cod without retracing their steps.

But that geographical advantage might never have been noticed by anyone had it not been for political and economic forces that were already shaping the outlines of Cape Cod's early twentieth-century tourist industry. Automobiles alone could not bring tourists to the Cape. That required roads—and good ones. New England's state governments were deeply involved in road development long before most vacationers even knew what cars were. Governor Rollins, the inventor of Old Home Week, had anticipated as early as the 1890s that state roads would become important tourist routes. But he, like other road enthusiasts, had expected the hordes of new tourists to arrive on *bicycles.*[10]

As it turned out, cars, not bicycles, changed the landscape of tourism—with a great deal of help from the states. The New England states launched massive state-funded road-building programs at the turn of the century, hoping to improve the commercial prospects of New England farmers and to encourage tourism.[11] (Indeed, it might almost seem that the inventors of automobiles were responding to a "need" already established by the New England states for some way of using their roads.) Massachusetts created its first Highway Commission in 1893, centralizing the control of highway expenditures once controlled by towns. Key tourist roads were opened in anticipation of the explosion of automobile touring. The Mohawk Trail, for example, opened in 1915; it connected Boston with the resorts and rural vacation areas of the Berkshires in western Massachusetts. Only the most intrepid auto travelers would have braved the locally maintained dirt roads that had served most rural areas before the state stepped in. The "natural" attractions of Cape Cod's old stagecoach roads would doubtless have been considerably less attractive to auto tourists had those roads not been transformed into "splendid state macadam, with red markers," as early as 1916.[12]

Cape Cod towns had often rejected innovations that threatened to bring large numbers of outsiders onto the Cape, or to jeopardize the independent towns' local control. In fact, the Old Colony Railroad itself had at first faced serious opposition from a number of Cape towns on the basis of those fears. (Street railways had run into similar obstacles in the town of Falmouth as late as 1910.[13]) If Cape Codders had known the uses to which the new state roads were to be put, perhaps they would have rejected them as well. But auto travelers, in contrast with resort vacationers who traveled by railroad or steamboat, had a tendency to appear in small numbers at first. A native's first encounter with auto tourists might be with only one or two harmless-looking strangers looking for a place to spend the night.

Hard evidence is difficult to come by, but Cape residents may have found such tourists harder to resist than earlier vacationers. A resident might begin by taking in a guest or two as they happened by, and end by running a full-scale boardinghouse or roadside restaurant. (Such a gradual progression had already softened the transition to the service economy for many former farming and sailing families in rural northern New England and even nearby Nantucket.) Then, too, such small-scale, informal innovations did not create the community upheaval and town-meeting debates that large-scale hotel or resort projects often caused.

On top of that, by 1920 Cape Cod was entering its sixth decade of depression; its population had declined to the level of a century earlier. Whatever remained of its former pursuits—commercial fishing, cranberries, farming—was hanging on in increasingly attenuated forms. (And those marginal industries were also falling into the hands of the growing numbers of Portuguese immigrants who now made up about ten percent of the population.) For those "Yankees" who remained, the choices had narrowed considerably in the first decades of the twentieth century. The temptation to hang out a Tourists Accommodated shingle may simply have grown too great to pass up.

In any case, the new automobile-oriented tourist industries—small-scale, informal, and dispersed along the roadsides—broke through the barriers of resistance to change and found their place on Cape Cod. Tea shops, guest houses, and tourist camps quickly sprang up to cater to rapidly increasing numbers of automobiles. One summer Sunday as early as 1936, the state police counted fifty-five thousand "motor cars" crossing over just *one* of the two canal bridges.[14] And the numbers have not diminished since. The Cape's tourist industries are still shaped by the automobile—still informal, scattered, and relentlessly road-oriented. Today, hundreds of thousands of automobiles come over the two bridges in July and August of each year, enough cars to cause mammoth traffic jams on every summer weekend, to harden the arteries of traffic in every town on the lower Cape, and to cause long-term residents to save their shopping trips for mid-afternoon on sunny days, when the tourists' cars are all parked at the beaches.

The Twentieth-century Tour

From the beginning, auto tourism on Cape Cod—and everywhere else—fostered a particular style of touring. It encouraged small-scale tourist services, scattered across widely dispersed areas. It helped to shape a new tourist's landscape, sharpening some boundaries that had once been vague, blurring some distinctions that had once been clear. And auto touring also transformed the experiences of tourists, not by breaking directly with earlier trends, but by carrying them to unheard-of extremes. These extremes—in mobility, in informality, and in the search for "privacy"—have become typical of twentieth-century tourist experiences.

The old-fashioned Victorian hotels had been designed with public interaction with strangers in mind. Private rooms were small and crowded, while public rooms were elaborately decorated and imposing. But alternative forms of tourism had already emerged in the second half of the nineteenth century, all of which emphasized their greater privacy and family domesticity in comparison with the hotels. The little cottages of Wesleyan Grove, the great "cottages" of Newport, the rented farmhouses in the Berkshires, and even boardinghouses from Nantucket to Vermont, were all said to provide greater privacy for the tourist.

Automobiles simply took that consumer preference one step further: They made it possible to frame the entire touring experience, even getting there, in complete privacy. And automobiles fostered industries that provided greater privacy on arrival. The motor cabins and auto camps that eventually became "motels" offered a complete reversal of the traditional hotel's use of space. Motels were judged by the luxuries and amenities available in one's *private* room, rather than in the often almost nonexistent public space.[15] Late twentieth-century innovations have gone further still. Now, tourists can secure almost total privacy in time-share condominiums, where they can live completely sealed off even from the workers, "quaint" or otherwise, who once made up such an important part of the touring experience.

But privacy meant more than being alone, or alone with one's family. It also meant greater segregation—the assurance that one would not meet people who were not one's "sort," not of the same social class (except as "naturally hospitable" workers or quaint locals). When the great hotels were abandoned by elite tourists in the late nineteenth century, it was not simply because they had come to be seen as too public but because they could not guarantee the kinds of exclusivity they had once promised. Here, again, the automobile offered an acceleration of a change already in progress. Automobiles provided tourists of all the vacationing classes with an even more extreme version of what they had been seeking for generations: an insulated, socially homogeneous vacation environment.[16]

That search has not been abandoned in the late twentieth century. In fact, contemporary tourists have gone far beyond the social stratification of nineteenth-century resorts. Whole regions of the vacation landscape today are divided by social factors like age, profession, and "lifestyle," in addition to the more traditional barriers of class, ethnicity, and religion. Nineteenth-century resorts were used as "marriage markets" (at least until the later part of the century, when they gained a reputation for "manlessness," as William Dean Howells termed it), but they were not nearly as homogeneous as a twentieth-century "singles" resort.

On Cape Cod, town lines often serve to delineate these all-important vacation borders: Students go to Hyannis for college-style nightlife; psychologists meet each other in Wellfleet; and Provincetown attracts gay and lesbian tourists (and curious observers) from all over the Northeast. These very sharp geographical boundaries, among other things, make possible the late twentieth-century vacation styles that seem to offer a more public, socially open experience. Bed-and-breakfasts, for example, are not really an exception to the highly stratified vacationscape: They work socially because they can provide an unspoken assurance that in their open and informal world one will encounter only tourists (and hosts) of a select, usually upper-middle-class, professional background.

But if tourist destinations have become ever more narrowly specialized in the twentieth century, the tourist *season* has spread out. Nineteenth-century tourists occupied the landscape only in July and August, but the twentieth-century tourist industry has colonized the rest of the year. The first incursion into the "off-season" occurred when Dartmouth College students began skiing in the White Mountains. The sport became widely popular in the 1930s, when college students from all over the Northeast began to take it up, and with that popularity came the need for skiing instructors, skiing equipment, and winter accommodations.[17] Since then, northern New England has come to rely increasingly on its winter tourist population as well as its summer people.

Even more recently, what was once called autumn has been transformed into "foliage season," in an attempt to keep the tourist dollars rolling in through the slow period of September and October. On flat Cape Cod, with its warm winters and pitch pine forests, skiing and leaf-peeping do not make much sense. But even there, tourist promoters have begun to make the attempt to bring tourists to the Cape "off-season." The spread of tourists through time and space has made for a much more permeable tourist environment. It has also blurred distinctions between tourists and residents, as "summer people" and "winter people" invest in property, get involved with local politics, and retire to the tourist region.

Nowhere is this blurring of boundaries more apparent than on Cape Cod. After World War II, the Cape became the vacation destination of choice for thousands of southern New Englanders who were reaping the benefits of a postwar economic boom. Since then, Cape Cod's population, summer and winter, has exploded: Between 1955 and 1980, the year-round population nearly tripled. The numbers reflect not only the exponential growth of the vacation industry, but also a change in its direction. Those twenty-five years brought a massive influx of second-home buyers and re-tirees, whose impact on the region's population, economy, and environment has proved to be even more dramatic than that of more transient tourists.

The new immigrants have changed the age structure of the region. Barnstable County (which is Cape Cod) now contains seven of the ten Massachusetts towns with the largest populations of residents over sixty-five.[18] They have also helped to link Cape tourism inextricably with the "boom-bust" cycle of the larger economy and with the ups and downs of the construction industry that builds those second homes and retirement communities. One quarter of Cape Cod's income is now generated by re-tirees; one quarter derives from "seasonal residents," summer people who own houses on the Cape; only another quarter still comes from transient "tourists."[19] While the region has become almost wholly dependent on the activities of people "from away," the distinction between natives and tourists has been almost completely obscured.

New England Revisited

The structure of the tourist industry has changed dramatically in the twentieth century; so too has the region that hosts that industry. New England's tourist industries in the early twentieth century began to face increasing competition from the ever more popular and accessible attractions of the West. As more and more tourists made the lengthy trek west to the Rockies, Yellowstone Park, and the Pacific Coast, New England could hardly claim to offer a comparable wilderness experience. Yet at the same time, New England's landscape was visibly "wilder," more wooded and less farmed, than it had been in the middle of the nineteenth century. The region that in mid–nineteenth century was more than three-quarters cleared land is today more than two-thirds reforested. The tourist landscape has changed along with the changing environment: Both the encroaching woodland and the endangered farm landscape have become objects of attention.

Wilderness and its preservation became a major impetus for touring in the early twentieth century. The roots of that interest went as far back as the camping tours of the Adirondacks popularized by the controversial Boston clergyman "Adirondack" Murray as early as 1869, and the preservation movement, which had its first victory with the creation of Yellowstone National Park in 1872.[20] In the first decades of the new century, wilderness and the "outdoors" became an important part of the tourist experience even in relatively tame New England. In the White Mountains, the hiking trails of the Appalachian Mountain Club replaced the bridle paths and carriage roads. Children's summer camps sprouted everywhere: By the 1920s, Vermont had 75 summer camps, New Hampshire had 185, and Maine, with its countless forested lakes, boasted 230.[21] (Almost overnight, Cape Cod, too, developed children's camps—thirteen in the 1920s.)

The appreciation of wild nature has become more and more central to the tourist experience over the past fifty years. Before World War II, for example, Cape Cod's promotional literature had focused primarily on its "quaint" remnants of an earlier Yankee life. Many of the tourists who drove through the towns and villages of the Cape in the 1920s and 1930s were looking for a special rural experience. An explosion of travel literature, most of it deeply nostalgic, let tourists know that a treasury of old Yankee artifacts and folkways were to be found "off the beaten track." Books like *Cape Cod Yesterdays* and *Cape Cod and the Old Colony* instructed the tourist in local landmarks, legends, and relics, retelling bits of history to accompany the roadside sites.[22]

After the 1940s, nostalgic guides to lost Yankee virtues were gradually superseded by guidebooks and literature that focused on the natural beauties of the Cape. As Cape Cod's vacationers increased in number, they became increasingly intrigued by the region's unique landscape. In the 1960s, naturalist John Hay, the founder of the Cape Cod Natural History Museum, wrote evocatively about the natural life of the Cape. Accompanied by popular scientific works like Arthur N. Strahler's *A Geologist's View of Cape Cod*, such writing helped to foster a new appreciation for the area's rich natural diversity. In 1961, Congress created the Cape Cod National Seashore, signaling the official arrival of a new attitude toward the region, along with the need to protect the still undeveloped parts of the Cape from the rapid growth that accompanied the newfound enthusiasm.

Over the past two decades, both the value and the fragility of Cape Cod's natural environment have become even more apparent. Most recently, the "Massachusetts miracle" of the mid-1980s fostered yet another wave of building expansion on the Cape. As housing tracts, malls, and hotels rapidly advanced over the remaining open land, an uneasy sense overtook many regional enthusiasts that the Cape was being "loved to death." By the end of the building boom of the 1980s, that sense had become so urgent that in 1990, Cape Cod voters gave a countywide Cape Cod Planning Commission the power to protect the dwindling natural resources of the

Cape. Along with other groups like the Association for the Preservation of Cape Cod, the Massachusetts Audubon Society, and the Cape Cod Natural History Museum, the Commission has worked to balance the Cape's need for revenue with its need to protect limited resources. These groups have pioneered in the development of "green" tourist activities, from whale-watching to marsh walks.

Concern for vanishing landscapes has motivated tourism all over New England, taking other forms in other settings. After World War II, New England's remaining farm landscapes came to have a new significance for tourists of the region. The disappearance of farms, and the mechanization that grew out of the war, gave new life to the already long-established vision of farms as the repositories of old-fashioned virtue and rural simplicity. The desire to escape from urbanism and its discontents has remained constant among tourists over the past fifty years. During the boom of the 1980s, one northern Vermont real estate company used a pitch that could have been lifted straight from the Vermont Board of Agriculture's turn-of-the-century promotional campaigns. In their brochure, the potential home buyer is portrayed as a refugee from urbanism, "escaped/From the vast city, where I long had pined/A discontented sojourner: now free,/Free as a bird to settle where I will." Perhaps not all late twentieth-century real estate brokers are literate enough to manipulate Wordsworth so effectively, but most would recognize the sentiment. It has now been a powerful motivation for vacation-home buyers for a hundred years.

At least in regard to these sentiments, the nineteenth-century alliance between Vermont farms and Vermont pastoral tourism seems to have held fast. Even today, when Vermont's farms are competing for land with time-share condominiums for skiers and a vastly increased summer-housing market, many of those who hope to preserve farming attempt to associate it with the pastoral tourist's landscape for which Vermont is famous. The Natural Organic Farmers' Association in Vermont put out bumper stickers several years ago that pleaded with tourists to "Help Keep Vermont Beautiful—Save Its Farms."

And Vermont's farms are apparently still of all farms the most virtuous. A wide variety of businesses have built on the foundation provided by the Vermont Board of Agriculture at the turn of the century. From Ben & Jerry's and the Cabot Cheese Cooperative to the smallest companies marketing salsa and chutneys, the state's producers rely on their consumers' deep faith in the purity and moral value of rural Vermont. But if those businesses have brought a measure of prosperity to the state, they have also helped to intensify the paradox at the heart of such development. As Vermont has become increasingly attractive to ex-urbanites, the very charm that attracts them has become endangered. In the summer of 1993, the director of the National Register of Historic Places placed the entire state at the top of its endangered list, citing the rapid loss of distinctive rural and village landscapes to malls and shopping strips.

The twentieth century has seen an intensification of such efforts to preserve (and market to tourists) the "oldness" of New England. On Nantucket, the first of New England's historic districts was formed in 1955, protecting most of the town's oldest neighborhoods from architectural change. In the decades that followed, the intensive reworking and "preservation" of Nantucket's waterfront and commercial center have continued to generate controversy over the balance of preservation, beauty, and profit—between Nantucket as architectural goldmine and Nantucket as coastal resort.[23]

Such feats of historic preservation are now no longer limited to the picturesque "colonial" streetscapes of places like Nantucket or Portsmouth. The great industrial cities, many of them still suffering from the effects of the massive deindustrialization of the region during the 1920s, have uncovered stirring histories and fascinating architecture of their own. When the city of Lowell's downtown "millscape" was transformed into Lowell National Park in 1978, it marked the coming of age of an entirely new attitude toward a part of New England's history that had been ignored by the region's tourists since the mid–nineteenth-century turn toward nostalgia. And if the mills have a legitimate history, so may the thousands of immigrants and industrial workers who have for so long been excluded from the collective regional past by champions of "Anglo-Saxon" exclusivity. Now Irish millworkers, African American artisans, and French-Canadian farmers may find a place in historical reconstructions of "old New England."

That vision of "old New England" has been somewhat modified by the addition of these "other" New Englanders, but it has remained a powerful and appealing myth. In some ways, it has grown stronger over time. It now seems entirely natural to perceive New England as old. The shock is in the discovery that New England was ever "new," that tourists might once have looked to the region for an experience not unlike what we seek out when we visit NASA or Disney's Future Land. For twentieth-century tourists, much of the landscape of New England belongs unambiguously to the past. When modern New Englanders read of a struggle over whether to replace a Berkshire town's factory buildings with an art gallery, or an old Lowell textile mill with a new microchip factory, they may be startled to think of these places as having a future at all, not simply as storehouses for ways of life that have disappeared.

Some of the conflicts at the heart of nineteenth-century tourism have thus been resolved for us. New England is unambiguously old from a twentieth-century perspective, and the only challenge is to travel in such a way as to avoid seeing the car dealerships and video stores that would undermine that vision. Similarly, most of us no longer have any trouble reconciling our vacations with religious and moral convictions; leisure is an accepted part of life for all who can afford it. If we share some of the "antimodernist" sentiments of late nineteenth-century tourists in search of the quaint, these nostalgic feelings are so pervasive that they no longer seem to conflict with faith in "progress." But some of the nineteenth century's incongruities are still very much with us.

The Road from Cape Cod

For all the enthusiastic commitment the tourist industry has received in recent years from regional governments and business groups, tourism has been almost completely invisible in public policy debates. That is all the more strange since it has become increasingly clear in the twentieth century that tourism, like any industry, can endanger the environment, the culture, or the health of the community it supports. Nowhere is that fact more obvious than in a heavily traveled region like Cape Cod. Many of the advocates of limits to growth on Cape Cod would argue that the Cape is in danger of becoming a regional sacrifice area—not to nuclear waste, but to the side effects of tourism.

Cape Cod's water resources have been profoundly jeopardized by the uncontrolled growth of the 1980s. Its economy has over the past forty years become heavily dependent on part-time, low-paying, dead-end jobs that ebb and flow with every season. When social scientists turn their attention to Cape Cod society, they find a state of affairs not perceptibly different in some ways from the social distortion of Third World tourist countries. Constant contact with outsiders whose only goal (at least for the moment) is pleasure, perhaps temporarily liberated from the ethical restraints that control their behavior at home, seems to have spawned some serious social problems in Cape communities, ranging in seriousness from a vague sense of alienation to epidemic alcoholism.[24]

Perhaps no other business *would* work better on Cape Cod, or generate fewer side effects. But that question is rarely discussed publicly. There are a number of reasons for the silence, several going back as far as the origins of tourism in this country. For one thing, few of the side effects of any kind of business are usually investigated with any care, particularly if the business provides the sole means of livelihood in a region. But tourism has another protection as well: A highly diffuse, apparently "clean" industry is a difficult one to confront.

Then there is the question of power. In the late nineteenth century, the power relations between hosts and guests were both explored and hidden by notions of "natural" hospitality, or of going "home" to the farm. Today, they can be obscured by the impersonality of hotels, condominiums, and automobile travel, or by the segregation which prevents personal contact with the wrong kinds of people. But at the heart of tourism is an experience of power differences, perhaps temporary but nevertheless intense: an experience of luxurious ease, of control over one's time, of access to cultural or natural resources, combined with a largely unacknowledged sense that the workers providing these services have, for the moment at least, none of these things.

One of the marks of a successful tourist attraction is its success in hiding all of that—making the production process, its workers, and their lives invisible. But the impact of those power differences is not really difficult to see, if one is looking. Part of the price of the tourist industry is often a loss of control over one's community. On Nantucket, year-round residents are evicted from their apartments during the summer months so that landlords may rent to summer people willing to pay triple the normal price. In Vermont, second homes spread out over prime farm land that embattled dairy farmers can no longer afford.

The questions of whether Nantucket's workers would prefer to attract fewer tourists and stay in their own houses, or whether Vermont's farmers would choose to risk lower property values along with fewer wealthy land investors, are not frequently asked.[25] One group that did ask such questions, the Cape Cod Commission, found in a 1991 survey that the great majority of Cape Cod residents favored a limit to further growth in the tourist industries, preferring that the Commission encourage the development of light industry instead. (Three-quarters of the respondents rejected development of the classic tourist businesses—miniature golf courses, factory outlet malls, restaurants and hotels—in favor of proposed alternatives.)[26]

Perhaps the most important reason why tourism is not more often subjected to public scrutiny is that the changes wrought by tourist industries are understood to be "natural," unavoidable—beyond the reach of policy. If tourism is the product of the workings of nature, questions like those framed by the Cape Cod Commission seem at best naive, at worst absurd, like asking residents what kind of weather they want. Even one severe critic of the impact of tourism on Cape Cod has stated flatly that tourism in the region is "structural, deeply rooted not only in decades of policy decisions, but also in the nature of humankind."[27] I disagree: Tourist industries are no more a product of the "nature of humankind" than are factories—microchip or potato chip. Twentieth-century promoters and tourists alike have reasons to cherish the illusion that tourism simply grows naturally from the physical or cultural "attractions" of a region. But that is all it is—an illusion. Tourist industries, like all industries, can be shaped and controlled by those who must live with the consequences. And they should be.

NOTES

Introduction

1. Auto World closed after six months, along with the bankrupt Hyatt-Regency Hotel, into which the desperate city had poured $13,000,000 in tax funds (at a time when one-half of its citizens were receiving some sort of public assistance). This sad and funny story was explored with devastating wit in *Roger and Me*, Michael Moore's brilliant 1989 documentary of the destruction of the city of Flint.

2. Adolph B. Benson, ed., *America of the Fifties: Letters of Frederika Bremer* (New York: The American Scandinavian Federation, 1924), 323.

3. Raymond Williams referred to this process as "conspicuous aesthetic consumption" in his groundbreaking discussion of the origins of scenic tourism in eighteenth-century England. Raymond Williams, *The Country and the City* (New York: Oxford University Press, 1973), 121, 128.

4. Ralph Waldo Emerson, *The Complete Essays* (New York: Random House, 1950), 5–6.

5. A wide variety of consumer goods in mid-century provide parallel histories, earmarked as gateways to a higher life, aesthetically, culturally, or morally. Thomas Richards has labeled such transactions pious consumption. Thomas Richards, *The Commodity Culture of Victorian England: Advertising and Spectacle, 1851–1914* (Stanford, Calif.: Stanford University Press, 1990), 104. The best example I have encountered of the mid-century commodification of

religion—and of the sanctification of consumption—is the story of little Ellen Montgomery's Bible-shopping expedition in Susan Warner's best-selling 1853 novel, *The Wide, Wide World.*

6. William Dean Howells, "The Problem of the Summer," in *Literature and Life* (New York: Harper and Brothers, 1902), 216–17.

7. George E. Street, *Mount Desert: A History* (Boston: Houghton, Mifflin & Co., 1905), 326.

8. Gary Kulik has most influenced my understanding of the nature of this imaginative reinvention of New England. I first heard him speak on the subject at the University of Massachusetts in Amherst in 1986, at a talk called appropriately "The Invention of New England."

9. On the origins and meaning of the myth of the Old South, see William R. Taylor, *Cavalier and Yankee: The Old South and American National Character* (Cambridge, Mass.: Harvard University Press, 1957).

10. Two studies of this process are David E. Whisnant, *All That is Native and Fine: The Politics of Culture in an American Region* (Chapel Hill, N.C.: University of North Carolina Press, 1983); and Henry D. Shapiro, *Appalachia on Our Mind: The Southern Mountains and Mountaineers in the American Consciousness, 1870–1920* (Chapel Hill, N.C.: University of North Carolina Press, 1978).

11. Henry David Thoreau, *Cape Cod* (Cambridge, Mass.: Riverside Press, 1894), 224, 330.

12. The Catskills offer the clearest parallel development, beginning some years earlier. Their location along the heavily traveled Hudson River route between New York City and Albany made them the most accessible romantic mountains in the east and brought them as early as the 1820s into a web of development that included scenic tourism, industrial development, shipping, and suburbanization. For the best account of the Catskills, see Kenneth Myers, *The Catskills: Painters, Writers, and Tourists in the Mountains, 1820–1895* (Hanover, N.H.: The Hudson River Museum of Westchester, University Press of New England, 1987).

Chapter 1: Tours, Grand and Fashionable

1. Nathaniel P. Willis, "Niagara—Lake Ontario—the St. Lawrence," in *Dashes at Life with a Free Pencil*, part 2: "Inklings of Adventure," reprinted from the 1845 edition in The American Short Story Series (New York: Garret Press, 1968), 30:10–12 (original pagination).

2. Willis, "Larks in Vacation," 76.

3. Jane Mesick, *The English Traveller in America* (New York: Columbia University Press, 1922), 8–9.

4. On the Grand Tour of Europe, see Jeremy Black, *The British and the Grand Tour* (London: Croom Helm, 1985).

5. Henry Wansey, *Journal of an Excursion to the United States of North America* (New York: Johnson Reprint Corporation, 1969), vii–ix.

6. For an interesting discussion of such motives in tours of New York State, see Roger Haydon, ed., *Upstate Travels: British Views of Nineteenth-Century New*

York (Syracuse, N.Y.: Syracuse University Press, 1982). For a general discussion of English travelers in America, see Mesick, *English Traveller.*

7. David John Jeremy, ed., *Henry Wansey and His American Journal* (Philadelphia: American Philosophical Society, 1970), 33.

8. George A. Bonnard, ed., *Gibbon's Journey from Geneva to Rome: His Journal from 20 April to 20 October 1764,* quoted in Christopher Hibbert, *The Grand Tour* (New York: G. P. Putnam's Sons, 1969), 87.

9. Basil Hall, *Travels in North America in the Years 1827–1828* (Edinburgh: Cadell, 1830), 2:145.

10. Robert Hunter, *Quebec to California in 1785–1786,* ed. Louis Wright and Marion Tinling (San Marino, Calif.: The Huntington Library, 1943), 123–24.

11. Wansey, *Journal,* 43–47.

12. Ibid., 14. Apparently, it was actually a recounting of his *father's* "eyewitness" experience of the battle. Anthony Lukas reported in his study of the roots of the Boston busing crisis that Charlestown's Irish "townies" still, as of 1976, hung around tourists offering to recite accounts of the Battle of Bunker Hill for tips. Anthony Lukas, *Common Ground: A Turbulent Decade in The Lives of Three American Families* (New York: Knopf, 1985), 143.

13. Una Pope-Hennessy, ed., *The Aristocratic Journey: Being the Outspoken Letters of Mrs. Basil Hall Written during a Fourteen Month's Sojourn in America, 1827–1828* (New York: Putnam, 1931), 91–92; Anne Royall, *Sketches of History, Life, and Manners, in the United States, 1826* (1826; reprint, New York: Johnson Reprint Corporation, 1970), 297.

14. Royall, *Sketches,* 369.

15. J. Q. P., "Extracts from Gleanings on the Way," *Southern Literary Messenger* 4 (April 1838): 251.

16. Royall, *Sketches,* 278.

17. Ibid., 331, 347–48, 387.

18. Ibid., 295–96.

19. Wansey, *Journal,* 122.

20. These were published as Una Pope-Hennessy, ed., *The Aristocratic Journey: Being the Outspoken Letters of Mrs. Basil Hall Written during a Fourteen Month's Sojourn in America, 1827–1828* (New York: Putnam, 1931).

21. Hall, *Travels in North America,* 2:122.

22. Ibid., 1:132.

23. Ibid., 1:109.

24. Timothy Dwight's observations were published posthumously as *Travels in New-England and New-York,* a defense of the culture of New England against attacks from English travelers.

25. Hall, *Travels in North America,* 1:93.

26. Seymour Dunbar, *A History of Travel in America,* (Indianapolis: Bobbs-Merrill Co., 1915), 2:851.

27. Hall, *Travels in North America,* 2:8.

28. This discussion of the transition from inns to hotels is based on information in Donna-Belle and James L. Garvin, *On the Road North of Boston: New Hampshire Taverns and Turnpikes, 1700–1900* (Concord, N.H.: New Hampshire Historical Society, c. 1988).

29. Willis, "Larks in Vacation," 79–80.

30. James K. Paulding, *The New Mirror for Travellers; and Guide to the Springs* (New York: G. and C. Carvill, 1828), 67.

31. Hall, *Travels in North America*, 1:195.

32. Gideon M. Davison, *The Fashionable Tour for the Summer of 1822* (Saratoga Springs, 1822), 53.

33. William L. Stone, *Reminiscences of Saratoga* (New York: Virtue and Yorston, 1875), chapter 1.

34. Kenneth Myers, *The Catskills: Painters, Writers, and Tourists in the Mountains, 1820–1895* (Hanover, N.H.: The Hudson River Museum of Westchester, University Press of New England, 1987), 30.

35. Hall, *Travels in North America*, 1:190.

36. Elkanah Watson, *Men and Times of the Revolution; or, Memories of Elkanah Watson* (New York: Dana and Company, 1856), 351.

37. Theodore Dwight, *The Northern Traveller, and Northern Tour: With the Routes to the Springs, Niagara, and Quebec, and the Coal Mines of Pennsylvania* (New York: J. and J. Harper, 1831), 154.

38. Ralph Greenhill and Thomas D. Mahoney, *Niagara* (Toronto: University of Toronto Press, 1969), 109–10.

39. Hall, *Travels in North America*, 1:125–26.

40. Horatio Gates Spafford's *Gazetteer of the State of New-York* (Albany: H. C. Southwick, 1813) was being used as a guidebook in the 1820s, and books of road descriptions were published as early as the 1740s. But guidebooks specifically designed for tourists were new in the 1820s.

41. Stone, *Reminiscences*, 185–86 and chapter 31, esp. 313–17.

42. *Saratoga Sentinel*, 15 August 1821; *Boyd's Saratoga Springs Directory*, 1868.

43. The National Union Catalog lists *Maria Monk* under Dwight's name.

44. Journal of Alexander Bliss, 22 June 1825, American Antiquarian Society manuscript collection. The wedding journey was only beginning to come into style as the fashionable tour was being created in the 1820s, and the "honeymoon" provided one of the most important motives for the fashionable tour. See Ellen Rothman, *Hands and Hearts, a History of Courtship in America* (New York: Basic Books, 1984), 82, 175.

45. The "great leap forward" was taken in the 1828 edition, which nearly doubled the size of the book, from 169 to 322 pages, primarily by including a whole set of new routes through New England's "rich mountain scenery."

46. William L. Stone, "A Trip from New York to Niagara in 1829: The Unpublished Diary of Colonel William L. Stone," *Magazine of American History* 20:490.

47. Haydon, *Upstate Travels*, 50.

48. Theodore Dwight, *The Northern Traveller*, 330.

49. Stone, "New York to Niagara," 321.

50. Paulding, *The New Mirror*, 180, 166, 179, 84.

51. For a somewhat different reading on the meaning of Saratoga Springs (over the entire nineteenth century), see Janice Zita Grover, "Luxury and

Leisure in Early Nineteenth-Century America: Saratoga Springs and the Rise of the Resort" (Ph.D. diss., University of California, Davis, 1973).

52. *Saratoga Sentinel*, 7 August 1821. Although it was located almost on the frontier, Saratoga was in a sense a substitute city, and in that sense, too, it fit into a traditional urban elite touring itinerary. In the summer of 1832, when cholera raged in northeastern cities, the streets of this isolated rural village were completely empty: Whatever the hotel keepers claimed, tourists did not believe crowded Saratoga was exempt from urban health risks.

53. Jeremiah Fitch, "An Account and Memorandum of My Journey to Saratoga Springs, 1820," *Massachusetts Historical Society Proceedings* 50 (February 1917): 196.

54. Fitch, 189–96.

55. *Saratoga Sentinel*, 9 August 1820.

56. Grover, "Luxury and Leisure," 18. Gideon M. Davison, *The Traveller's Guide: Through the Middle and Northern States, and the Provinces of Canada* (New York: G. and C. and H. Carville, 1833), 150–51.

57. Theodore Dwight, *The Northern Traveller*, 154–55.

58. Nathaniel P. Willis, "Meena Dimity; or, Why Mr. Brown Crash Took the Tour," 160.

59. Fitz-Greene Halleck, *The Poetical Works* (New York: D. Appleton and Co., 1865), 190.

60. James Silk Buckingham, *American Historical, Statistical, Descriptive* (London: Fisher, Son & Co., 1841), 2:100, 435.

61. Caroline Gilman, *The Poetry of Travelling in the United States* (New York: S. Colman, 1838), 84.

62. Paulding, *The New Mirror*, 228–29.

63. Ibid., 96.

Chapter 2: The Uses of Scenery

1. Nathaniel Hawthorne, "Sketches from Memory," *Nathaniel Hawthorne* (New York: Library of America, 1982), 339.

2. Excerpts from the diary of Joseph T. Buckingham, in Kenneth Walter Cameron, *Genesis of Hawthorne's "The Ambitious Guest"* (Hartford: Thistle Press, 1955), 6–8.

3. See, for example, Malcolm Andrews, *The Search for the Picturesque: Landscape Aesthetics and Tourism in Britain, 1760–1800* (Stanford, Calif.: Stanford University Press, 1989); Esther Moir, *The Discovery of Britain: The English Tourists, 1540–1840* (London: Routledge and Kegan Paul, 1964).

4. Franklin B. Sanborn, ed., *Memoirs of Pliny Earle, M. D.* (Boston, 1898), 45–46.

5. Lucy Crawford, *The History of the White Mountains from the First Settlement of Upper Coos and Pequawket* (1845; reprint, Portland: F. A. and A. F. Gerrish, 1946) 136–37. Crawford seemed uncertain whether wild animals were more interesting to tourists alive or dead; he often attempted to capture them alive

and bring them home but usually had to settle for displaying their dead bodies—and displaying himself instead as a great hunter.

6. For an analysis of the meaning of the Willey tragedy to American tourists, see John F. Sears, *Sacred Places: American Tourist Attractions in the Nineteenth Century* (New York: Oxford University Press, 1989), 72–86. Robert McGrath has pointed out the peculiar usefulness of the Willey tragedy as an "instant ruin" in the creation of interest in White Mountain scenery. Robert McGrath, "The Real and the Ideal," in *The White Mountains: Place and Perception* (Hanover, N.H.: University Press of New England, 1980), 59.

7. Crawford, *History*, 105.

8. Theodore Dwight, *The Northern Traveller, and Northern Tour: With the Routes to the Springs, Niagara, and Quebec, and the Coal Mines of Pennsylvania* (New York: J. and J. Harper, 1831), 352.

9. The best account of the Crawfords' story is still Lucy Crawford's 1845 *History of the White Mountains*.

10. The names are taken from Ethan Allen Crawford's visitors' albums, now lost. See Frederick Tuckerman, "Gleanings from the Visitors' Albums of Ethan Allen Crawford," *Appalachia* 14, no. 4 (June 1919): 377–82.

11. Nathaniel Hawthorne *The Letters, 1813–1843* (Columbus, Ohio: Ohio State University Press, 1984), 224.

12. J. Bard McNulty, ed., *Correspondence of Thomas Cole and Daniel Wadsworth* (Hartford: Connecticut Historical Society, 1983), 12.

13. For an insightful discussion of Cole's relationship with the Catskills and their development as a tourist region, see Kenneth Myers, *The Catskills: Painters, Writers, and Tourists in the Mountains, 1820–1895* (Hanover, N.H.: The Hudson River Museum of Westchester, University Press of New England, 1987). Myers says Cole probably left the Catskills for the White Mountains because the Catskills had already become too "touristy" by the late 1820s.

14. Sarah Josepha Hale, "The Romance of Travelling," in *Traits of American Life* (Philadelphia: Carey and Lea, 1835), 189–91.

15. Ralph Waldo Emerson, *The Complete Essays* (New York: Random House, 1950), 5–6.

16. This entire passage was intended by Emerson to establish definitions of the "poet" and "nature" that are not unrelated to my point here but that served other purposes. For the best discussion of what Emerson did mean, see R. Jackson Wilson, *Figures of Speech: American Writers and the Literary Marketplace, from Benjamin Franklin to Emily Dickinson* (New York: Knopf, 1989), chapter 4, esp. 177–78.

17. In 1864, Fabyan was bought out by Sylvester Marsh, a wealthy investor and former resident, as part of his scheme to build a cog railway to the top of Mount Washington. Within a few years, the hotel was in the hands of a corporation made up of Marsh and his friends. Corporate ownership became the norm in the resort hotel business by the 1870s, as explored in more detail in Chapter 3. Information on Horace Fabyan comes from Peter Bulkley, "Horace Fabyan, Founder of the White Mountain Grand Hotel," *Historic New Hampshire* 30, no. 2 (1975): 53–77. Bulkley reconstructed the life of this leg-

endary, but almost unknown, figure from court records, tax lists, and census reports.

18. Fabyan left his mark on the region, though. The train station that was later built near his hotel site was named for him, and even today the train depot—now abandoned in its turn—houses a restaurant called Fabyan's.

19. Frederick Kilbourne, *Chronicles of the White Mountains* (Boston: Houghton Mifflin & Co. 1916), 174.

20. Bulkley, "Horace Fabyan," 63.

21. Adolph B. Benson, ed., *America of the Fifties: Letters of Frederika Bremer* (New York: The American Scandinavian Federation, 1924), 323.

22. Anthony Trollope, *North America* (Philadelphia: Lippincott, 1863), 35.

23. Sylvester Breakmore Beckett, *Guide Book of the Atlantic and Saint Lawrence Rail Roads* (Portland: Sanborn and Carter, 1853), 2.

24. The publisher Daniel Appleton produced national tour guidebooks beginning in 1846. In the early years they had different titles and different authors, but they became standardized in the 1860s. Willis Pope Hazard, *American Guide Book* (New York: D. Appleton and Co., 1846), 190–92; T. Addison Richards, *Appleton's Illustrated Hand-book of American Travel* (New York: D. Appleton and Co., 1857), 9.

25. Harriet Martineau, *Retrospect of Western Travel* (London, 1838), 2:112, 115.

26. Excerpts from the diary of Joseph T. Buckingham, in Cameron, *Genesis*, 6–8.

27. Although these conventions were generally consistent over twenty years or so, there was a gradual shift in emphasis toward what is sometimes referred to as the "Christian sublime." A later visitor to the Notch, for example, compared it to a "vast cradle" and was inspired by the thought of "what a mighty power . . . upheaved these 'everlasting hills'!" Diary of Caroline Barrett White, vol. 5, 8 September 1854, American Antiquarian Society manuscript collection.

28. There is an extensive literature on the aesthetic of the sublime, beginning with Edmund Burke's *A Philosophical Enquiry into the Origin of Our Ideas of the Sublime and Beautiful.* Paul Shepard's *Man in the Landscape: A Historic View of the Esthetics of Nature* (New York: Knopf, 1967) gives a historical analysis of changing attitudes toward landscape, as does Ronald Rees, "The Scenery Cult: Changing Landscape Tastes over Three Centuries," *Landscape* 19 (May 1975). Elizabeth McKinsey's *Niagara Falls: Icon of the American Sublime* (Cambridge, England: Cambridge University Press, 1985) provides an interesting analysis of the category of the sublime as it was applied to the greatest of all American prototypes.

29. Alan R. Booth, ed., "Francis Silsbee's August Odyssey, 1831," *Essex Institute Historical Collections* 100, no. 1 (January 1964): 62.

30. Mary A. Hale, "A Trip to the White Mountains in 1840," *Essex Institute Historical Collections* 83, no. 1 (January 1947): 28.

31. Booth, "Francis Silsbee," 63.

32. Bryant F. Tolles, Jr., ed., "Journal of a Tour to the White Hills: An 1842

Chronicle by Samuel Johnson," *Essex Institute Historical Collections* 120, no. 1 (January 1984): 30.

33. Caroline Barrett's prose may have been a little overdone by contemporary standards. By 1849 her rapturous expressions and reliance on Byron were perhaps a little dated—not surprisingly for a young woman from a small northern New England town. Diary of Caroline Barrett (White), vol. 1, June and October 1849.

34. It went on: "'My feeling I cannot express. I gasped, yet hardly dared to breathe, as I viewed for the first time the monarch of the mountains.'" This from one of his most unfeeling and hardhearted characters in a withering indictment of Victorian culture. Samuel Butler, *The Way of All Flesh* (London: Penguin Books, 1987), 45.

35. George Byron, *Don Juan*, Canto V, verse 52, ed. T. G. Steffan, E. Steffan, and W. W. Pratt (London: Penguin Classics Edition, 1986), 232. *Don Juan* lampooned not only the scenic sensibility, but also romantic heroism, faithful love, and religious piety—everything sacred to early nineteenth-century readers. In all likelihood, a young woman like Caroline Barrett, who committed page after page of "Childe Harold" to memory, would have been prevented from ever encountering a copy of the incendiary *Don Juan*.

36. Allan Nevins and Milton Halsey Thomas, eds., *Diary of George Templeton Strong* (New York: McMillan, 1952), 1:212–13, 18 September 1843.

37. Diary of Caroline Barrett (White), vol. 1, 1 September 1849.

38. William L. Stone, "A Trip from New York to Niagara in 1829: The Unpublished Diary of Colonel William L. Stone," *Magazine of American History* 20:321. This is a quotation from a poem by Fitz-Greene Halleck that satirizes the responses of tourists to Niagara Falls.

39. Hawthorne, "Sketches of Scenery," 342.

40. Hawthorne, "My Visit to Niagara," 246–49.

41. Raymond Williams has argued that in England, the taste for romantic scenery originally grew out of an overall increase in consumption among eighteenth-century gentry landowners. It rested, as he argued, on a separation of "productive" land—now intensively managed to generate profit—from land that was to be "consumed"—now designated "landscape" (a word that had formerly applied only to paintings). Landscape could be "consumed" either in the form of the newly shaped ("landscaped") parks of gentry estates, or in the form of tourists' landscapes in wild or remote regions. In its earliest form, the cult of scenery was thus entwined with the changing consumption styles of the English aristocracy. Raymond Williams, *The Country and the City* (New York: Oxford University Press, 1973), 121, 128.

42. Nathaniel P. Willis, "Pedlar Karl," in *Dashes at Life with a Free Pencil*, part 2: "Inklings of Adventure," reprinted from the 1845 edition in The American Short Story Series (New York: Garret Press, 1968), 30:5 (original pagination).

43. This was before Willis discovered there was a market in writing about American scenery, after which he began to find many redeeming features in the "unmeaning" landscape. See, for example, the introduction to *American Scenery*, in which Willis carves out a very clever middle ground between the

usual criticisms of American scenery and an emerging new line of praise for it. Nathaniel P. Willis, *American Scenery, or Land, Lake, and River: Illustrations of Transatlantic Nature* (London: George Virtue, 1840), esp. 1–2.

44. Una Pope-Hennessy, ed., *The Aristocratic Journey: Being the Outspoken Letters of Mrs. Basil Hall Written during a Fourteen Month's Sojourn in America, 1827–1828* (New York: Putnam, 1931), 69.

45. Basil Hall, *Travels in North America in the Years 1827–1828* (Edinburgh: Cadell, 1830), 1:123–25; 2:3.

46. Quoted in Rees, "The Scenery Cult," 42.

47. Allan Wallach has argued that these wealthy patrons of Thomas Cole shared a perception that the old aristocratic power had been defeated in politics and business and that their only remaining influence was in the realm of culture. By the 1830s, they (and Cole with them) had placed their faith in the Whig party, in the hope of creating a new gentry. Allan Wallach, "Thomas Cole and the Aristocracy," *Arts Magazine* 56 (November 1981): 94–106.

48. Thomas Cole, "Lecture on American Scenery," *Northern Light* 1 (1841): 25–26. Thomas Cole himself appears to have hoped that scenery and art would do something far more radical than simply train a new gentry. As Allan Wallach argues, his opposition to the vulgar rich was part of his larger opposition to the entire industrial capitalist order. See previous note.

49. Kenneth Myers has argued that the scenic sensibility was inextricably linked with the attitude of a new *business* class: "Just as an aesthetic judgment necessitates the objectification of a part of the natural world as an attractive or ugly *view* or *landscape*, so a business decision requires the objectification of natural goods as marketable commodities." Myers, *The Catskills*, 19.

50. Peter Bulkley, "Identifying the White Mountain Tourist: Origin, Occupation, and Wealth as a Definition of the Early Hotel Trade, 1853–1854," *Historic New Hampshire* 35, no. 2 (1980): 107–59.

51. Thomas Starr King, *The White Hills: Their Legends, Landscape, and Poetry* (Boston: Crosby, Nichols and Co., 1860), vii.

52. Ibid., 72.

53. Ibid., 58.

54. In this regard, scenic tastes followed the pattern explored by Karen Halttunen in her study of advice literature from the same period, *Confidence Men and Painted Women*. Halttunen argues that this literature required of those who wished to be considered genteel both a completely "transparent" heartfelt sincerity and an adherence to a rigorous and complex etiquette to fit every occasion. This contradiction, Halttunen argues, was at the root of the sentimental culture of the 1840s—and I would add, at the heart of the cult of scenery, which was an important part of that culture. Karen Halttunen, *Confidence Men and Painted Women: A Study of Middle-Class Culture in America, 1830–1870* (New Haven, Conn.: Yale University Press, 1982).

55. Samuel C. Eastman, *The White Mountain Guide Book* 3d ed. (Concord, N.H.: Edson C. Eastman, 1863), 271.

56. It differed in one important sense: It was only part of a much longer and

less routine journey the Whites made in the hope of restoring Frank's health. The whole journey included other forays into the White Mountain region, a long stay in nearby Fryeburg, Maine, and a tour through Vermont. Diary of Caroline Barrett White, vol. 5, August to October 1854.

57. In fact, two mountain peaks in the White Mountains were named after Indian leaders not even remotely connected with the region: Mount Tecumseh and Mount Osceola, both apparently named sometime during the 1850s, referred respectively to Indian leaders from the Ohio River Valley and from Florida. Robert and Mary Hixon, *The Place Names of the White Mountains* (Camden, Maine: Down East Books, 1980), 128, 165–66.

58. Ibid., 19.

59. Tolles, "Journal of a Tour," 27.

60. King, *The White Hills*, 28.

61. Hixon, *Place Names*, 174, gives the literal interpretation; and Benjamin Willey gives the romantic interpretation in *Incidents in White Mountain History* (Boston: Nathaniel Noyes, 1856), 14.

62. Henry David Thoreau, "Cape Cod," in *Henry David Thoreau* (New York: Library of America, 1985), 851.

63. Thoreau's "associations" never quite fit the pattern, though. He used too many obscure classical references. See, for example, his extended quotation from Virgil (in Latin) in relation to a hike up Mount Wachusett, published as "A Walk to Wachusett" in *The Boston Miscellany* in 1843. William Howarth, ed., *Thoreau in the Mountains* (New York: Farrar, Strauss, Giroux, 1982), 28–36.

64. His experiences on Mount Katahdin or on Cape Cod cannot be categorized simply as encounters with the sublime. In fact, they are a direct repudiation of the language of the sublime, since he described nature as having *no human meaning:* the sublime in nature, though frightening in its power and "otherness," was understood to be filled with significance, even messages, for its human viewers. Thoreau, "Ktaadn," 645; "Cape Cod," 979.

65. *The White Mountain and Winnipisiogee Lake Guide Book* (Boston: Jordan and Wiley, 1846), 26.

66. William Oakes, *Scenery of the White Mountains* (Boston: 1848), plate 3, n.p.

67. Peter Bicknell, ed., *The Illustrated Wordsworth's Guide to the Lakes* (Exeter, England: Webb and Bower, 1984), 110–11.

68. Willey, *Incidents*, 306.

69. King, *White Hills*, 222.

70. Ibid., 220.

71. John Spaulding, *Historical Relics of the White Mountains* (Boston: Nathaniel Noyes, 1855), 16–17.

72. Moses F. Sweetser, *Here and There in New England and Canada: Among the Mountains* (Boston: Boston and Maine Railroad, 1889), 20.

73. John Anderson, *The Book of the White Mountains* (New York: Minton, Balch, & Co., 1930), 56.

74. Kilbourne, *Chronicles*, 103.

75. Theodore Dwight, *The Northern Traveller*, 340.

76. She reported that she had seen the Profile in the Crawford Notch. Martineau, *Retrospect*, 2:112.
77. Oakes, *Scenery of the White Mountains*, plate 10, n.p.
78. King, *White Hills*, 112.
79. Willey, *Incidents*, 36.
80. Eastman, *White Mountain Guide Book*, 81.
81. F. Allen Burt, *The Story of Mount Washington* (Hanover, N.H.: Dartmouth Publications, 1960), 237.
82. Diary of Caroline Barrett White, vol. 5, 9 September 1854.
83. Eastman, *White Mountain Guide Book*, 106.
84. King, *White Hills*, 351.
85. Eastman, *White Mountain Guide Book*, 79.
86. David Strauss, "Toward a Consumer Culture: 'Adirondack Murray' and the Wilderness Vacation," *American Quarterly* 39, no. 2 (Summer 1987): 270–83.
87. Thoreau, "Cape Cod," 1,039.

Chapter 3: Cottage Heaven

1. Samuel Devens, *Sketches of Martha's Vineyard and Other Reminiscences of Travel at Home, by an Inexperienced Clergyman* (Boston: J. Munroe and Co., 1838).
2. The architectural history of Wesleyan Grove is a fascinating story in its own right. For a detailed and imaginative exploration of that history and its meaning, see Ellen Weiss, *City in the Woods* (New York: Oxford University Press, 1987).
3. Hebron Vincent, *History of the Camp-Meeting and Grounds at Wesleyan Grove, Martha's Vineyard (for the eleven years ending with the meeting of 1869)* (Boston: Lee and Shepard, 1870), 23–27.
4. *Providence Journal*, 8 August 1864.
5. *Christian Advocate*, 1865, quoted in Henry Beetle Hough, *Martha's Vineyard, Summer Resort after 100 Years* (Rutland, Vt.: Tuttle Publishing Co., 1936), 52.
6. *Vineyard Gazette*, 31 August 1866.
7. *New York Times*, 31 August 1866.
8. *Vineyard Gazette*, 27 August 1869.
9. Bayard Taylor, "Travel in the United States," *Atlantic Monthly* 19, (April 1867), 477.
10. *Providence Journal*, 9 August 1865, 1
11. Thomas Starr King, *The White Hills: Their Legends, Landscape, and Poetry* (Boston: Crosby, Nichols and Co., 1860), 72.
12. Daniel Rodgers attributes to Beecher a key role in the creation of such new attitudes toward work and leisure and explores the relationship of these ideas to the transformation of the middle class from a "producer's ethic" to a "consumer's ethic," in *The Work Ethic in Industrial America, 1850–1920* (Chicago: University of Chicago Press, 1974), esp. chapter 3.

13. Henry Ward Beecher, "The Mountain Farm to the Sea-Side Farm," *Eyes and Ears* (Boston: Ticknor & Fields, 1862), 53.

14. In a similar controversy over recreation—the question of novel-reading—Nina Baym found, out of twenty-one mid-century magazines, only one that completely rejected novel-reading: It was the "leading Methodist journal," Cincinnati's *Ladies' Repository*. They capitulated in 1859, around the same time that Methodists began to consider the possibility of summer vacations as well. Nina Baym, *Novels, Readers, and Reviewers: Responses to Fiction in Antebellum America* (Ithaca, N.Y.: Cornell University Press, 1984), introduction and chapter 1.

15. Vincent, 128–29.

16. Reverend B. W. Gorham, *Camp-Meeting Manual, a Practical Book for the Camp Ground* (Boston: H. V. Degen, 1854), 45, 49.

17. The annual income of most industrial workers in the 1860s was calculated by Daniel Horowitz to be between $250 and $400. Daniel Horowitz, *The Morality of Spending* (Baltimore: Johns Hopkins University Press, 1985), 10.

18. The names of these cottage owners are taken from several sources, but primarily from the records of the Martha's Vineyard Camp Meeting Association's applications to put each surviving cottage on the National Register of Historic Places; these reported the first owner of the cottage where it is known. (Copies were consulted at the Dukes County Historical Society.) I have taken from these records the list of all the first cottage owners, with construction dates ranging from 1862 to 1872, for six neighborhoods in Wesleyan Grove. I have also added the names of cottage owners from other sources—newspaper articles that listed the names of contributors to funds, for example—which has probably skewed the results slightly upward in class.

19. These include seven men listed as "merchants," two with no occupation listed (who appeared to be wealthy), and four with "professional" titles (a senator, an engineer, an editor, and an architect). There were also six ministers, which among the Methodists was no indication either of elite training or of substantial leisure.

20. Stuart Blumin, *The Emergence of the Middle Class: Social Experience in the American City, 1760–1900* (Cambridge, England: Cambridge University Press, 1990), 74–76. Blumin says that directory designations in the mid–nineteenth century were inconsistent because of a confusion resulting from the emergence of new kinds of middle-class occupations out of more traditional trades—the mirror image of the process of "proletarianization." This was especially true for Wesleyan Grove's most common occupations. Blumin estimates that perhaps fifteen percent of those listed as artisans in directories were really businessmen and perhaps factory owners (p. 71). Blumin points out, too, that many white-collar jobs—clerks, bookkeepers, and so on—were also newly created during these years, and of indeterminate status.

21. Information from city directories for New Bedford, 1856, 1865, 1869–70, 1875–76.

22. Moses Scudder, *American Methodism* (Hartford: S. S. Scranton, 1867), 569.

23. Donald B. Marti, "Rich Methodists: The Rise and Consequences of Lay

Philanthropy in the Mid-Nineteenth Century," in Russell E. Richey and Kenneth E. Rowe, eds., *Rethinking Methodist History: A Bicentennial Historical Consultation* (Nashville: Kingswood Books, 1985), 161.

24. These cottage-owning clergy showed up in their home city of New Bedford. The Reverand James D. Butler was listed in the 1856 directory as a "mariner," and later as the clergyman of the Seaman's Bethel Methodist church; Abraham P. Robinson was listed in 1856 as a dealer in "fruit, etc.," in 1865 as a "laborer," in 1869 as the Reverend Abraham P. Robinson; the Rev. George W. Stearns was the pastor of the Elm Street Methodist church in New Bedford, and also advertised himself as "physician," "surgeon," and "homeopathic physician."

25. Hebron Vincent, unpublished autobiographical sketch, manuscript application for membership in the New England Methodist Historical Society. Dukes County Historical Society.

26. David Clark, *The Way Reverend Moses Scudder Secured a Cottage at Martha's Vineyard* (Hartford, 1870), 9.

27. Newport was a foil for many new vacation places and vacationing styles in the second half of the nineteenth century. Henry Ward Beecher, for example, contrasted the "artificiality" and haste of a Newport vacation with the privacy and quiet of his vacations in the Berkshires. Henry Ward Beecher, "Inland v. Seashore," *Star Papers* (New York: J. C. Derby, 1855), 111.

28. John S. Gilkeson, *Middle Class Providence, 1820–1940* (Princeton: Princeton University Press, 1986), chapter 2.

29. *Harper's New Monthly Magazine* 5 (July 1852): 267.

30. In 1868, for example, roughly four thousand people "stopped permanently" for the summer, with as many as ten thousand to fifteen thousand there for a week or two of camp meeting. During that year there were about 600 tents and cottages on the grounds (and also, of course, a number of boardinghouses and small hotels). See Vincent, *History*, 189, 210–11.

31. Weiss, *City in the Woods*, 58–59.

32. James Jackson Jarves, "A New Phase of Druidism," *The Galaxy* 11 (December 1870): 781.

33. Charles Dudley Warner, "Their Pilgrimage," *Harper's New Monthly Magazine* 73 (July 1886): 174.

34. Jarves, "A New Phase," 780.

35. *New York Times*, 31 August 1866.

36. Karen Halttunen has suggested that middle-class Victorian houses were segregated into "back-regions," where all preparations for self-presentation were made, and public space, where the "genteel performance" took place. Wesleyan Grove seems to have presented the illusion that these separations had been done away with—that there was no "performance" going on, and no preparation necessary. Karen Halttunen, *Confidence Men and Painted Women: A Study of Middle-Class Culture in America, 1830–1870* (New Haven, Conn.: Yale University Press, 1982), 92–123.

37. Richard Luce Pease, *A Guide to Martha's Vineyard and Nantucket* (Boston: Rockwell and Churchill, 1876), 35.

38. British historians have made this point particularly clear in regard to

the development of English seaside resorts in the early and mid–nineteenth century. See especially J. K. Walton, *The English Seaside Resort: A Social History* (New York: St. Martin's Press, 1983), 43; and J. A. R. Pimlott, *The Englishman's Holiday: A Social History* (Sussex, England: Harvester Press, 1976), 121.

39. Jarves, "A New Phase," 779.

40. *New York Times*, 31 August 1866.

41. On inexpensive ways to make the home beautiful, see, for example, Harriet Beecher Stowe, "House and Home Papers," *Household Papers and Stories* (Boston: Houghton, Mifflin & Co., 1896), 54–68; or Catharine E. Beecher, *The American Woman's Home* (Hartford: The Stowe-Day Foundation, 1985), 84–103.

42. Vincent, *History*, 182.

43. *Camp Meeting Herald* 3, no. 1 (21 August 1866).

44. *Vineyard Gazette*, 27 August 1869.

45. Vincent, *History*, 182.

46. A wealthy merchant, William Hathaway, Jr., first moved to the edge of town to an address near the new "rural cemetery." Then, in 1875, he was no longer in New Bedford; the 1876 Vineyard Grove directory listed him as a resident of North Dighton.

47. Ellen Weiss interprets Wesleyan Grove as a prototype for "that pervasive American residential habit, the suburb." Weiss, *City in the Woods*, xiii–xiv.

48. *Providence Journal*, 20 August 1868.

49. *New York Times*, 20 August 1867, 2.

50. Vincent, *History*, 133–34.

51. Clark, 15.

52. Ibid., 14.

53. Vincent, *History*, 170.

54. *Vineyard Gazette*, 31 August 1866.

55. Advertisement in *Providence Journal*, 22 August 1867.

56. It was also, of course, a way of saying that it *was* Newport. Weiss, *City in the Woods*, 96–98.

57. *The Cottage City, or The Season at Martha's Vineyard* (Lawrence, Mass.: S. Merrill and Crocker, 1879), 33.

58. Jarves, "A New Phase," 779.

59. Dukes County Land Grants Records, Baker, vol. 53, nos. 37, 39, and 41; and vol. 50, nos. 41 and 42. Land Grants Records, Scudder, vol. 47, no. 2.

60. Marti, *Rich Methodists*, 159–64.

61. Vincent, *History*, 225.

62. Warner, "Their Pilgrimage," 170.

63. Old Colony Railroad, *The Old Colony: or Pilgrim Land, Past and Present* (Boston, 1887), 29.

64. That vacation community, and Howells's experiences as a vacationer, are the subject of Chapter 6. William Dean Howells, "Confessions of a Summer Colonist," *Atlantic Monthly* 81 (December 1898): 44.

65. Ibid., 52–53.

66. Warner, "Their Pilgrimage," 173.

67. Ibid., 172.

Chapter 4: "Manufactured for the Trade"

1. Jane G. Austin, *Nantucket Scraps* (Boston: Houghton Mifflin & Co., 1893), 9, 13.

2. Ibid., 13.

3. Michael Kammen locates a major turning point in American enthusiasm for tradition in the 1870s. Before that transformation, he found only sporadic interest in the past, primarily in the form of interest in the "founding fathers" and founding events of the Republic. Michael Kammen, *Mystic Chords of Memory: The Transformation of Tradition in American Culture* (New York: Knopf, 1991).

4. T. J. Jackson Lears brings together many of these cultural trends in one analytical framework as the "antimodernist" impulse, the manifestation of a cultural crisis among old Yankee elites confronting modern industrialized society. T. J. Jackson Lears, *No Place of Grace: Antimodernism and the Transformation of American Culture, 1880–1920* (New York: Pantheon Books, 1981).

5. This use of region as preserver of the past played a key role in the South as well. Almost as soon as the Civil War ended, a nostalgic literature emerged to celebrate the virtue, heroism, and purity of the antebellum slaveholders' culture. See, for example, the discussion of the work of Thomas Nelson Page in Chapter 6.

6. Moses F. Sweetser, *Here and There in New England and Canada: Among the Mountains* (Boston: Boston and Maine Railroad, 1889), 66.

7. See Edward Byers, *The Nation of Nantucket: Society and Politics in an Early American Commercial Center, 1660–1820* (Boston: Northeastern University Press, 1987). Byers stresses the freewheeling aspects of Nantucket's social and economic life—its highly developed mercantile capitalism, weak communal ties, and religious tolerance—in contrast with notions of colonial New England's village homogeneity.

8. Herman Melville, *Moby Dick* (Evanston, Ill.: Northwestern University Press, 1988), 64.

9. Edwin P. Hoyt, *Nantucket: The Life of an Island* (Brattleboro, Vt.: The Stephen Greene Press, 1978), 136. Harry B. Turner, *Argument Settlers* (Nantucket, Mass.: Inquirer and Mirror Press, 1917), 31.

10. William F. Macy, *The Story of Old Nantucket*, 2d ed. (Boston: Houghton Mifflin & Co., 1928), 142. This 1915 account by the president of the Nantucket Historical Association is typical in its attention to the whaling industry and its lack of interest in what followed (after all, it is the story of "old Nantucket").

11. *Nantucket Inquirer and Mirror*, 31 March 1866.

12. Edward K. Godfrey, *The Island of Nantucket, What It Was and What It Is* (Boston: Lee and Shepard, 1882), 269.

13. *Nantucket Inquirer and Mirror*, 30 September 1865.

14. Ibid.

15. Ibid., 24 February 1866.

16. Will Gardner, *The Coffin Saga* (Nantucket: Whaling Museum Publications, 1949), 194–98.

17. Byers, *The Nation of Nantucket*, 273–74.

18. Clay Lancaster, *The Far-Out Island Railroad* (Nantucket, Mass.: Pleasant Publications, 1972), 1–7.

19. This information comes from the Nantucket Registry of Deeds for these years. The *Nantucket Inquirer* reported that the Surfside Land Company had sold more than three hundred lots by November 1882. The only way that this number can be squared with the Registry of Deeds information is if one includes a June 1882 sale of most of the company's land to the *trustees* of the company for $120,000, in a transaction that was apparently designed to put up front money for the company, and to empower the trustees to sell bonds to recoup their losses—obviously not a sale of cottage lots at all.

20. Sherburne Bluffs papers, Peter Foulger Museum and Library of Nantucket Historical Association; Hoyt, *Nantucket*, 136.

21. Henry Beetle Hough, *Martha's Vineyard, Summer Resort after 100 Years* (Rutland, Vt.: Tuttle Publishing Co., 1936), 165–67.

22. *Nantucket Journal*, 13 August 1879, quoted in Lancaster, *Far-Out Island Railroad*, 4.

23. *Nantucket Inquirer and Mirror*, 22 August 1868.

24. *Providence Journal*, 30 July 1881.

25. Register of Sherburne Hotel, 1879–1881, Peter Foulger Museum and Library of Nantucket Historical Association.

26. Homer Socolofsky, ed., "The Private Journals of Florence Crawford and Arthur Cappen, 1891–1892," *Kansas Historical Quarterly* 30 (1964): 41, 44.

27. A. Judd Northrup, *'Sconset Cottage Life: A Summer on Nantucket Island* (New York: Baker, Pratt and Co., 1881), 147–48.

28. Socolofsky, "Private Journals," 41.

29. Edward Bellamy, *Six to One: A Nantucket Idyl* (New York: G. P. Putnam's Sons, 1878), 11–12.

30. D. H. Strother, "A Summer in New England," *Harper's New Monthly Magazine* 21 (November 1860), 745–46.

31. Samuel Adams Drake, *Nooks and Corners of the New England Coast* (New York: Harper Brothers, 1876), 336.

32. Charles Sweetser, *Book of Summer Resorts* (New York: J. R. Osgood, 1868), 69.

33. Old Colony Railroad, *The Old Colony: or Pilgrim Land, Past and Present* (Boston, 1887), 66–67.

34. Byers, *The Nation of Nantucket*, 93–101, 159–70.

35. In the White Mountains, for example, a similar notion was expressed in the anecdote of the Old Man of the Mountains, which God had supposedly erected as a sign to show that "in New Hampshire, he made men." The Connecticut Building at the Chicago Exposition had the same sentiment carved on its facade: "Connecticut's best crops are her sons and daughters."

36. "Nantucket," *Scribner's Monthly Magazine* 6, no. 4 (August 1873): 385–99.

37. *Scribner's* and the guidebooks were using a reproduction of an oil painting by Hermione Dassel, which was probably intended to express the pathos

of being the "last" Indian. The guidebooks, of course, presented the "last Indian" as a tourist attraction.

38. In fact, both Billy Clark and Fred Parker, the "Hermit of Quidnet," are featured in the latest edition of the current *Guide to Nantucket!* Polly Burroughs, *Guide to Nantucket, 4th ed.* (Chester, Conn.: The Globe Pequot Press, 1988), 20–21, 123.

39. For an account of the transformation of visual images of Nantucket, see Robert A. di Curcio, *Art on Nantucket* (Nantucket, Mass.: Nantucket Historical Association, 1982). On Eastman Johnson, see Patricia Hills, *Eastman Johnson* (New York: Clarkson N. Potter, Inc., 1972), esp. 87–101.

40. Godfrey, *The Island of Nantucket*, 7–8.

41. Ibid., 6.

42. Ibid., 72.

43. Drake, *Nooks and Corners*, 326.

44. Frank Sheldon, "Nantucket," *Atlantic Monthly* 17 (March 1866): 300.

45. Ibid.

46. Ibid., 301.

47. *Nantucket Inquirer and Mirror*, 31 March 1866.

48. Macy, *The Story of Old Nantucket*, 144–45.

49. Bellamy, *Six to One*, 39.

50. Austin, *Nantucket Scraps*, 53.

51. Northrup, *'Sconset Cottage Life*, 69.

52. Drake, *Nooks and Corners*, 331.

53. Strother, "A Summer in New England," 745.

54. *The Old Colony*, 66.

55. Ibid.

56. *Nantucket Inquirer and Mirror*, 15 September 1877.

57. Ibid.

58. Isaac H. Folger, *Handbook of Nantucket* (Nantucket, Mass.: Island Review, 1874), 10–12.

59. *Nantucket Inquirer and Mirror*, 27 August 1881, 1 July 1876.

60. Ibid., 1 July 1876.

61. Bellamy, *Six to One*, 39.

62. *Nantucket Inquirer and Mirror*, 21 July 1877.

63. Godfrey, *The Island of Nantucket*, 57.

64. Printed sources reported that five hundred people were in evidence at the reunion, so it is possible that local guests did not sign the register.

65. The Coffin reunion was reported on at length in many newspapers; the *Nantucket Inquirer and Mirror* printed a supplement called the *Daily Memorial* to commemorate the event on 17 August 1881. (Even though so much detail was reported, however, they did not manage to convey that it rained heavily for the entire three-day period, as Jane Austin later reported in her book *Nantucket Scraps.*)

66. *Daily Memorial*, 17 August 1881 (supplement for *Nantucket Inquirer and Mirror*).

67. Henry S. Wyer, "Ye Second Coffyn Reunion," flyer, Coffin Reunion col-

lection, Peter Foulger Museum and Library of Nantucket Historical Association.

68. This story is told in a centennial edition of the *Inquirer and Mirror, One Hundred Years on Nantucket, 1821–1921,* a supplement printed on 23 June 1921, in an article called "Facts about . . . the Veranda House," by Henry B. Worth, Peter Foulger Museum and Nantucket Historical Association Library. In Chapter 5, I explore the relationship between boardinghouse keepers and their visitors in another context.

69. Austin, *Nantucket Scraps,* 213. This was Jane Austin, a writer who achieved minor renown with a series of "colonial revival" novels based on the history of the Plymouth Bay Colony. Her attitude toward Nantucket's racial heritage fits well with attitudes of other "colonial revival" summer people who are discussed in Chapter 6.

70. Macy, *The Story of Old Nantucket,* 146.

71. Drake, *Nooks and Corners,* 330.

72. It was not until 1923, when the Nantucket Historical Association took over the ownership of the house, that it was restored to a seventeenth-century style.

73. This is a paradox explored at length by David Lowenthal *The Past is a Foreign Country* (Cambridge, England: Cambridge University Press, 1985). See especially page xxiv: "Manipulation makes the past both more and less like the present—less because we set it apart, more because we put our own stamp on it."

74. William Root Bliss, *Quaint Nantucket* (Boston: Houghton, Mifflin & Co., 1896), v–vi.

75. William Butler, "Another City Upon a Hill: Litchfield, Connecticut, and the Colonial Revival," in Alan Axelrod, ed., *The Colonial Revival in America* (New York: W. W. Norton and Co., 1985).

76. David C. Bryan, "The Past as a Place to Visit: Reinventing the Colonial in Deerfield, Massachusetts" (Senior honors thesis, Amherst College, 1989).

77. Everett U. Crosby, *95% Perfect* (Nantucket: Inquirer and Mirror Press, 1937).

78. The contrast is especially clear if one compares the people who inhabited the imaginary Nantucket with the people who inhabited the imaginary Deerfield. In Deerfield those who did most to create its new image romanticized themselves and their own families; it was C. Alice Baker's friends who were dressed in "colonial" garb and photographed in ancient doorways. In Nantucket, picturesque figures like Billy Clark, the town crier, were photographed by outsiders for their own purposes. For contrasting visual images from Deerfield, see Susan Mahnke, ed., *Looking Back: Images of New England, 1860–1930* (Dublin: Yankee Books, 1982).

Chapter 5: That Dream of Home

1. Hal Barron, *Those Who Stayed behind: Rural Society in Nineteenth Century New England* (Cambridge, England: Cambridge University Press, 1984), 69–74.

2. Ibid., 59–64. Barron points out that the shift to dairying required more labor than was available to most northern farmers.

3. Harold Fisher Wilson wrote an economic history of the region in *The Hill Country of Northern New England: Its Social and Economic History, 1790–1930* (New York: Columbia University Press, 1936). He shared the contemporary perspective on the decline of the region. For a revision of this view and a review of the data, see Barron, *Those Who Stayed Behind*, a study of the town of Chelsea, Vermont, and a general revision of the decline framework.

4. Census information, as arranged in Wilson, 102–108.

5. Barron, *Those Who Stayed*, 11–15.

6. In other regions a similar sense of crisis fueled the Populist movements during these same years.

7. Charles R. Corning, "Governor Rollins," *The Granite Monthly* 27, no. 3 (September 1899): 126.

8. The census takers of the 1890 census were aware of the difficulties of defining "rural" and "urban" in New England; they used a special regional cut-off figure of only 2,500 to define "urban."

9. Dwight had been disposed to hope that time would improve the northern settlements, diminish the influence of dissolute lumbermen and sailors, increase the number of sober and hard-working farmers, and disseminate religion and education in the north—little of which he saw in his turn-of-the-century travels. On Maine's social problems, for example, see Timothy Dwight, *Travels in New-England and New-York*, ed. Barbara Miller Solomon (Cambridge, Mass.: Belknap Press of Harvard University Press, 1969) 2:161–63.

10. New Hampshire Old Home Week Association, *Annual Report of Old Home Week in New Hampshire* (Manchester, Vt.: Arthur E. Clarke, 1900), 9.

11. William H. Burnham, "Old Home Week In New Hampshire," *New England Magazine* 22 (August 1900): 649.

12. John Anderson, *The Book of the White Mountains* (New York: Minton, Balch, & Co., 1930), 680.

13. New Hampshire Old Home Week Association, 73.

14. Ibid., 10.

15. That would be just under a third of all towns in each state. For Vermont, "The First Observance of Old Home Week," *The Vermonter* 7, no. 2 (September 1901): 1; for New Hampshire, Burnham, "Old Home Week in New Hampshire," 647.

16. New Hampshire Old Home Week Association, 94.

17. "Vermont Old Home Week," *The Vermonter* 6, no. 10 (May 1901): 166–67.

18. New Hampshire's Board of Agriculture, and to a lesser degree Maine's Board of Agriculture, undertook almost exactly the same work, but in both those states, a variety of other forms of tourism already existed, and indeed dominated the landscape—scenic mountain resorts, coastal resorts, wilderness camping. That makes Vermont's industry a better case study for the purposes of this chapter.

19. Victor I. Spear, "Farm Management," *Vermont State Board of Agriculture Report, 1892–1893* (Montpelier, Vt.: 1893), 56–57.

20. Arthur H. Gleason, "What New Hampshire Can Do; Why It Should Abandon Its Plan of Attracting Summer Boarders," *Country Life in America* 9 (1905): 76–78. Gleason also pointed out that the interests of summer vacationers clashed with the interests of other industries, such as paper mills, which necessarily ruined the scenery the vacationers prized.

21. The state was extremely successful at creating and protecting its "brand name" status: Maple syrup producers in both Massachusetts and Quebec have been sued in recent years for labeling their syrup with the word *Vermont*—clear testimony that the state's name carries connotations of rural purity to a far greater extent than the names of other places.

22. C. T. Wiltshire, "The Summer Boarder As An Asset," *The New England Homestead* 64 (18 May 1912): 623.

23. John W. Titcomb, "The Fish and Game Supply of Vermont," *Vermont State Board of Agriculture Report, 1891–1892* (Burlington, Vt.: Free Press, 1892), 158.

24. New Hampshire and Vermont have characteristically been imagined as opposites of each other in one way or another: masculine crags versus feminine hills—or more recently as conservative "Live Free or Die" New Hampshire versus the progressive "People's Republic of Vermont." Vermont's landscape artists and earlier promoters had attempted to bring in a share of the scenic tourist trade that had come to New Hampshire in mid-century. But their efforts to portray the Green Mountains as craggy, picturesque, and awe-inspiring—like the White Mountains, in short—were largely unsuccessful. See William C. Lipke and Philip N. Grime, eds., *Vermont Landscape Images, 1775–1976* (Burlington, Vt.: Robert Hall Fleming Museum, 1976).

25. [Victor Spear], *Vermont, A Glimpse of Its Scenery and Industries* (Montpelier, Vt.: Argus and Patriot, 1893), 1, 5.

26. E. R. Towle, Esq., "How to Make Farm Life Pleasant," *Vermont State Board of Agriculture Report, 1872* (Montpelier, Vt.: 1872), 542. The sorts of reforms they had in mind were clearly designed to make farm families resemble the ideal urban middle-class Victorian family, centered in a powerful but benevolent father who protects his wife from overwork and provides gentle nurturing for his children.

27. Barron, *Those Who Stayed*, 31–36.

28. Thomas C. Hubka has noted the mixed conservatism and progressivism in the familiar attached-house-and-barn arrangement of many New England farms, which was designed as an improvement in efficiency that would make it possible to compete with western farmers, and also to continue a traditional mixed agricultural system. Thomas C. Hubka, *Big House, Little House, Back House, Barn: The Connected Farm Buildings of New England* (Hanover, N.H.: University Press of New England, 1984), 180.

29. Information on Victor Spear was gathered from these sources: Albert Nelson, ed., *Who's Who in New England* (1909), 872; Jacob Gullery, *Men of Vermont* (1894), n.p.; and Prentiss C. Dodge, *Encyclopedia of Vermont Biography* (1912), n.p.

30. Spear, "Farm Management," 55.

31. Ibid., 57.

32. Victor Spear, "Attractions of Vermont" (excerpts from *Resources and*

Attractions of Vermont) Vermont Board of Agriculture Report, 1891–1892 (Montpelier, Vt.: 1892), 102.

33. Clarence Deming, "Broken Shadows on the New England Farm," *The Independent* 55 (30 April 1903), 1,018–20; W. A. Giles, "Is New England Decadent?" *The World Today* 9 (September 1905), 991. For a bibliography of such articles, see Wilson, *The Hill Country of Northern New England*, 403–37.

34. Hal Barron contrasted these two perspectives in *Those Who Stayed*, 31.

35. This was written by Rollin Lynde Hartt about the town of Belchertown, Massachusetts, where he had apparently been robbed at a town fair. Rollin Lynde Hartt, "A New England Hill Town," *Atlantic Monthly* 83 (April 1899): 571–72.

36. In the next few decades, reformers in both the country life and the eugenics movements attempted to attack the problems of "degeneration" in rural New England through a variety of means ranging from consolidating rural churches to sterilizing rural "defectives." For an intriguing account of the Vermont eugenics crusade, see Kevin Dann, "From Degeneration to Regeneration: The Eugenics Survey of Vermont, 1925–1936," *Vermont History* 59, no. 1 (Winter 1991).

37. *New England Homestead* 35 (24 July 1897), 89. For a summary of farmers' responses to the rural-reform aspects of the Country Life movement, see chapter 7 of William L. Bowers, *The Country Life Movement in America, 1900–1920* (Port Washington, N.Y.: Kennikat Press, 1974), 102–27. Bowers finds widespread resentment of the assumptions of the movement and a general consensus that the farmer needed economic justice, not moral uplift.

38. See, for example, Stowe's *Oldtown Folks, The Minister's Wooing, The Pearl of Orr's Island,* or *Poganuc People*—all novels that display Stowe's gift for memorializing without trivializing the world she had lost (often idealized, but rarely sentimentalized).

39. Hartt, *A New England Hill Town*, 571–72.

40. New Hampshire Old Home Week Association, 72.

41. Herbert Wendell Gleason, "The Old Farm Revisited," *New England Magazine* 22 (August 1900): 678.

42. Edith Wharton, *Summer* (New York: D. Appleton & Co., 1917), 170, 173.

43. L. H. Carroll, "One State and the 'Summer People' Industry," *The World's Work* 4 (August 1902): 2,383.

44. In 1894, Victor Spear published a *Report on Summer Travel for 1894* (Montpelier, Vt.: Vermont State Board of Agriculture, 1894), in which he reported that 54,236 summer guests had been in Vermont. That total was based on a very rudimentary reporting system, and probably seriously underestimated the total. The Vermont Board of Agriculture's *Agricultural Report for 1896* reported sixty thousand visitors for the summer of 1895 (p. 110) Its *Agricultural Report for 1897* reported 36,502 visitors with only about half the usual hotels and summer boarding places responding (p. 195); 650 is the largest number of places which took advantage of the free advertising in the board's pamphlets, reported in the Vermont Board of Agriculture's *Report for 1895*, 171. Spear's opinion is recorded in his *Report on Summer Travel for 1894*, 7.

45. Kitty Kent, "Varied Menu for Boarders," *New England Homestead*, (11 August 1900): 139.

46. Wiltshire, "The Summer Boarder," 623.

47. Mrs. A. J. Gibbs, "A Talk with Farmers' Wives," *Vermont Board of Agriculture Report, 1889–90* (Montpelier, Vt.: 1890), 118.

48. Frank W. Rollins, "New Hampshire's Opportunity," *New England Magazine* 16 (July 1897), 539–40.

49. Wiltshire, "The Summer Boarder," 623.

50. Now, of course, New England "plain country fare" brings to mind the very doughnuts, pie, and baked beans rejected by these turn-of-the-century tourists.

51. Sarah Wood, "An Ideal Hostess," *American Agriculturist* 66, no. 2 (14 July 1900): 42.

52. William Dean Howells, letters to his father, in *Selected Letters of W. D. Howells* (Boston: Twayne Publishers, 1979), vol. 2, 18 June 1876 and 30 July 1876.

53. William Dean Howells, *The Vacation of the Kelwyns* (New York: Harper and Bros., 1920), 5, 32–33.

54. Alvan F. Sanborn, "The Future of Rural New England," *The Atlantic Monthly* 79 (1897): 79–80.

55. Wiltshire, 623.

56. Sally McMurry has described one element of this struggle in an article on rural rejections of conventional urban parlors. Sally McMurry, "City Parlor, Country Sitting Room: Rural Vernacular Design and the American Parlor, 1840–1900," reprinted from *Winterthur Portfolio* 20, no. 4 (Winter 1985): 273.

57. Howells, *Vacation*, 26.

58. Central Vermont Railroad, *Summer Homes among the Green Hills of Vermont* (St. Albans, Vt., 1894), 21.

59. Mrs. A. M. Lewis, "Pie a Standard Dessert," *New England Homestead* 43 (20 July 1901), 71.

60. Ibid.

61. Ibid.

62. George W. Perry, "The Summer Boarder Garden," in Fifteenth Report of Vermont State Horticultural Society, *Ninth Report of the Vermont Commissioner of Agriculture, 1916–1918* (St. Albans, Vt., 1918), 62.

63. Susan Warner, *Nobody* (New York: Carter and Brothers, 1882) 255–61.

64. Wood, "An Ideal Hostess," 42.

65. Evangeline [pseud.], "The Other Side," *New England Homestead* 41 (18 August 1900): 20.

66. Warner, *Nobody*, 248–58. Warner's testimony on rural household economy is probably far more reliable than that of many novelists of her generation: She lived a more or less hand-to-mouth rural existence for most of her life, and certainly knew the price of apples and winter clothing, as well as the consequences of a cash-poor existence.

67. Mary Gray, "A Charming Boarding Place," *New England Homestead* 41 (4 August 1900): 116.

68. "Aids to Guests' Comforts," *New England Homestead* 43 (12 July 1901): 44.

69. "First Class Boarders," *American Agriculturist* 66, no. 1 (7 July 1900): 18.

70. "To the Summer Boarder," *New England Homestead* 41 (25 August 1900): 186.

71. Howells, *Vacation*, 6.

72. Kent, "Varied Menu for Boarders," 139.

73. *Burlington Free Press*, 10 April 1930, 9, as quoted in Wilson, *The Hill Country of Northern New England*, 279.

Chapter 6: The Problem of the Summer

1. Howells, *Selected Letters of W. D. Howells* (Boston: Twayne Publishers, 1979), 1:330.

2. Ibid., 2:60–61.

3. Ibid., 1:328.

4. Ibid., 2:102.

5. Ibid., 2:130–133.

6. Ibid., 4:107.

7. Ibid., 110, 130–31.

8. Ibid., 244. This vacation at Annisquam actually came after the Howellses' first summers at York and Kittery, in 1902, but it seems to have confirmed the Howellses in their decision to stay up north.

9. Ibid., 178.

10. Ibid., 182.

11. Ibid., 211.

12. After his wife's death, Howells gave the Kittery Point house to his son and moved back to York. Ibid., 5:170–71.

13. William Dean Howells, "My Mark Twain," in *Literary Friends and Acquaintances* (New York: Harper Brothers, 1911), 394.

14. Howells, *Letters*, 4:213–14.

15. *The Wave*, 18 July 1888, 3.

16. Howells, *Letters*, 4:52–53.

17. William Dean Howells, "The Beach at Rockaway," in *Literature and Life* (1902; reprint, Port Washington, N.Y.: Kennikat Press, 1968), 161.

18. Sarah Orne Jewett wrote to Horace Scudder, for example, that York "reminds me of my dear Deephaven though that was 'made up' before I had ever stayed overnight in York or knew and loved it as I do now." Sarah Orne Jewett, *Letters* (Waterville, Maine: Colby College Press, 1967), 32.

19. Mildred Howells, ed., *Life in Letters of William Dean Howells* (Garden City, N.Y.: Doubleday, Doran and Co., 1928), 2:159.

20. Timothy Dwight, *Travels in New-England and New-York*, ed. Barbara Miller Solomon (Cambridge, Mass.: Belknap Press of Harvard University Press, 1969), 2:138–39.

21. Thomas Bailey Aldrich, *The Story of a Bad Boy* (New York: Houghton Mifflin & Co., 1923), 28.

22. Sarah Orne Jewett, "River Driftwood," in *Deephaven and Other Stories* (New Haven, Conn.: College and University Press, 1966), 183.

23. Ibid., 171.

24. *Biographical Review* (Boston: Biographical Review Publishing Co., 1896), 352–53.

25. E. D. Twombly, *The Old York Transcript*, 16 November 1899, 2.

26. Moses F. Sweetser, *Here and There in New England and Canada: Among the Mountains* (Boston: Boston and Maine Railroad, 1889), 192.

27. Ibid., 32.

28. [H. E. Evans], *York, Maine* (York, Maine: York Bureau of Information, 1896), front cover.

29. *Old York Transcript*, 27 July 1899, 2.

30. In the following section on the appeal of the "colonial" for the affluent visitors of the Piscataqua River towns, I have benefited from the work of many contributors to Sarah Giffen and Kevin Murphy, eds., *"A Noble and Dignified Stream": The Piscataqua Region in the Colonial Revival, 1860–1930* (York, Maine: Old York Historical Society, 1992). This was a project so closely collaborative and richly interdisciplinary that it is difficult for me to delineate any single contribution, including my own. Citations are listed hereafter as *ANDS*. For a social analysis of the "colonial revival" and its relation to the political and social controversies of the Gilded Age, see the essays collected in Alan Axelrod, ed., *The Colonial Revival in America* (New York: W. W. Norton and Co., 1985). Michael Kammen analyzes a variety of impulses toward the past in the period from 1870 to 1915 in *Mystic Chords of Memory: The Transformation of Tradition in American Culture* (New York: Knopf, 1991). Particularly relevant are his discussions of the colonial revival, ancestor worship, and historic preservation, in part 2, chapters 5 to 10.

31. That difference was apparent to some people even at the time. The editor of the *Old York Transcript* distinguished the "colonial" spirit of inquiry from a more generalized nostalgic interest in the past in 1899, when he wrote that it had been recognized for years that York was "historically wonderful," but until recently that fact had been passively "felt . . . in the atmosphere, and in a few tangible old landmarks," rather than enhanced by "concerted action in bringing relics to the light of modern days." *Old York Transcript*, 17 August 1899, 1.

32. Amy Wilkinson Hufnagel, "Emma Lewis Coleman (1853–1942), Photographer," *ANDS*, 152–54.

33. The best analysis of the transformation of such "summer colonials" is Richard Candee, "Restoring the Colonial Home," *ANDS*, 35–47.

34. *Old York Transcript*, 17 August 1899, 1.

35. This story was reported in the *Boston Sunday Herald* and in a variety of local newspapers and printed accounts. Kevin Murphy argues that the story was basically a legitimizing device for a project conceived and executed largely by women. See Kevin Murphy, "The Politics of Preservation: Historic House Museums in the Piscataqua Region," *ANDS*, 196.

36. Earle G. Shettleworth, Jr., "Lady Pepperrell House," *ANDS*, 55–57.

37. T. J. Jackson Lears, *No Place of Grace: Antimodernism and the Transformation of American Culture, 1880–1920* (New York: Pantheon Books, 1981).

38. Thomas Nelson Page, "Miss Godwin's Inheritance," in *The Novels, Stories, Sketches and Poems of Thomas Nelson Page* (New York: Charles Scribner's Sons, 1910).

39. Jewett, "River Driftwood," 173.

40. William Dean Howells, "Staccato Notes of a Vanished Summer," in *Literature and Life*, 258–59.

41. Ernest Ingersoll, *Down East Latch-Strings, or Sea Shore, Lakes and Mountains by the Boston and Maine Railroad* (Boston: Boston and Maine Railroad, 1887), 232–35.

42. Jewett, "River Driftwood," 179.

43. It is not stretching the category too far to say that some "summer people" no longer "summered" in the region at all. Thomas Bailey Aldrich and his family no longer maintained a presence in Portsmouth by the time the Howellses came to Kittery Point. When Aldrich's grandfather died in 1870, they had stopped using Portsmouth as their summer base. In 1893, the Aldriches built a summer house farther "down east" in Tenant's Harbor, Maine, leaving Aldrich's ancestral home in Portsmouth for more casual visiting. But for all that, Aldrich remained an important presence in the network: Aldrich's vision of the region loomed large in the imagination of scores of influential visitors, and his connections with key culture shapers remained equally close. Sarah Orne Jewett, for example, visited Tenant's Harbor often and wrote that "Dunnet Landing," the location of her finest stories, collected as *The Country of the Pointed Firs*, "must be somewhere 'along shore' between the region of Tenants Harbor and Boothbay." Jewett, *Letters*, 116.

44. As quoted in Jane C. Nylander, "Jacob Wendell House," *ANDS*, 24.

45. Aldrich's list here is not in the proper order because he had to make it scan; it probably ought to have read "Malayan, Scythian, Slav, Kelt, and Teuton"—but that would never have rhymed.

46. Thomas Bailey Aldrich, "Unguarded Gates," *The Writings of Thomas Bailey Aldrich: Poems* (Boston: Houghton Mifflin & Co., 1911), 2:71–72.

47. Albion W. Tourgée, "The South as a Field for Fiction," *The Forum* 6 (December 1888): 405.

48. *Agamenticus, Bristol, Gorgeana, York: An Oration by the Hon. James Phinney Baxter . . . on the 250th Anniversary of the Town of York, August 5, 1902* (York, Maine: Old York Historical and Improvement Society, 1904), 116, 117, 114, 115.

49. *Old York Transcript*, 8 June 1899.

50. Nantucket's enthusiasts sometimes described islanders in similar terms, contrasting the hardy, virile mariners of old with the "full-fledged lackeys" they feared would replace them. But for business reasons, promoters of Nantucket found it necessary to reconcile Yankee "character" with the "natural" hospitality they needed.

51. William Dean Howells, "Confessions of a Summer Colonist," *Atlantic Monthly* 81 (December 1898): 50.

52. Page's support for the Spanish-American War was clearly rooted in racial politics, as he made clear in his poem "The Dragon of the Seas," published in the *Washington Post* in 1898.

53. In stories like "A Little Captive Maid" (1891) and "Bold Words at the Bridge" (1899), she wrote about Irish people in terms similar to those she used to capture the spirit of native-born Maine locals; in "Mère Pochette" (1888) and "Little French Mary" (1895) she defended French-Canadian immigrants from local resentment.

54. From *Red Rock*, a novel intended to depict the horrors of Reconstruction, as quoted in Theodore L. Gross, *Thomas Nelson Page* (New York: Twayne Publishers, 1967), 79–80.

55. Jewett, *Deephaven*, 55.

56. Especially in "The Mistress of Sydenham Plantation" (1888) and "A War Debt" (1895), Jewett's plots seem almost indistinguishable from those of Page. Her clear motive—to present the possibility of a sensitive and cultured elite joining hands across sectional rivalries—mirrors Page's, too.

57. Page, "Miss Godwin's Inheritance," 5.

58. Ibid., 19.

59. Ibid., 33–34.

60. Kevin Murphy has argued that the colonial revival movement provided a unique opportunity to exercise skills and creative energy for the wealthy and influential women who pioneered in the creation of museums. See Murphy, "The Politics of Preservation," *ANDS*, 193–204.

61. Howells, "The Problem of the Summer," in *Literature and Life*, 220.

62. Ibid.

63. Ibid., 221.

Epilogue: Tourism in the Twentieth Century

1. Henry David Thoreau, *Cape Cod* (Cambridge, Mass.: Riverside Press, 1894), 224, 35, 75, 330.

2. [Anna Warner], *The Little Nurse of Cape Cod* (Philadelphia: American Sunday-School Union, 1863), 46–47.

3. Drake warned his readers not to try to imitate Thoreau's visit to Cape Cod: "no one ought to attempt [such a tramp as Thoreau's] who cannot rise superior to his surroundings, and shake off the gloom the weird and widespread desolateness of the landscape inspired." *Appleton's Illustrated Hand-Book of American Summer Resorts* (New York: D. Appleton and Co., 1876), 91.

4. Statistics for the summer of 1887 illustrate something of the difference between a major resort, a minor resort, and a place with no tourist industry: The island of Nantucket listed twenty-eight hotels and boarding houses in that year, twenty-three of which were open in summer only; together they accommodated over two thousand tourists. Falmouth, the Cape's most developed tourist town, had at that point eight hotels and boardinghouses, accommodating between five hundred and six hundred travelers. Orleans, farther down

the Cape, had three boardinghouses that would sleep a total of twenty people (and these, revealingly, were open all year). Old Colony Railroad, *The Old Colony: or Pilgrim Land, Past and Present* (Boston, 1887).

5. The economic history of Cape Cod can be read in detail in its one and only full-length history, Henry C. Kittredge, *Cape Cod: Its People and Their History* (1930; reprint, Orleans, Mass.: Parnassus Imprints, 1968). This information comes from Paul Donham, "The Twisting Track of Cape Cod's Economic History," *Cape Cod Business Journal* (March 1984): 10–13.

6. Herman A. Jennings, *Chequocket, Provincetown* (Provincetown, Mass., 1890), 11.

7. *Souvenir of Old Home Week, Harwich, Massachusetts* (Harwich, Mass.: Old Home Week Association, n.d.), n.p.

8. *Massachusetts: A Guide to Its Places and People. The WPA Guide to Massachusetts*, written by the Federal Writers' Project of the Works Progress Administration for the State of Massachusetts, with a new Introduction by Jane Holtz Kay (New York: Pantheon Books, 1983; first published in 1937), 406.

9. Harold Fisher Wilson, *The Hill Country of Northern New England: Its Social and Economic History, 1790–1930* (New York: Columbia University Press, 1936), 279.

10. Frank W. Rollins, "New Hampshire's Opportunity," *New England Magazine* 16 (July 1897), 538. One guidebook argued in 1916 that it was their touring experiences on bicycles that convinced most New Englanders to support greater state expenditures on roads; jolting around on the rutted dirt roads "resulted in the discovery that good roads paid." *A Handbook of New England*, Sargent's Handbook Series (Boston: Porter E. Sargent, 1916), 45.

11. *WPA Guide to Massachusetts*, xl; Sargent's *Handbook of New England*, 45.

12. *Handbook of New England*, 10.

13. Josef Berger (Jeremiah Digges), *Cape Cod Pilot* (Boston: Northeastern University Press, 1985; first published in 1937), 361.

14. Ibid., 3.

15. The development of motels is explored in John A. Jakle, *The Tourist: Travel in Twentieth-Century North America* (Lincoln, Neb.: University of Nebraska Press, 1985), 163–66.

16. Some historians have argued that the automobile had a "democratizing" effect on the tourist experience by providing new opportunities for inexpensive, short vacations that were practical for lower-middle-class and even working-class Americans. It is true that vacationing did "trickle down" into the ranks of the established working classes in these years, but the transition to auto travel was not primarily a transition from elite tourism to "democratic" tourism. More traditional forms of travel, especially trolley lines, had also provided opportunities to lower-income Americans, running from the centers of eastern industrial cities to nearby beach towns and rural retreats—and these were far less expensive than buying a car. Greater numbers of working-class vacationers did take to the roads in the 1920s, but that was due much more to their ability to gain paid vacation leave from modern corporations than to the effects of the automobile.

17. F. Allen Burt, *The Story of Mount Washington* (Hanover, N.H.: Dartmouth Publications, 1960), chapter 11.

18. Lee Cuba, "Retiring to Vacationland," *Generations* (Spring 1989): 63.

19. *The Cape Codder* 46, no. 40, Special Section (17 May 1991): 8.

20. David Strauss, "Toward a Consumer Culture: 'Adirondack Murray' and the Wilderness Vacation," *American Quarterly* 39, no. 2 (Summer 1987): 270–83; Roderick Nash, *Wilderness and the American Mind* (New Haven, Conn.: Yale University Press, 1977).

21. Wilson, *The Hill Country of Northern New England*, 292.

22. I am indebted to Jim O'Connell, Economic Development Officer for the Cape Cod Commission, for his exploration of these different varieties of travel and regional literature on Cape Cod. My discussion here is based on his research and analysis.

23. Jane Holtz Kay offers a thoughtful analysis of these Nantucket controversies in Jane Holtz Kay and Pauline Chase-Harrell, *Preserving New England* (New York: Pantheon Books, 1986), 61–65.

24. There has not yet been a great deal of research on the industry's effects in tourist regions in the "developed" world, but a fascinating discussion of the implications of other studies for the Cape can be found in David J. Damkoehler, "The Hidden Human Costs of Economic Dependence," *Cape Cod Business Journal* (June 1984): 18–23. The *Business Journal* sponsored a survey of a fifth-grade class in South Yarmouth that revealed startling levels of anger at tourists, whom the students characterized as "rude, mean, disgusting, and selfish," "pushy," and "like animals." (A number of students also attempted to defend tourists, pointing out that "your relatives are tourists if they don't live on Cape Cod.")

25. That is, these questions have not been discussed when the industries are located in the "developed" world; there is a great deal of open discussion of control, power, and money among anthropologists, economists, and political scientists who study the tourist industry in poor countries.

26. The methods used to get these results were fiercely challenged by pro-tourist forces on the Cape. Published in *The Cape Codder*, 9.

27. Damkoehler, "The Hidden Human Costs," 18.

INDEX